Freemasonry's

Royal Secret

Also from Westphalia Press
westphaliapress.org

Brethren: Behold Your Supreme Council: Bio-Bibliographical Dictionary of the SGIG and Deputies of the Supreme Council, 33°

A Study in American Freemasonry

ESOTERIKA by Albert Pike: The Symbolism of the Blue Degrees of Freemasonry

Ancient Mysteries and Modern Masonry: The Collected Writings of Jewel P. Lightfoot

Essay on The Mysteries and the True Object of The Brotherhood of Freemasons

James Hoban's Secret Society

Female Emancipation and Masonic Membership: An Essential Collection

The Rosicrucian Philosophy in Questions and Answers

Freemasonry, Heir to the Enlightenment

Grand Crosses of the Court of Honour: Concise Scottish Rite Biographical Dictionary

Masonic Myths and Legends

A Radical In The East

Brought to Light: The Mysterious George Washington Masonic Cave

Worlds of Print: The Moral Imagination of an Informed Citizenry, 1734 to 1839

History of the Grand Orient of Italy

Why Thirty-Three?: Searching for Masonic Origins

A Place in the Lodge: Dr. Rob Morris, Freemasonry and the Order of the Eastern Star

The Great Transformation: Scottish Freemasonry 1725-1810

The 33 Principles Every Mason Should Live By: The True Meaning of Being a Mason

Masonic Regularity and Recognition: A Global Issue

Getting the Third Degree: Fraternalism, Freemasonry and History

Dudley Wright: Writer, Truthseeker & Freemason

Freemasonry: A French View

Freemasonry's *Royal Secret*

THE JAMAICAN "FRANCKEN MANUSCRIPT" OF THE HIGH DEGREES

By
ARTURO DE HOYOS, 33°, GRAND CROSS, KYCH
Past Master, McAllen Lodge No. 1110, AF & AM of Texas
Grand Archivist & Grand Historian

With an Introduction Co-Authored by
ALAIN BERNHEIM, 33°
Past Master, Ars Macionica Lodge No. 30, R.·.G.·.L.·. of Belgium
Albert Gallatin Mackey Awards for Excellence and Lifetime Achievement

Westphalia Press
An imprint of Policy Studies Organization

Freemasonry's Royal Secret: The Jamaican "Francken Manuscript" of the High Degrees

Westphalia Press
An imprint of Policy Studies Organization
1527 New Hampshire Ave NW
Washington, DC 20036
info@ipsonet.org

ISBN: 978-1-63391-947-1

Book layout by Elizabeth A. W. McCarthy

Cover design by Jeffrey Barnes
jbarnesbook.design

Daniel Gutierrez-Sandoval, Executive Director
Policy Studies Organization & Westphalia Press

Contents

Introduction

ALTHOUGH MUCH HAS BEEN WRITTEN about Freemasonry as a social phenomenon, the academic study of its ritual is a comparatively recent practice in the English language. It owes its genesis primarily to the works of Quatuor Coronati Lodge No. 2076, London, and their annual transactions, *Ars Quatuor Coronatorum*. Subsequent to the creation of this premiere research lodge in 1884, a myriad of others have emerged, but few have had the resources to provide the authentic and complete texts of disused and outdated ritual. The works of Douglas Knoop, G. P. Jones, Douglas Hamer, Harry Carr, Colin Dyer, A. C. F. Jackson, and Jan Snoek, to name but a few, have become essential to understanding the evolution of Masonic ritual. Although Europeans have been quick to embrace ritual research, in the United States there have been only two Masonic organizations which have consistently focused on ritual studies. Since 1932 the Grand College of Rites, U.S.A., has privately printed the rituals of extinct and unrecognized Masonic and quasi-Masonic rites, orders, and systems, and the Scottish Rite Research Society, founded in 1991 by the Supreme Council, 33°, S.J., has published works on both Craft Masonry and the high degrees, to aid an understanding of the development of its ritual and symbolism, with a focus on the Ancient and Accepted Scottish Rite. By providing source texts to researchers, we hope to arrive at a more accurate understanding of how Masonic ritual developed—a branch of study which has been hindered by the limited availability to authentic texts.

The Jamaica Manuscript

The document which is transcribed *in toto* in this book is a *ca.* 1790–1800 bound manuscript of the rituals of the twenty-five degrees of the "Order of the Royal Secret"[1] (ORS) a "high degree" system of Freemasonry, created around the mid-1760s, which is best known for being the parent of the Ancient and Accepted Scottish Rite (AASR, Scottish Rite), now the most successful branch of Freemasonry in the world. As explained elsewhere, the Scottish Rite absorbed the degrees of the Order of the Royal Secret and added several of its own to create a rite of thirty-three degrees. The original transcriber of the 439-page *Jamaica*

1. This system was previously and mistakenly called the "Rite of Perfection" until its correct name was discovered by Alain Bernheim.

Manuscript is unknown, but its language reveals that it is a copy of an undiscovered *Francken Manuscript*—a name given to several known similar manuscripts, named for their translator/transcriber, Henry Andrew Francken, an enthusiastic Dutch Mason who received the degrees from Estienne Morin, a French Mason who brought the degrees to the New World.

The *Jamaica Manuscript* is unique for having more ritual information than other known copies of Francken's manuscripts. In addition to the twenty-five degrees of the Order of the Royal Secret it includes three "detached degrees [which were] given in different parts of the world ... free of expence [*sic*], to those Brethren who are high enough to understand them."[2] The three degrees were the "Select Master of 27" (now called "Select Master" and a part of the York Rite), the "Knight of the Royal Arch" (reputedly an Irish version), and the "Grand Master Ecose" (which was also among Frederick Dalcho's rituals of the Charleston Supreme Council).

These additional degrees where not among those Francken received from Morin, but were appended to the *Jamaica Manuscript* by its transcriber. These additional degrees include occasional phonetic errors, such as "hail Puissant" for "all Puissant." A notable phonetic error is unfortunate and problematic. It obligates the member to keep the secrets of a Brother Royal Arch Mason, "even those of murder and Treason not excepted." A letter from Samuel F. Bradford to Le Barbier Duplessis (written October 20, 1809) includes what is likely the correct form: "but those of murder and treason not accepted."[3] The confusion of *excepted* for *accepted* in faulty manuscripts (exposed by anti-Masons) was likely responsible for the comments of Jeremy L. Cross, General Grand Lecturer of the United States:

> In regard to my giving any oath whatever, requiring the initiated to swear to conceal all *crimes* of a companion R. A. Mason, Murder and Treason not excepted, or authorized others so to give it, IS WITHOUT THE LEAST FOUNDATION OF TRUTH. I never gave such an oath, nor have I ever authorized others so to give one; and furthermore, I have never given myself, nor authorized any person to give, any oath in masonry, whereby the person so taking it is required to conceal *any crime whatever*, which may be committed by any mason against the laws of God and his country; and so far from that being the case, every mason is required to keep and obey the moral laws of God; "to be a quiet and peaceable citizen; true to his government, and just to his country." He is *forbid* to countenance disloyalty or rebellion, but is patiently to submit to the legal authority of the country in which he lives.[4]

Even honest ex-Masons recognized that this was not part of the ritual. For example, seceding Mason William L. Stone wrote, "The obligation has never been so given,

2. *Circular throughout the Two Hemispheres* (Charleston, S.C.: Supreme Council, 33°, December 4, 1802).

3. Samuel F. Bradford, Philadelphia, October 20, 1809, to Le Barbier Duplessis. This letter, which was the property of the late Kent Logan Walgren, was seen by Arturo de Hoyos in 1995.

4. Jeremy Cross, *Boston Masonic Mirror* vol. 3 (Sat., Jan. 28, 1832), no. 31, pp. 241–42.

within the range of my masonic experience, and is not sanctioned or allowed by the Grand Chapter, having jurisdiction in the premises. Nor have I, as yet, found a Royal Arch Mason who recollects ever to have heard the obligation so given."[5]

The provenance of the *Jamaica Manuscript* is unknown. The earliest known reference states that it "belonged to an old Jewish family in Jamaica."[6] How and when the manuscript became the property of the Supreme Council, 33°, Southern Jurisdiction, is also unknown. Arturo de Hoyos first saw it as a researcher in its archives in the early 1990s, when he was allowed to make a copy for study. A couple of years later he transcribed the copy and shared it with fellow members of the board of directors of the Scottish Rite Research Society, when there was some informal discussion about publishing it in the future. After accepting the position of Grand Archivist and Grand Historian of the Supreme Council in 1999, he was distressed to learn that a few months earlier the original manuscript had been sent to a bookbinder to be case-bound, but that it had somehow been misplaced, and the binder has been unable to relocate it. Fortunately, since we possess copies of the entire document, and have herein reproduced the entire manuscript, we will be able to reclaim it when it resurfaces. Unfortunately, we have not been able examine the original paper for water marks, which might identify the paper maker, and give us a more precise date.

The Evolution of Masonic Ritual

The Order of the Royal Secret, and its place in the history of high degree Masonry, can only be appreciated within the broader context of Masonic ritual history. The story of how Freemasonry evolved from a simple system to a complex one is long and involved, but a brief outline of the events which led to the creation of the Order of the Royal Secret will help provide a context for the rituals herein transcribed.

The earliest traditions of Freemasonry are preserved in a collection of documents known as the "Old Charges," or "Gothic Constitutions." The two earliest known copies of these constitutions are the *Regius MS* (ca. 1410) and the *Cooke MS* (ca. 1420).[7] All of the oldest known copies of the Old Charges are of English origin. About 127 copies are known to survive, and they entail the Mason's code of conduct,

---

5. William L. Stone, William L. Stone, *Letters on Masonry and Anti-Masonry, Addressed to the Hon. John Quincy Adams* (New York: O. Halsted, 1832), pp. 74–75.

6. Eugene E. Hinman, Ray V. Denslow and Charles C. Hunt, *A History of the Cryptic Rite* 2 vols. (General Grand Council, R.·. & S.·.M.·., U.S.A., 1931), vol. 2, p. 99. The authors call it "the Panama Ritual" because it came to them from Panama, but on p. 100 they provide a facsimile of manuscript p. 367, and the caption reads "Jamaica Ritual." Inasmuch as the Order of the Royal Secret was practiced in Jamaica, and came from there, I have called it the *Jamaica Manuscript.*

7. Douglas Knoop, G. P. Jones, and D. Hamer, *The Two Earliest Masonic MSS* (Manchester: Manchester University Press, 1938) and Andrew Prescott, "The Regius and Cooke Manuscripts: Some New Contexts," in *Collected Studies in the History of Freemasonry, 2000–2003* (Sheffield: University of Sheffield, 2003).

his regulations, and a traditional or mythical history.[8] The rituals from which modern Freemasonry derived, on the other hand, are likely of Scottish origin. In fact, Scotland played such a substantial and vital role in Freemasonry's origins that even the common names of its earliest degrees derive from Scottish origin.[9]

The appointment of William Schaw as "Maister of Wark" by James VI of Scotland in 1583 played a significant role in the development of organized Freemasonry. His issue of the first and second "Schaw Statutes" in 1598 and 1599 introduced many concepts which continue today. These statutes were founded on the Old Charges. They together formed the basis of government for modern Masonic Grand Lodges. The Schaw Statutes defined a hierarchy of "wardenis, dekynis, and maisteris in all thingis concerning thair craft." Lodges were to be presided over by a "generall Wardene," while William Schaw himself presided over all the Masonic lodges in his country, as Grand Masters do throughout most of the world today.

Be that as it may, England established the world's premiere Grand Lodge in 1717 (the "Grand Lodge of London and Westminster," later called the "Grand Lodge of England"). At first the fledgling Grand Lodge of England practiced a simple two-degree system (Entered Apprentice and Fellow Craft). We are fortunate that several early documents exist which give us some understanding of early Freemasonry.[10] Then, as now, the degrees were simply levels of membership. At this early period a "Master" was a Fellow Craft who presided over his brethren. We discover hints of secrets reserved for Masters as early as the *Trinity College Dublin MS.* (1711), which allocates specific signs to the "Enterprentice," the "fellow craftsman," and the "Masters." The secrets of the latter came to be called the "Master's part."

By February 1725 the existing Apprentices' Degree was divided into two parts (creating the ancestors of today's Entered Apprentice and Fellow Craft degrees),[11] and content of the former Fellow's Degree was included in a new degree, called Master Mason. A degree bearing that name is first known to have been conferred on May 12, 1725, when Charles Cotton and Papillon Ball "Were regularly passed Master,"[12] however we ignore its contents.

Remarkably, in a note appended to *A Dialogue between Simon and Philip* (ca. 1725), we read:

---

8. See Wallace McLeod, *The Old Gothic Constitutions* (Bloomington, IL: Masonic Book Club, 1985).

9. David Stevenson, *The Origins of Freemasonry: Scotland's Century, 1590–1710* **(Aberdeen: 1988).**

10. Many of these are included in Douglas Knoop, G. P. Jones and Douglas Hamer, *The Early Masonic Catechisms* 2d ed. (Manchester: Manchester University Press, 1963).

11. Lionel Vibert, "The Evolution of the Second Degree," in *The Collected Prestonian Lectures: 1925–1960* (1965; reprinted, London: Lewis Masonic, 1984), pp. 47–61.

12. R. F. Gould, "Philo-Musica et Architectura Societas Apollini. [A Review.]," in AQC 16 (1903), pp. 112–28.

> And the Junior Prentice takes you by the hand and knocks three times at the Door. The Master askes who's there. And the Prentice answers. One that has a desire to be made a Mason. The Master reply's Bring him in. N.B. The reason of those three Knocks is not known to Prentices but to the Master, which is from HIRAM the Grand Master in SOLOMON'S TEMPLE. Being murdered by his three Prentices and was dispatch'd by the third Blow the last Prentice gave him and this because he would not discover the secrets to them.[13]

Thus, the Master Mason Degree was actually the first of our "high degrees." However, when its first description appeared in Samuel Prichard's pamphlet, *Masonry Dissected* (October 20, 1730) Hiram was murdered by Fellow Crafts.[14] Be that as it may, other high degrees developed about the same time. We know that in 1732 Joseph Laycock was appointed Provincial Grand Master of the Harodim (later "Heredom") body in London, which gave birth to the Royal Order of Scotland, and, by 1734–35 other degrees were invented, two of which were the "Excellent Mason" and "Grand Mason."[15]

Scots Masonry

In a broad sense the high degrees stand apart from the Craft rituals, although some may be dependent upon them. Their origin lies primarily in two main types of Masonry: Scots/Scotch/Scottish Masonry[16] (now known as *Ecossais* Masonry) which arose in London, and Templar Masonry, which arose in France. As early as 1733 a reference to a "Scotch Masons' Lodge" appears in one of Richard Rawlinson's manuscripts; it appeared as "Scotts Masons Lodge" in an engraved list of lodges in 1734, and yet again, on an engraved plate, in 1735.[17] The Lodge met at the Devil Tavern, Temple Bar, London, and was active until 1736. It's been noted that from 1735–46 there were at least four lodges conferring the Scots Master Degree in Southern England. We do not know much about this early degree. We know only that its conferral required three officers and that multiple persons

13. AQC 57, 1946, p. 9. Text corrected by J. H. Lepper after the photographs of the original MS p. 7n1.

14. The complete texts of the Trinity College Dublin MS., as well as *Masonry Dissected*, are included in Douglas Knoop, G. P. Jones, and Douglas Hamer, eds., *The Early Masonic Catechisms*, 2d ed. (Manchester: Manchester University Press, 1963).

15. Hugo O'Kelly was made a Mason in Ireland before arriving in Portugal about 1734–45. On August 1, 1738, he told the Inquisition that "there are two more classes which they call Excellent Masons, and Grand Mason, which are above all others and superior...." Quoted in S. Vatcher, "A Lodge of Irishmen at Lisbon, 1738," AQC 84 (1971), p. 88.

16. On Scots Masonry and the early high degrees see J. Fairbairn Smith, "A Commentary. D'Assigny's Enquiry—Serious, Impartial" in Fifield D'Assigny, *A Serious and Impartial Enquiry into the Cause of the Present Decay of Free-Masonry in the Kingdom of Ireland* (Bloomington, IL: Masonic Book Club, 1974); Alain Bernheim, "Did Early 'High' or Ecossais Degrees Originate in France?" in *Heredom* 5 (1996), pp. 87–113.

17. Eric Ward, "Early Masters' Lodges and their Relation to Degrees. Part 2—Scots Masters and the Embryo R.A.," AQC 75 (1962), p. 155.

could receive it at a single ceremony. In 1740 we find the Scotch Master Masons Degree conferred on "normal" Master Masons, as we read that at the Lodge at the Rummer, Bristol, on July 18, 1740, it was "Order'd & agreed That Bro. Tomson & Bro. Watts & any other member of this L[odge]. that are already Master Masons may be made Scotch Master...."[18]

Whether *Ecossais* Masonry was influenced in any way by early Scottish Masonic practices is unknown. Of course, it is not impossible that elements of Scottish traditions were introduced into English Masonry (as had the names of the degrees). *Ecossais* Masonry became particularly popular in France, as René Guilly explains:

> It is the extraordinary importance taken by the Ecossaise degree in France in the 1740s which gave the word an unequalled fate. The Ecossais, that is those Masons who owned the degree, were the heads of the Lodges, far before Craft degrees became differentiated through rites. It is this, and this only, the first meaning of *Ecossisme*, a word which was to become an exceptional fate. Let us add the (legitimate) prestige of Freemasonry from Scotland, we can then understand how words such as Ecossais and Ecossisme became the French equivalent of learned Mason and of good Freemasonry. The actual direct geographic tie was nil, as it has been perfectly demonstrated, and the notion of rite was then inexistent.[19]

In 1732 *Loge L'Anglaise* was founded in Bordeaux, mostly by Irish Masons.[20] It was the first lodge founded in that city. First chartered in March 1766 by the English Modern Grand Lodge, it still exists today. In 1740 *Loge L'Anglaise* created *Loge la Française* which worked in French.

By December 1743 the Scots Masters had gained sufficient strength that the final article (No. 20) of the General Regulations adopted by the Grand Lodge meeting in Paris began, "As we learn that some brothers recently announce themselves as Scots Masters (*maîtres Ecossois*)...", and within two years we see a first diversification noted in the Statutes of St John of Jerusalem, dated June 24, 1745, in Paris, which stipulated that "the ordinary Masters will gather with the Perfect and Irish Masters three months after St John's Day, the Elect Masters six months later, and those possessing higher degrees when they deem expedient" (Article 40).[21]

Estienne Morin

In 1717, the same year in which the Premiere Grand Lodge was founded, Estienne (Stephen) Morin was born in Cahors, France.[22] And, as the Premiere Grand Lodge

---

18. Eric Ward, "Early Masters' Lodges and their Relation to Degrees. Part 1—English Masters Lodges and the Dissection of Masonry," AQC 75 (1962), p. 131.

19. René Désaguliers [pseudonym of René Guilly], *Renaissance Traditionnelle* 54–55 (1983), p. 93.

20. Alain Bernheim, "Notes on Early Freemasonry in Bordeaux (1732–1769),"AQC 101 (1988), pp. 33–131.

21. Alain Bernheim, *Une certaine idée de la Franc-maçonnerie* (Dervy, 2008), pp. 183–85, 446–59.

22. Alain Bernheim, "Estienne Morin—New Information about his Birth," in AQC 105 (1992), pp. 255–6.

would shape Craft Masonry worldwide, so too would Morin exercise a substantial influence on the development of high degree Freemasonry. Morin's influence can be compared with that of three others: Carl Friedrich Eckleff, Carl Gotthelf von Hund, and Jean-Baptiste Willermoz, synthesizers of the Swedish System, the Rite of Strict Observance, and the Rectified Scottish Rite. Morin's creation, the 25-degree "Order of the Royal Secret," would itself lay the foundation for the creation of the Ancient and Accepted Scottish Rite which is, in terms of numbers and geographic distribution, the most successful Masonic system today.

We know little about him as a person, other than that he was Catholic,[23] and a merchant.[24] We don't yet know what year he was made a Mason, but according to a letter written in May 1750, in 1744 he "was initiated into the mysteries of the Scots perfection" by a lawyer named Petit de Boulard.[25] He was the driving force behind the creation of the *Ecossais* Mother-Lodge in Bordeaux, and was among the signers of the *Reglements of the Parfaite Loge d'Ecosse* (dated "eighth of the second month of the year 5746," meaning July 8, 1745, according to its dating code).[26] During the time of his known Masonic activity, 1744–71, the national authority of the Grand Lodges in London, Paris, and Berlin was limited. The degrees beyond Master Mason had not been codified, in the sense that they are today, with a more precise correlation between degrees of a given rite or system throughout the world. Morin would contribute greatly to the stabilization of the high degrees.

In 1744 or 1745, a book called *Le Parfait Maçon* was published. This work is of particular importance to those interested in the development of high degree Freemasonry. In a section on the "Secret of the Scottish Masons" (*Secret des maçons ecossois*) its description of Scottish Masonry reveals that it was an ancestor of many subsequent degrees, including the Holy Royal Arch,[27] and the Scottish Rite's 15° Knight of the East, and 16° Prince of Jerusalem:

23. Morin's religion appears on his passport application filed in Bordeaux on March 27, 1762, at the time of leaving France to return to the Islands. He was then "45 years old, of medium height, black hair, wearing a wig, a native of Cahors in the Quercy [and] an old Catholic." Johel Coutura, "Deux Quercinois aux origines du Rite Ecossais," in *Chroniques d'histoire maçonnique* (Institut d'Etudes et de Recherches Maçonniques [IDERM]), No. 44, pp. 91, 93. Facsimilé of the original document in Trebuchet, *De l'Écosse à l'*Écossisme, Tome 2—Vol. 2 [2014], pp. 508–511. However Trebuchet writes that the family name Morin does *not* appear between 1690 and 1750 on any document belonging either to the Cahors parish or to any village situated 35 miles around Cahors (*ibid.*, p. 157).

24. Letter from Morin, August 28, 1764, in: Nicolas Choumitzky, "Étienne Morin", *St-Claudius No 21, Compte rendu 1927–1928*, p. 45.

25. Sharp Doc. 15.

26. Alain Bernheim, "Notes on Early Freemasonry in Bordeaux (1732–1769)". *AQC* 101 (1988), pp. 110–113 ; dating code described pp 81–82. "Estienne Morin et l'Ordre du Royal Secret", *Acta Macionica* (Bruxelles) vol. 9 (1999), p. 20.

27. A connection to the Holy Royal Arch may further be suggested by a letter (Sharp Doc. 2) written in 1746 by a Brother Dutillet, which stated "by inspection of my letter, you can easily know that I am indeed a S[cot]. In any case, I should be able to prove it to you *by the words that are under the vault* [or *arch*]" (emphasis added).

> It is said among the Masons that there are still several degrees above that of the masters, of which I have just spoken; some say there are six in all, & others go up to seven. Those called *Ecossois* [Scottish] *Masons* claim that they form the fourth grade. As this Masonry, different from the other in many ways, is beginning to gain favour in France, the Public will not be annoyed if I relate what I have read about it in the same manuscript which seems indeed to give the *Ecossois* the degree of superiority above the Apprentices, Fellows, & ordinary Masters.
>
> Instead of weeping over the ruins of the Temple of Solomon, as their brethren do, the *Ecossois* are concerned with rebuilding it.[28]

France was not alone in embracing Scots Masonry. An Ecossais lodge *De l'Union* had been founded in Berlin on St. Andrew's Day, November 30, 1742,[29] and its continued activity is evinced by a certificate in French presented to Frederic Dahle, a Danish gentleman, on October 2, 1747, by "the Most Sublime Scots Lodge de l'Union of Berlin," certifying that he had been received "Scots Master in our Most Sublime Sanctuary of Elder Brethren [*frères ainés*] and created a Knight of St. Andrew."[30]

Masonic Rites, Orders, and Systems

In the most fundamental sense Scots Masonry could be considered a very primitive "rite," even though it consisted of a single degree. In modern use, Masonic rites are enlarged.

> The word 'rite', from the Latin *ritus, is cognate* with the Greek αριθμός [*arithmos*], *meaning* 'number'. In masonic as in liturgical use, the word 'rite' refers to an event, or sequence of events, which govern(s) the prescribed actions or practices of a ceremony or organized group. There are two main types of rites in Freemasonry: (1) a procedure with a symbolic or defining nature, such as the rites of circumambulation, discalceation, or investiture, which may be grouped to form a larger ceremony (or degree), and (2) the linking of masonic degrees, for initiation or instruction, under administrative or governmental authority.... The words 'system' and 'order' also have similar meanings and use in Freemasonry.[31]

It is not possible to describe precisely how the first Masonic rite coalesced. Much of what we surmise about the early rites is conservative supposition supported by fragmentary evidence. We might assume, for example, that there was some logical development; i.e., degrees with common motifs or themes might be

---

28. *Le Parfait Maçon ou les Veritables Secrets des quatre Grades d'Aprentis, Compagnons, Maîtres ordinaires* et Écossois *de la Franche Maçonnerie—Imprimé cette année*, pp. 97–98.

29. Werner Schwartz & Reinhold Dosch (Schiftleitung und Zusammenstellung) 1990, 250 *Jahre Große National-Mutterloge „Zu den drei Weltkugeln,"* p. 36.

30. The words of the certificate are reproduced in Alain Bernheim, *Les Débuts de la Franc-Maçonnerie à Genève et en Suisse* (Genève: Slatkine, 1994), pp. 68–69, from Schröder *Materialien, Erster Theil*, (1806), p. 144.

31. Arturo de Hoyos, "Masonic Rites and Systems," in Henrik Bogdan and J. A. M. Snoek, *Handbook of Freemasonry* (Leiden: Brill, 2014), p. 355.

grouped together, and (quasi-)historical events might be placed in chronological order, although such is not always the case. However, we can gather some idea as to how the degrees were collated by considering the *Conversations Allégoriques*[32] (*CA*), a series of thirteen pamphlets published by Erasme Pincemaille in Metz, France, in 1763 and 1766, each giving the catechism of a Masonic degree. This thirteen-degree collection—from *Apprenti* (Apprentice) to *Parfait Maître Anglais* (Perfect English Master)—has several degrees in common with *Les Plus Secrets Mystères des Hauts Grades de la Maçonnerie Dévoilés*[33] (*LPSM*), the 1766 exposé of fully developed hauts grades rituals with costumes, props, and dialogues. These two small works (or fourteen, if each of the *Conversations* is counted as a separate publication) are the earliest printed sources for several of the degrees which eventually became the Ancient and Accepted Scottish Rite. *Conversations* can be thought of as loosely-allied degrees worked in Metz in the mid-1700s, while *Les Plus Secrets Mystères* represents a later development—a coherent rite, a system of ceremonies that both teach morals lessons and advance a story arc.

CONVERSATIONS ALLÉGORIQUES (1763–66)	*LES PLUS SECRETS MYSTÈRES* (1766)
1° Apprentices	1° Perfect Elect
2° Fellowcrafts	2° Elect of Pérignon
3° Masters	3° Elect of the Fifteen
4° Perfect Masters	4° Junior Architect
5° Irish Masters	5° Senior Architect
6° English Masters	6° Knight of the Sword & of Rose Croix
7° Masters Elect	7° Noachite or Prussian Knight
8° Masters Elect of the Stranger	
9° Masters Elect of the Fifteen	
10° Illustrious Masters	
11° Scots	
12° Sublime Scots	
13° Perfect English Masters	

It is interesting to compare the following of contemporary corresponding degrees, in Lyons and Metz.[34]

32. For the Complete text see Arturo de Hoyos and S. Brent Morris, trans. and eds., *Allegorical Conversations Arranged by Wisdom* (Washington, DC: Scottish Rite Research Society, 2012).

33. For the complete text see Arturo de Hoyos and S. Brent Morris, trans. and eds., *The Most Secret Mysteries of the High Degrees of Masonry Unveiled* (Washington, DC: Scottish Rite Research Society, 2011).

34. From Alain Bernhein, "Avatars of the Knight Kadosh in France and in Charleston," *Heredom* 6 (1997), 152–58.

DEGREES OF THE BRETHREN OF LYONS, May 1761	DEGREES OF THE BRETHREN OF METZ, June 1761
1. Apprentif	1. Apprentif
2. Compagnon	2. Compagnon
3. Maître	3. Maître
	4. Fendeur
4. Me Elu	5. M^{e} parfait irlandois prévôt et juge
	6. Maître Elu ou petit Elu
5. Second grade d'Elu	
6. Elu des 15	
7. M^{tre} illustre	7. M^{tre} illustre
8. M^{tre} parfait	
9. M^{tre} Irlandois. Prévôt et juge	
10. M^{tre} secret	
11. M^{e} anglois	8. M^{e} anglois
12. M^{e} favory	
13. Apprentif	9. Ecossois apprentif
14. Compagnon	10. Ecossois Compagnon
15. Maître	11. Ecossois Maître
16. Ecossois des 3 J. ou Ecossois de Paris	12. Ecossois de Clermont
17. Ecossois Trinit^{re} d'Edimbourg	13. Ecossois de Prusse
18. Petit architecte 19. Grand architecte	14. Apprentif architecte 15. Compagnon architecte 16. M^{e} architecte
20. Ecossois des 5 Lettres	
21. Sublime Ecossois	17. Sublime Ecossois
22. Elu suprême	
23. Chev^{er} de l'Orient	18. Chev^{er} de l'Orient
24. Chevalier du soleil et des adeptes	
25. Chevalier de l'aigle, du pélican, chev^{er} de St André ou maçon d'Heredon	
	19. Chevalier d'Occident
	20. Royal arche

DEGREES OF THE BRETHREN OF LYONS, May 1761	DEGREES OF THE BRETHREN OF METZ, June 1761
	21. Chevalier Grand Insp^eur^ Grand Elû d^er^ grade suspecté d'être celuy de l'Aigle de Lyon [Knight Grand Inspector Grand Elect last degree which we believe could be that of the Eagle of Lyons]

The Order of the Royal Secret

The status of Scottish Masonry was raised in 1745 when the French *Grand Master, Louis* de Bourbon, comte de *Clermont*, adopted new statutes for the Grand and Sovereign Lodge of St. John of Jerusalem. Issued for use throughout the kingdom, they elevated the prominence of high-grade Scottish Masonry by giving Scottish Masters special rights. In 1748 Morin founded an *Ecossais* lodge in Le Cap Français, in the French colony of Saint–Domingue (Santo Domingo, now Haiti). The *hauts grades* lodges in Bordeaux introduced concepts and terms which would become part of later systems. For example, they used the expression "admitted to perfection" in 1750.[35]

On August 27, 1761, the Grand and Sovereign Lodge of St. John of Jerusalem (the French Grand Lodge at Paris) together with the Grand Council of Regular Lodges issued a patent to Morin to promulgate Masonry in the New World. Although the original cannot be found the surviving copies—which differ slightly from each other—all agree that Morin was created a Grand Inspector, and that his patent "authorize[ed] and empower[ed] him to establish perfect and sublime Masonry in all parts of the world."[36]

By the mid-1760s Morin created and began promulgating a Masonic rite of twenty–five degrees, which he called the "Order of the Royal Secret" or "Order of Prince of the Royal Secret"[37] (sometimes mistakenly called the "Rite of Perfection"), named for the rite's final degree, "The Royal Secret, or the Knights of St Andrews, and the Faithful Guardians of the Sacred Treasure." The authority and laws of the rite are the *Constitutions and Regulations of 1762*.[38] There is now

35. Alain Bernheim, *"Notes on Early Freemasonry in Bordeaux (1732–1769),"*AQC 101 (1988), p. 114.

36. Since Charles Porset published the correspondence between Mathéus, Constant de Castelin, and Fleuret de Turville (Bibliothèque Nationale de Paris, FM2 544, fol. 7–36) in *Chroniques d'Histoire Maçonnique* No 48 (IDERM, Paris 1997), pp. 10–47, the existence of Morin's patent cannot be doubted anymore.

37. The Supreme Council's first official document, the *Circular throughout the Two Hemispheres* (dated December 4, 1802), refers to the system as "the order of Prince of the Royal Secret."

38. For a transcription, see Albert Pike, *Ancient and Accepted Scottish Rite of Freemasonry: The Constitutions and Regulations of 1762. Statutes and Regulations of Perfection, and Other Degrees....* (New York: Masonic Publishing Co., A.M. 5632 [1872]; new edition, J. J. Little, &c., 5664 [1904]).

substantive evidence that, to bolster his authority, he created and backdated these *Constitutions.*[39]

Although it was once commonly believed that the Council of the Emperors of the East and West created the Order of the Royal Secret, research by Alain Bernheim provides substantial evidence that Morin was personally responsible for its organization. The Order of the Royal Secret included many of the most popular degrees worked at the time, many of which are preserved in the ca. 1764–68 *Saint–Domingue MS.* (Baylot FM⁴ 15).[40]

About this same time efforts were made to bring Bordeaux's version of the high degrees to the American continent. A lodge in New Orleans, Louisiana, called *Grande et Magnifique Loge de Parfaits d'Écosse*, was the first, being founded on April 12, 1764, by Louis-François Tiphaine.

Morin remained in Saint Domingo until 1765 and travelled thereafter between Jamaica and Saint-Domingue. In 1770 he created a Grand Chapter of his Order in Kingston, Jamaica, and the following year he died and was buried there. It is known that Morin created at least six Deputy Inspectors General, who extended the Rite by further appointments. According to research by the History Committee, Supreme Council, 33°, Northern Masonic Jurisdiction, the following Deputy Grand Inspectors General of the Order of the Royal Secret were appointed.

The Degrees of Estienne Morin's "Order of the Royal Secret"

The twenty-five degrees of his Masonic rite were divided into seven classes. It was a complete Masonic system, although the Craft degrees were not worked. The titles which follow are as they appear in Francken's 1783 manuscript.

1st Class

1° Entered Apprentice
2° Fellow Craft
3° Master

39. Morin based his 1762 *Constitutions* on the 1763 *Statutes and Regulations of the Grand Lodge of France.* See Alain Bernheim, "Une Découverte Étonnante Concernant les Consitutions de 1762," in *Renaissance Traditionnelle* No. 59 (July 1984), pp. 161–97. A. C. F. Jackson, "The Authorship of the 1762 Constitutions of the Ancient and Accepted Rite," Ars Quatuor Coronatorum 79 (1984), pp. 176–91. A. C. F. Jackson, *Rose Croix: A History of the Ancient and Accepted Rite for England and Wales* rev. & enl. (London: Lewis Masonic, 1980, 1987), pp. 46–54. For the opposite view see Jean-Pierre Lassalle, "From the Constitutions and Regulations of 1762 to the Grand Constitutions of 1786," in *Heredom* 2 (1993), pp. 57–88.

40. Pierre Molliere, "Nouvelles Lumières sur la Patente Morin et le Rite de Perfection," in *Renaissance Traditionnelle* No. 110–111 (April-July, 1997), pp. 111–57. For transcriptions of the rituals, see Louis Trebuchet, *De l'Écosse à l'Ecossisme: Fondements historiques du Rite Écossais Ancien Accepté. Tome 2—Volume 1 & 2, 1745–1761. Floraison des grades écossais.* (Marseilles: Ubik editions; Collection Fondations, 2014)

2D CLASS

4° Secret Master
5° Perfect Master
6° Perfect M[aste]r by Curiosity, or Intimate Secretary
7° Provost & Judge, or Irish Master
8° Intendant of the Buildings, or M[aste]r in Israel[.] Many French Lodges, called this degree, Scotch M[aste]r of the three J. J. J.

3D CLASS

9° Chapter of Master Elected of Nine
10° Illustrious Elected of 15
11° A chapter called Sublime Knights Elected

4TH CLASS

12° Grand Master Architect
13° Royal Arch
14° Perfection[.] The Ultimate of Symbolic Masonry

5TH CLASS

15° Kn[igh]ts of the East or Sword
16° Grand Council of the Illustrious & most valiant Princes of Jerusalem
17° Knights of the East & West
18° Knights of the white Eagle or Pelican, known by the name of perfect Mason, or knight of the Rose Cross

6TH CLASS

19° Sublime Scotch Masonry, Called by the name of gr[an]d Pontif
20° Venerable gr[an]d M[aste]r of all symbolic lodges, Sovereign princes of masonry, or M[aste]r ad vitam
21° Prussian Kn[igh]t or Noachite, In Two Degrees—otherwise Called, The Masonic Key
22° Knights of the Royal Ax—or the Gr[an]d Patriarchs By the Name of Princes of Libanon

7TH CLASS

23° The Key of Masonry[.] Philosophical Lodge of the Kn[igh]ts of Eagle, or Sun
24° Chapter of the grand Inspector of Lodges, grand Elected Knights of Kadoch, Now by the Title of knights of the white & black Eagle
25° The Royal Secret, or the knights of St Andrews, and the Faithful guardians of the Sacred Treasure

As might be expected several degrees printed in the *Conversations Allégoriques* and *Les Plus Secrets Mystères* appear in more developed and sophisticated form in the rituals of the Order of the Royal Secret. For example, the Elu (Elect) degrees of the *CA*, *LPSM*, and the ORS roughly correspond to each other; the Knight of the Sword and of Rose-Croix of *LPSM* corresponds to the 15°and 16° ORS, and the Noachite or Prussian Knight in *LPSM* corresponds to the 21° ORS. But we also find content exported from some sources and integrated to another, as is the case with "golden ring" of 6° English Master (*CA*), which becomes an important part of the 14° Perfection (ORS).

Francken Brings the Order to the United States

Three years after Louis-François Tiphaine brought Bordeaux's high degrees to New Orleans, Francken embarked upon a similar venture in 1767 when he began to confer in Albany the high degrees he received in the West Indies. Fortunately, he also transcribed several manuscript copies of the rituals of the Order of the Royal Secret, some of which survive today. These are generically known as the *Francken Manuscripts*. His zeal to propagate the high degrees caused him to appoint Moses Michael Hays in 1768 a Deputy Inspector General for the West Indies and North America. Hays, in turn, appointed other deputies which ensured the Order's survival until the early 1800s, when it faded after its absorption into the "Rite in 33 Degrees," known since 1804 as the Ancient and Accepted Scottish Rite.

[1]

Secret Master

THIS LODGE OUGHT TO BE spread with black and strewed with Tears.—The Master represents Solomon and is stiled most powerfull, and comes to the Temple to repair the loss of Hiram Abiff by seven Experts;—There is only one Warden who is called Adoniram: It is he who had the Inspection of the workmanship at Mount Libanus: He was the first Secret Master.

The Form of the Lodge.

Solomon, holds a Scepter in his hand and is cloathed in mourning, lined with Ermine, placed in the East, before a triangular Alter on which is a Crown with laurel and Olive Leaves.

Order.

Adoniram the Inspector in the West, who does not make use of any Iron tool, because the work was suspended by the death of Hiram Abiff. Solomon is decorated with a large blue Ribbon from the Right shoulder to the left hip, to which hangs a Triangle; Adoniram is decorated with a large white Ribbon bordered with black, round his neck in a Triangular form—an Ivory key suspended with the letter *Z* thereon. All the brethren the same with white Aprons and Gloves, black strings to the apron the flap blue with an Eye painted in gold, the white signifies the Candor and Innocence of the Master, the black the mourning of the Chief. This Lodge ought to be enlightened with 81 Candles lighted and distributed by 9 times 9, but may be done with 3 times 3.

To Open.

QUESTION: Brother Adoniram, are you a Secret Master?

ANSWER: Most powerfull I have past from the square to the Compass—I have seen the Tomb of the respectable Hiram Abiff, I have in Company with my Brethren shed

[2]

my tears.

Q: what is the O Clock?

A: The Dawn of the day has drove darkness away and the Light begins to shine in this Lodge.

Q: If the great Light has drove away darkness and we are all Secret Masters it is high time to begin our work. Give notice that I am going to open this Lodge of secret master.—Then the most Powerfull strikes 7 times with his hands and the Inspector and all the Brethren also, When the most Puissiant makes the sign of Silence, with the 2 first fingers of his right hand on his lips, Which is answered by the brethren with their left When the most Puissiant says this Lodge is opened.

The Reception

The Blue Master or Candidate must be well examin[d] by an Expert brother in his former 3 degrees when the examiner knocks 7 times; The same is given to the grand Inspector Adoniram who reports the same to the most powerfull, and desires the candidate to be introduced as he will be answerable for his Capacity zeal and Constancy—when the Candidate is introduced—he is ordered to be conducted to Adoniram to whom he is to give an Account of himself. Afterwards he advances near the Altar with his right knee on the ground, his head bound as if blinded: with a great Light in his hand a square placed on his forehead and whilst in this position the most powerful speaks to him as follows, "You have seen till now, but the thick Veil which covers the Sanctum Sanctorum of Gods Temple your Fidelity Zeal and Constancy, hath gained you to the favor I now

[3]

Grant you. It is to show you our treasure, and to Introduce you to the holy and secret place: Come and Contract your Obligation." When Adoniram raises him in order to lead him to kneel at the foot of the Altar, where he takes the obligation of the blue Master with this addition, never to reveal to any Person below him this degree; to be an Exact Observer of all such laws as shall be Prescribed to him and to Obey and fulfill all orders and decrees from this Royal Lodge under the Penalty of his former Obligations: After which Adoniram raises him and the Most Powerfull invests him with the Ribbon, key, Apron, the Crown of Laurel and Olive leaves and tells him Viz[t]—"My dear Brother, I receive you Secret Master and give you rank among the Levites, this Laurel represents the Victory you are to gain over your Passions; the Olive is the Symbol of peace and Union, which ought to reign among us, it belongeth to you to deserve that favor. That God may enable you one day to arrive in the Secret place, to Contemplate the Pillar of Beauty I decorate you with this Ivory key, hung to a white and black Ribbon, Symbols of your fidelity, Innocence and discretion, the Apron and the Gloves are the marks of the Candor of all the secret Masters in the number of which you have deserved to be introduced My Dear Brother I give you in Quality of Secret Master a rank among the Levites to become a faithfull Guardian at the Sanctum Sanctorum and put you in the number of 7 to fulfill the loss of our Dear Master Hiram Abiff, and one of the Conductors of the works which were raised to the Divinity: The Eye on your Apron is to remember that you shall have a careful Eye and

[4]

Watch the Conduct of the workmen in general."

Sign.

Your sign is that of Silence repeated by one putting the 2 first fingers of the right hand on the lips; The other Answer with the 2d: of the left; Pass word:

Word: the pass word is *Zizon* a hebrew word Signifying Balustrade.

Token: The token is first that of the Master and creep up reciprocally to the Elbow and ballance 7 times with the other; During the ballancing Cross your Legs—

Secret Words: The Secret words are *Job, Adonai* and *Jua*. These are the 3 first names which God gave himself when he Manifested himself to Moses on the Mountain of which you see the 3 Initials traced on the plane of the Triangle: Go brother pass the brethren and then listen to our Doctrine

Lecture.

Q: 1st: are you a Secret Master?
A: 1st: yes I am and glory in it.
Q: 2d: How was you received a Secret Master?
A: 2d: I passed from the square to the Compass.
Q: 3d: Where was you made a Secret Master?
A: 3: Under the Laurel and Olive tree.
Q: 4th: In what place was you received?
A: 4: In the Sanctum Sanctorum.
Q: 5: Who made you?
A: 5: Solomon with Adoniram the Inspector of the works.
Q: 6: Did you perceive any thing on Entering the Sanctum Sanctorum?
A: 6: The Character of the Divinity.
Q: 7: Did you perceive any thing Else on Entering

[5]

the Sanctum Sanctorum?

A: 7: I perceived the great Circle in the middle of which is inclosed the blazing Star which blinded me with holy respect and Contemplation.

Q: 8: What signifies the Hebraic Character in the Triangle?

A: 8: A thing above the Common knowledge of human, that I cannot Pronounce.

Q: 9: We are in the Lodge and that is permitted?

A: 9: I have seen the great Light dazling without knowing it.

Q: 10: What did Inclose that great brightness?

A: 10: The Enefable name of the Grand Architect of the Universe, Moses alone has seen it <he had> the first Pronounciation from the Grand Architect of the Universe when he appeared to him on the Mountain, it was forbid by a Law Moses made publick never to pronounce it, by which <means> we lost the true pronounciation.

Q: 11: What did you perceive more?

A: 11: Nine other words in the Hebraic Characters.

Q: 12: Where were they placed?

A: 12: In 9 Beams that came from the Luminous blazing.

Q: 13: What signifies the 9 names?

A: 13: The 9 names which god gave himself when he spoke to Moses on mount Sinai, making him hope one day his future, Issue, should, know his real name.

Q: 14th: Give them to me with their significations?

A: 14: *Eloah, Adonai, Jehivah, Javhe, Job,*

[6]

Aloim, Achab, Osem and *Jesays* which altogether Compose those Letters which Inclose 72 names who are taken like the name of the Divinity to the Cabalistical Tree, and the Angels Alphabet.

Q: 15: What signifies the Circle that surround the △?

A: 15: It represents the Immensity of the Person of God which hath neither beginning nor End.

Q: 16: What signifies the Blazing Star?

A: 16: It is a Meteor which ought to guide is to the Divine Providence.

Q: 17: What signifies the G in the Center of the blazing <Star?>

A: 17: Glory, Grandeur and Gomer.

Q: 18: What do you mean by those?

A: 18: By glory, God, by Grandeur, I mean the man that might be great by perfection; Gomer a hebrew word Signifies thanks to God for his Supreme power it was the first word that was pronounced by Adam at his beholding Eve.

Q: 19: What signifies the 5 beams of the blazing Star?

A: 19: The 5 Order of Architecture which was used at the Construction of the Temple, The Senses of nature without which men would not be perfect.

Q: 20: What did you see more in the Sanct^{m} Sancto^{m}?

A: 20: The Ark of Alliance; The Golden Candlestick with 7 branches and the Table with bread of proportion.

Q: 21: Where was the Ark of Alliance placed?

[7]

A: 21: In the middle of the Sanctum Sanctorum under the blazing Star.

Q: 22: What doth the Ark and blazing Star represent?

A: 22: As the Ark was the Emblem of Alliance which God had made with his people, it was put under the shadow of the wings of Cherubims, in the like manner is the Arch which Incloses the triangle in the Blazing Star, the Emblem of the Alliance of Brother Masons.

Q: 23: Of what form was the Arck?

A: 23: An Oblong Square.

Q: 24: Of what was it made?

A: 24: Of Shittim wood, Covered within and without with Gold. Topt with <a> Gold Crown and borne by 2 Cherubims of Gold.

Q: 25: What was the name of the cover of the Ark?

A: 25: The Propitiatory, or Place that served to appease gods Anger.

Q: 26: What did it contain?

A: 26: The Testimony which god gave to Moses, The Tables of the Laws.

Q: 27: What did they Contain and of what were they?

A: 27: They were of white Marble and Contained the 10 Commandments in Hebraic Characters.

Q: 28: What were the 10 Commandments?

A: 28: The Decalogue Engraved by Moses and

[8]

dictated by the Almighty: The first table contained the 4 divine and the 2^{d} the 6 human Commandments which ought to be regarded in the duty of Man to Man.

Q: 29: How do you distinguish them?

A: 29: By the divine laws and those of the human laws.

Q: 30: Of what use was the table?

A: 30: To put the 12 loaves of bread of proportion on Which ought always to be in the presence of God as he had ordered to Moses.

Q: 31: Of what were the 12 loaves made?

A: 31: Of the Purest flour.

Q: 32: How were they placed?

A: 32: Six on the right and 6 on the left forming two heaps.

Q: 33: What did they put above?

A: 33: A very bright and pure Ewer.

Q: 34: Why?

A: 34: In order that they should be a monument to the Obligation made to God.

Q: 35: What was the name of the Sanct^{m} Sanctorum in Hebrew?

A: 35: Dabir.

Q: 36: What signifies that word?

A: 36: Speech.

Q: 37: Why so?

A: 37: Because it was there the Divinity resided and where he delivered his Oracles.

Q: 38: Who constructed the Ark?

[9]

A: 38th: When Moses had received the orders from God to Construct the Ark, he made choice of Bezaleel the <son of Uri> the son of Hur of the Tribe of Judah and *Miriam*, Sister to Moses, and of *Aholiab*, son of Ahisimach of the tribe of Dan, the most learned of the people: The populace testified, so much Ardor, for the works and offered with so much Joy to carry the same on; That Moses made publick by sound of trumpet, that he wanted no more. They then began to work by the model God gave Moses and he also shewed the numbers of the sacred vessels that were to be put in the tabernacle to serve for the sacrifices.

Q: 39: What signifies the 7 branches of the Candlestick?

A: 39: The 7 Planets.

Q: 40: What was in the top of each of the 7 branches?

A: 40: A Lamp in each and all of them looked East & West.

Q: 41st: Of how many parts was the Candlestick with the 7 branches composed?

A: 41st: Of Seventy parts.

Q: 42^{d}: What Signifies the number of parts?

A: 42^{d}: The number represents the 12 Signs by which the planets made their Courses and the 7 lamps the 7 planets.

Q: 43: What does the Eye, always in our Lodge represent?

A: 43: An only Eye which enlightens us.

Q: 44: How did they go up to <the> galleries of the Temple?
A: 44: By a Stair Case in the form of a Screw that went up by the 3: 5 and 7 <Steps> fixed on the wall from the <north> side.

[10]

Q: 45: What was the name of the Stair Case?
A: 45: *Cocles* which is to say the form of a Screw.
Q: 46: How many doors were in the Sanct^{m} Sancto^{m}?
A: 46: Only one, on the East side and was called *zizon* and was covered with purple, hyacinth Gold and Azure.
Q: 47: What doth these Colours represent?
A: 47: The four Elements.
Q: 48: How old are you?
A: 48: Three times 27 accomplished 81.
Q: 49: What is the pass word?
A: 49: *Zizon* or Ballustrade.

To Close.

Q: Brother Inspector what is it O Clock?
A: The end of day.
Q: What doth remain to do?
A: To Practice virtue fly vice and remain in Silence.

(Then the Most Powerfull says,) "Since there remains no more to do, than to practice virtue and to fly from vice, Let us Enter into Silence, that the will of God may be done and accomplished. It is time to rest, Brother Inspector give notice by the mysterious number;" when he knocks 7 times, which is answered with their hands as at the opening and says, "this Lodge is closed."

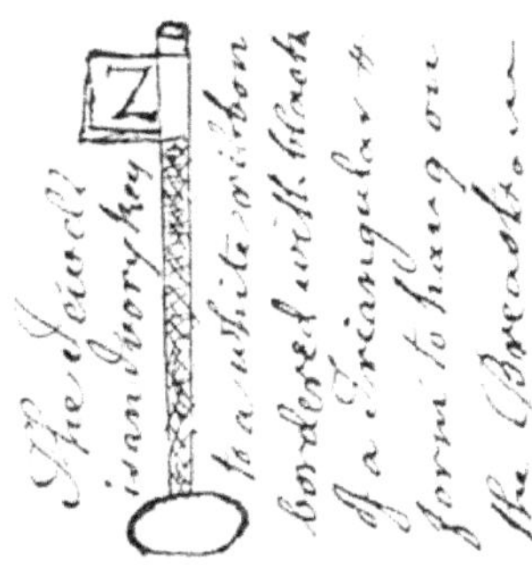

[11]

Perfect Master

The lodge of perfect master ought to be hung with Green; Four white columns of each side placed at equal distance. To be Illuminated with 16 Lights 4 in each Cardinal point. A table before the Canopy Covered with black cloth. Strewed with Tears.

Form of the Lodge

The Most Right Worshipful and respectable Master represents the noble Adoniram, being the first that was made Secret Master. He commanded the works of the Temple before Hiram Abiff: arrived at Jerusalem and afterwards had the Inspection over the workmen at Mount Lebanus. He is decorated with the Ornaments of perfection and if a Prince of Jerusalem with those decorations. He Occupies the Seat of Solomon, placed in the East under a Canopy.

2^d There is but one Warden who represents *Stolken* in the function of Inspector with the Ornaments of his highest Degrees, he is seated in the West.

3^d The other Brethren Assistants, being at least perfect Masters ought to be Decorated with a large green Ribbon on the neck with the Jewell of a Compass, extended to an angle of 60 Degrees.

4th A brother Conductor represents Lebuz,* Captain of the Guards, decorated as the others with a sword in his Hand.

5th All the Brethren must have Aprons of white leather, the flap down and of Green. On the middle of the Apron must be Embroidered or painted in 3

[12]

Circles a Square Stone in the middle of which is the Letter *J* 

* **Lebuz.** This is the copyist's misreading of *Zerbal.*

To Open.

Adoniram Interrogates as follows.

Q: Brother Inspector is the Lodge well Tiled and are we all perfect Masters?
A: Right Worshipfull we are well Tiled and are all Perfect Masters.
Q: Give notice I am going to open this Lodge of perfect Masters?
A: Brethren the Right Worshipfull master gives notice that he is going to open the Lodge.

Then the Right Worshipfull, Strikes with an Iron 4 times, the Brother Inspector in the West 4 the brother in the South 4 and a brother in the North 4 They then make the sign of Admiration altogether

Q: Brother Stocken whats the clock?
A: It is four: Then the Right Worshipfull says, "Since it is 4 tis High time to set the Workmen to work; Give notice that the Lodge of Perfect masters is opened." The Inspector Repeats the same.

Form of Reception

The Candidate must be decorated with the Order of the Secret Master in the Anti Chamber.

After the Lodge is opened, the master of ceremonies goes and Strikes 4 times on the shoulder of the Inspector and says: "There is in the Anti chamber a Brother a secret master and who is desirous to be received and admitted to the Degree of Perfect

[13]

Master." The Inspector reports the same to the Right Worshipful Adoniram, who says "is he well worthy and Qualified to receive that favour; Do you Answer for his zeal fervor and Constancy?" When the Inspector says, "I Answer for him"; Then the Right Worshipfull says, "let him be introduced according to the Ancient form:" When the Inspector orders the Master of Ceremonies to Instruct the Candidate: Who goes to him—Examines him in his former degrees and takes from him all offensive Arms and puts round his neck a string of Green Silk, holding the said string in his left hand, and a naked sword in his right. Conducts him to the door on which he knocks 4 times, which is repeated by the brother Inspector within, who Conveys it to the Right Worshipfull and tells him some Body knocks, the Right Worshipfull orders him to see who it is. When the Inspector orders the Tyler to open the Door halfway, in Order to see who has knocked! After the Tyler has asked; The Master of Ceremonies reports it to the Inspector and shuts the Door, who reports it to to [*sic*] the Right Worshipfull Master. Who gives orders to Introduce him: When the Candidate is Conducted to the Southward of the Tomb traced on the floor of the Lodge: As soon as the Right Worshipfull sees him with the sign of Secret Master on him, he asks him; "What do you demand Brother?" Answer: the favor of being received Perfect Master: Right Worshipfull (says,) "Brother Inspector

[14]

Teach this Brother to Travel." When the Inspector takes him by the Silk String from the South and makes him pass 4 times round the Lodge and then orders him to kneel; After which he passes through the Tomb on each side of the 2 Columns Saltiere.

In Crossing he steps from one to the other, the Candidate having all the while the Sign of Secret Master only, then he is placed opposite the Altar on his right knee a little Bent, after waiting a little while in this Posture he is ordered to kneel, put his right hand on the Bible and take the following Obligation

Obligation "I, A:B: do promise before the grand Architect of the Universe and this respectable Assembly, never to reveal or Communicate to any person whatsoever, to whom the same doth not belong the Secrets of this degree Under any pretence whatsoever, and not to converse but with true brothers known to be such and them Lawfully received. Under the penalty of being dishonored and to suffer what I did impose on myself by my former Obligations so pray God keep me in right and Equity. Amen, Amen, Amen, Amen."

After the Candidate has finished the Above the Right Worshipfull takes the string off his neck and says, "my Dear Brother I draw you from your Vicious Life, and by the power I have received from the most Powerful King of Kings, I raise you <to> the degree of perfect Master on Condition that you Observe what I shall prescribe to you by our Laws."

Sign 1st The sign to be known, in Quality of perfect Master

[15]

is that of Admiration, by Extending the Arms and Hands open, looking up to heaven, then letting them fall on the bottom of the belly and Cross them, then fixing your Eyes on the ground.

Sign 2d The second sign is to Advance reciprocally by degrees the points of your right shoes to each other, (when you wish to know one, who will do the same) then touch the knees mutually and bring your right hand on the heart and then bring it to the Right side in a square, the one as well as the other.

TOKEN The Token is that of the blue Masters Gripe putting the left hand on the others back and press the fingers as if you would enter them 4 times when the other answers *Mahabon,* then Gripe one anothers right hand with four fingers clinched in one anothers, the Thumb upwards form^{g} a Triangle

WORDS The pass word is *Acassia.*

The Secret word is *Jeva.*

Mahabon is the name of the Intendant of Solomon and was a great friend of Hiram Abiff.

THE HISTORY.

Solomon being informed that the Body of Hiram Abiff had been found and already deposited in the lower end of the Temple and being pleased to be able at least to gather the precious remains of so great a man, Ordered the noble Adoniram his grand Inspector to have the Funeral as pompous as possible, forbidding at the same time to Efface the marks of the blood that had been spilled in the Temple, untill Revenge should be performed

[16]

And to furnish themselves at the funeral with white Aprons and Gloves. The noble Adoniram Grand Master Architect and Chief of <the> works from that moment <set about and> gave a plan of a superb monument which was to be raised to his memory and was to be composed of black and white marble which was perfectly finished in 9 days. The heart of the respectable Hiram Abiff was inclosed in an Urn and deposited at the Top of an Obelisk which was placed near the West part of the Temple a little to the North side to shew his murderers had deposited him there first in a Ditch, before they had carried him to the place where the sprig of Cassia was—when Stocken Discovered him first. The Urn in which the heart of Hiram Abiff was deposited was pierced with a sword and every person Qualified went to testify their respect, and when Vengeance was compleat his Body was taken and Inclosed in the Obelisk and Covered with a Triangular Stone on which was engraved M:B and a Sprig of Casia at the Top <thus> . The letters was in Hebrew Characters and was buried in the middle of the great Hall in an Apartment seperated from the Temple where Solomon met to keep a Chapter and used to Confer with Hiram of Tyre and Hiram Abiff on the Sacred Mysteries. He was buried with all honors and solomon ordered that the blood which was spilt in the Temple should remain untill the traitors should be discovered. Three days after the Ceremony Solomon went with all his Court to the Temple, where all the workmen were in the same order as they were at the funeral

[17]

when Solomon directed his prayer to the Lord Examined the Tomb, Canopy *and Triangle, and repeated* the Letters that were Engraved in the Center When he raised his Eyes and hands to Heaven and said with Joy in his heart *It is Compleat,* And by a sign of Admiration the Brethren raised their hands on their right shoulder, stretching their arms and then Crossed and hanging over the Belly saying Amen, Amen, Amen, Amen.

The Lecture.

Q: 1st: Are you a perfect Master?
A: 1: I have seen the Circle and the square put upon the two Columns Across.
Q: 2d: Where were they placed?
A: 2: In the placed where was deposited the Body of our Right Worshipfull Master Hiram Abiff.
Q: 3: What doth the Columns represent?
A: 3: The Columns of Jackin and Boaz which I have passed to attain the Degree of Perfect Master.
Q: 4: What was Solomons intention in creating this degree?
A: 4: Solomon to Encourage the Brethren with a respectable Love and to execite them to a due Enquiry of those bloody ruffians our Dear Master Hiram Abiff: The names of whom they were Ignorant of, but having a suspicion that they were among them. Ordered a General search of the workmen, when they found that there were wanting three, supposed to be guilty; He directed *Adoniram* to raise a superb Tomb, at the west end of the Temple and Inclose thereon at the Top in an Urn, the Heart of Hiram

[18]

Abiff well embalmed of which none had any knowledge, But the perfect Masters. Accordingly, the heart of this respectable Chief was directly closed up in an urn, and the Urn exposed on the Top of the Obelisk untill Vengeance should be accomplished; There ~~appeared~~ appeared through the Urn, a sword, an Emblem of the desire of the brethren to assist and perform vengeance: The Body was buried in a separate Apartment from the Temple where Solomon kept his Chapter.

Q: 5: What did you learn from the Degrees you have past?
A: 5: To Rule my Actions and purify my heart in Order to deserve perfection.
Q: 6: What signifies the Square Stone in the Center of the Circles?
A: 6: It teacheth, that our Edifice ought to have for a foundation a perfect stone from which we are cut and constructed.
Q: 7: What do they represent altogether?

A: 7: The Creation of the Universe which was accomplished by the will of God. And the Action he has given to the primitive Qualities.
Q: 8: What do you mean by that?
A: 8: I mean Cold, heat, and dampness the mixture of which is enclosed in the 4 Elements.
Q: 9: Why are they found in this place?
A: 9: To learn us that God is all and every where and without his help there is no building with Solidity

[19]

Q: 10: What signifies the Letter *J*, which is in the Center of the square Stone?
A: 10: It is the Initial of the second word of the perfect Master.
Q: 11: Pronounce it?
A: 11: *Jeva?*
Q: 12: What doth it signify?
A: 12: It is the name of <the> Grand Architect of the Universe, as it is understood by me.
Q: 13: How was you received perfect Master?
A: 13: The point of a spear to my heart and a halter <round> ~~to~~ my neck.
Q: 14: Why the point to your heart?
A: 14: To make me remember that I have consented it should be snatched out of me, If I should infringe my Obligation and reveal the Secrets of Masonry.
Q: 15: Why the halter round your neck?
A: 15: To learn me that my humiliation ought to be great as I proceed in Masonry and Virtue.
Q: 16: How many signs have you?
A: 16: One by five.
Q: 17: Why one by five?
A: 17: To put me in mind of the degrees I have past.
Q: 18: How many Tokens have you?
A: 18: One by five.
Q: 19: Why one by five?
A: 19: In remembrance of the five points of my En<trance>
Q: 20: What do they signify?
A: 20: The four turns of my Entrance and the 5th of Admiration.
Q: 21: What is the Tomb you past by at your Entrance[?]
A: 21: It is the representation of the burial place

[20]

of Hiram Abiff in the Valley.

Q: 22: Why is it situated at the North East of the Sanct^{m}[?]

A: 22: To learn us that the man ought to be undefiled in Order to render him worthy to enter the Sanctum Sanctorum.

Q: 23: What Signifies the Rope that Comes from the Coffin which is spread as far as the Temple?

A: 23: A Rope that the Brothers used, to take up the Body of Hiram Abiff to put him into his Coffin which was made of green wyth.

Q: 24: Does it signify no more?

A: 24: It does; that we have broke the ties of Sin.

Q: 25: What did you learn on Entering?

A: 25: I have learnt to alter my Steps from Apprentice to fellow Craft from that to Master and to Cross the two Columns.

Q: 26: Why that?

A: 26: To call to my Memory that it has been by passing my first Degrees that I have attained to the Degree of Perfect Master.

Q: 27: Is there no mystery hid under that Signification?

A: 27: It teacheth us that we cannot attain the Sanct^{m} Sanctorum but by purity of manners, Righteousness of heart and Secrets of the first degrees of which there is a School.

Q: 28: Why did you Enter by the Sanctum Sanctorum?

A: 28: To learn me to abandon the Common road.

Q: 29: What Colour is your Collar?

A: 29: Green.

Q: 30: Why Green[?]

A: 30: To remember that being dead in Vice, I hope to revive in virtue and by that attain to the last Degree, in Order to make some progress in the Sublime sciences which I hope to attain and know one day.

Q: 31: Who can Communicate them <to> you?

[21]

A: 31st: God alone, to whom it belongeth to know all things.

Q: 32: What signifies the two pyramids that are seen in your picture?

A: 32: *Egypt*; where the Sciences first took their rise.

Q: 33: What signifies your Jewell?

A: 33: That a perfect master ought only to act with measure, and ought to be attentive always to every thing that is Just.

To Close.

Q: – What is it O Clock Brother?

A – Right worshipful Adoniram it is Five.

Q – "Since it is five and the work is ended; It is time to refresh ourselves: Give notice that I am going to Close this Lodge."

A – Take notice Brethren that this Lodge is going to be closed. Adoniram then knocks 4 times which must be repeated by Stokin; a brother in the South and a brother in the North: Adoniram then makes the Sign of Admiration; the brethren do the same and admire the Tomb; after which the Lodge is Closed.

Jewell: The Jewell of the Perfect Master is a Compass extended to 60 degrees, and hung by a green ribbon round the neck.

[22]

6th Degree.

Intimate Secretary.

There are only two brethren to be in this Lodge when a Reception is to be made—They represent Solomon, and Hiram King of Tyre; both of them are Covered with a Blue Cloak lined with Ermine; A Crown on each of their heads and a scepter in each of their hands: there are to be two drawn swords across the Table, and a roll of parchment. The place where this Lodge is kept represents the hall of Audience of Masons, furnished with black hangings, and strewed with Tears. This Lodge ought to be enlightened with twenty seven lights, in three Candlesticks of nine Lights each, fixed the same as in the Symbolic Lodge East, West and South. This Lodge is Opened and Closed by Twenty seven knocks; Nine at a time; with a little distance between the 8th and 9th.

To Open.

Solomon knocks the twenty seven as above; and Hiram answers the same; when all the Brethren present, bend their right knees, having their hands crossed in such a manner that the two thumbs touch their forehead, and all repeat in a low voice Jova! Jova! Jova! after which they rise; drawing their Swords. Solomon appoints a Captain and Lieutenant of the Guards; (and they all go by the Title of *the Guards.*) He then recommends them to behave themselves with decency, and take particular Care of the security of the Lodge; to keep off all Brethren that would come near: Then *the Guards,* disappear.

[23]

The Guards or Brethren of this Lodge are looked upon as Prefect Masters, and ought to have White Aprons, lined and bordered with a firey Colour; the figure of a Triangle to be painted on the flap of the Apron.

Jewell. The Jewel; Is a Triple Triangle to hang on the breast to a fiery red Ribbond, round the neck.

The Gloves are to be bordered with Red.

After the Guards go out, there remain only Solomon and Hiram of Tyre.

Form of the Reception.

The Candidate being in the Anti Chamber, the Captain of the Guards takes from him his Hatt and Sword; his Apron, Gloves, and the String of Perfect Master, And all Offensive weapons, and then places him by the Door of the Lodge, which is left half open on purpose; his hand across the door, and in this position he peeps, and listens to what passes within, so that Hiram of Tyre may perceive him; At the same time the Guards make a small noise at the door, which Occasions the King of Tyre to turn his head that way, and when he perceives the Cowan, he raises his Eyes upwards and exclaims "Heavens, there is a Listner!" To which Solomon answers, "That it cannot be; since the Guards are on the out side." On which Hiram arises without speaking and runs to the door; seizes

[24]

the Curious by the hand, and draws him into the Lodge; Then he says to Solomon "here he is," To which Solomon says, "What shall we do with him"; Hiram answers (putting his hand to his sword) "We must kill him," On which Solomon quits his place; puts his hands on the Guard of Hirams sword and says "Stop my Brother," He then Strikes a hard blow on the Table; On which the Captain and five or Six of the Guards enter and salute the King; Then Solomon says "Let that Guilty man come forth when wanted; you will answer for him." The Guards then depart with the Prisoner; And Solomon and Hiram of Tyre remain for some time by themselves, speaking very low; Then Solomon strikes a great blow again on the Table, and the Guards immediately enter, conducting the Candidate in the middle of Them and by a Sign of Solomon to the Guards they advance him to the foot of the throne, and then every person is seated; when Solomon speaks as follows; "I have prevailed by the Entreaties with the King of Tyre my Ally, whom your Curiosity had offended, and for which he had pronounced sentence of Death on you: I have not only obtained your pardon, but his consent also to receive you as an Intimate secretary to the cause of our new Alliance: Do you find yourself capable of keeping Inviolably secret the matters which we are willing to discover to you, and are you willing to take an Obligation in the most solemn

[25]

manner (when the Candidate answers, "I consent.") Then Solomon makes him kneel and putting his hands on the Bible, the Candidate takes the following Obligation "I: A:B. do promise and swear in the presence of the Grand Architect of the Universe, and this Right Worshipfull Assembly never to reveal direct or Indirectly, to any person under the Heavens, any matters or things that is now about to be communicated to me in this degree of the Intimate Secretary nor to any brother of a lower degree: I further promise that I will attend all summonses sent me from this Lodge; and strictly observe and keep as near as possible in my power, all the Laws and Constitutions of this Lodge: I further do promise and swear that I will always pay due regard and Submission to all sentences and Decrees, of the Grand Council of Jerusalem; under no less penalty than to have my body dissected my bowels torn from thence, and my heart into piece meal, and the whole thrown to the wild Beasts of the forest, So help me God to persevere in the same—Amen!"—After this Solomon shews the Candidate the Draft, and Explains the same to him as follows; "The Window that appears to be in the Cloud, represents the Vault of the Temple, and in the Glazing there is an (I.) which is the Initial of the name of the

[26]

Grand Architect of the Universe;—The Tears and Mausoleum refers to the Chamber of Audience of Masons in the palace, lined with Black Cloth, where Solomon used to retire and grieve the unhappy fate of Hiram Abiff, and where Hiram of Tyre found Solomon when he came to visit him: The letter *A.* in the Mausoleum signifies *Alliance*; the *P.* at the right of the Mausoleum signifies *Promise*: and the other P. to the left means *Perfection*."—After this Solomon says "Dear Brother, I receive you as an Intimate secretary; promise me to be faithfully cemented to the Order in which you have entered, as was that great man whose place you have supplied; The Colour of the ribbon which decorates you, ought to bring to your remembrance, the blows which the cruel Assassins gave him; and his blood, which he chose rather to have spilt to the last drop, than to reveal the Mysteries of Masonry; We hope my dear Brother, that your fidelity will be stedfast to every proof, and this sword with which I am arming you will defend <you> against the Temerity of any who dare to surprize you in what we are going to Instruct you."

1st: SIGN. The first sign is made by carrying your right hand to your left shoulder, and draw it down to your right hip in Token of your Obligation.

2d: SIGN. The second sign is by Crossing your hands and Arms, letting them fall on your sword side, and then raising your Eyes to heaven.

[27]

TOKEN. The Token is to take each others right hand, One says, *Birit*; turning the others hand with the back part downwards; then the other turns it up and says *Neder*; the first person turns it again and says *Selemoth*, which signifies *Alliance*; Promise (and) Perfection.

1st–PASS WORD, is Joabert, the name of the Candidate; or Curious Brother.

2d: PASS WORD, is *Zerbal*, the name of the Captain of the Guards.

THE GRAND WORD is Jova!

THE HISTORY.

Solomon in Consequence of the treaty which his Ambassadors had made with the King of Tyre, was to give him in return for the materials which had been taken from Mount Lebanus and the Quarries of Tyre for the building of the Temple (in part of which he had already furnished him with certain measures of Oil, Honey and wheat) a promise of Thirty Cities in Galalee, and which was to be complied with after the Temple was finished and Compleated: It happened that Solomon was one year, without granting them and Hiram having visited them and finding the Land Steril, the people rude, uncultivated and of bad Morals; and also considering, it would be more expence than profit to him; he resolved to go in person to Solomon and complain of his breach of promise and Agreement, being arrived

[28]

at Jerusalem; he made his Entry through the Guards, which were in the Court, and proceeded directly to the Kings Apartment where Solomon was giving himself up to Grief for Hiram Abiff. King Hiram went in, in a manner so hasty, that one of Solomons favorites named *Joabert*, perceiving it, and fearing he went with an Intention to Execute some bad design against Solomon, he followed him and went to the door to Listen; Hiram perceiving it, Exclaimed "Oh Heaven—they hear us," (or words to that Effect) and ran to the door immediately and pulled him into the Chamber, and said to Solomon "Here he is"; Solomon, seeing him could not doubt, and said, "What shall we do with him"; to which Hiram replied, "We must kill him," and putting his hand on his sword for that purpose, Solomon rising from the Throne and preventing him, says, "Stop your hand my Brother," and then gave a great knock on the Table, upon which the Guards entered, to whom Solomon said; "Seize, Joabert that wicked man, withdraw with him, and you will answer to me for his appearance." When Solomon was alone with Hiram, he thus addressed him; "Sire, Joabert is the greatest favorite I have, and of all the Lords in my Court, he is the most attached to me;—I am well convinced of his design; and what he has done, was to preserve me from your Anger;

[29]

The Alteration he saw in your countenance, when you came through the Court, he had excited his Curiosity; I therefore pray you to revoke your sentence, and I will answer for his zeal and discretion." The King of Tyre perceiving by the Intercession, Solomon made for his favorite how dear he was to him, freely gave his Consent to every thing which Solomon had desired; And before they seperated, they renewed their former Alliance, with promises that they would be Allies offensive and defensive, and signed the treaty which was kept unalterable with other matters; to which Joabert was the Intimate Secretary.

The Lecture.

Q: 1st. Are you an Intimate secretary?
A – I am! (and raises his Eyes to heaven.)
Q: 2d How was you received?
A – By Curiosity.
Q:–3 What danger did you risk?
A – The loss of my life.
Q:–4 What did they do with you after you was surprized?
A – They put me into the hands of the Guards and I received sentence of Death.
Q:–5 Were they Intimate secretarys or perfect Masters?
A – I then was Ignorant thereof; but by my resolution firmness and Stability, it proved to me that I was truly the first who had been Initiated into the Degree of an Intimate secretary.

[30]

Q:–6th What are the pass words?
A – *Joabert* and *Zerbal.*
Q: 7. What do you mean by Joabert and Zerbal?
A – Joabert was the name of Solomons favorite, who Listened at the door; and Zerbal is the name of the Captain of the Guards.
Q: 8 What is the Grand Word?
A – *Jova.*
Q: 9 What was you before you was received Intimate Secretary?
A – A favorite of Solomons.
Q: 10. Of what Province?
A – Of Capula.
Q: 11 Your Surname?
A – Capulist.
Q: 12 How many Governments did Solomon give the King of Tyre to recom-

pence him for the materials which he had furnished him with, for the Construction of the Temple?

A – Thirty.

Q: 13 Where was you received?

A – In Solomons Apartment lighted by Twenty seven Candles and hung with black.

Q: 14 What does the letter *I* signify, which you saw in the window?

A – It is the Initial of the third name of the Grand Architect of the Universe, which in this Degree signifies "Give thanks to God, the work is done."

Q: 15 What signifies the *A.* and 2 *Ps*: in the triangle?

A – The *A* means *Alliance*; the first *P.* signifies *promise*, and the second, stands for *Perfection.*

Q: 16 Why is this Lodge lighted by twenty seven Candles?

A – To represent the 2700 Candlesticks Solomon had made for the use of the Temple.

[31]

Q: 17th What represents the Grand Door?

A – The Entrance of Solomons Palace.

Q: 18 What signifies the Triple Triangle which hangs to the lower end of your Ribbon?

A – The three Theological Virtues of faith; Hope and Charity;—You may also give it another interpretation Solomon; Hiram of Tyre, and Hiram Abiff.

To Close.

Q: What is the hour?

A – It is Nine.

The Lodge is then Closed in the same manner as it was Opened by Twenty seven knocks, (that is) three times nine, a little distance or pause being made between the Eighth and the ninth.

[31]

7th Degree.

Prevost and Judge.

(by some called Irish Master.)

This lodge must be illuminated by 5 great lights one in each Corner; with one in the Center and adorned with Red. The Master is called Thrice Illustrious; placed in the East, under a blue Canopy, with a parcell of Stars round him; He represents Tito prince Herodim the Eldest of the Prevost and Judges, first Grand Warden and Inspector of the three Hundred Architects who Used to draw the plans for the workmen.

[32]

In this Lodge there are two Wardens.

To Open.

Q: Illustrious Brother Wardens are we tiled?
A. Thrice Illustrious we are well Tiled.
Q. Where is your Master placed?
A. Every where.
Q. Why so?
A. To supervise the Conduct of the workmen, and preside over their works; rendering Justice to every one.
Q. What is it O Clock?
A. Break of Day; Eight O Clock, two and seven.

Then the thrice Illustrious knocks 4 times quick and one separate; which is repeated by the 2 Wardens, after which the Thrice Illustrious says, "As it is 8 O Clock, two and seven, It is time to proceed to work"; which is repeated by the Wardens; After which all the Brethren Clap four and one separate; Then the Master says, "The Lodge is Opened."

Form of Reception.

In this Lodge is a Master of Ceremonies, who proceeds to the preparing room; and Conducts the Candidate to the door of the Lodge, on which he knocks four and one separate, which is repeated within by the Thrice Illustrious and the two Wardens: The thrice Illustrious then Orders a brother to go and see who knocks, when the Tyler informs that brother "That Brother N.N. desires to pass to the Degree of Prevost and Judge," which he reports to the Thrice Illustrious, who gives orders that the Master of Ceremonies must examine the Candidate, and then Introduces him in the Antient form; Whereupon

[33]

the Master of Ceremonies Introduces the Candidate, and brings him between the Wardens; The Senior Warden takes him by the hand and directs him to kneel, When the Candidate is Ordered to say "*Civi*," The Senior Warden lays a naked sword on his left shoulder; After about a minutes pause; The Thrice Illustrious says "Ky," on which the Senior Warden raises the Candidate, and leads him seven times round the Lodge – It is to be Observed, that at every turn, when opposite to the Thrice Illustrious he pays his Obedience in making the signs of his preceeding degrees, beginning with that of "Entered Apprentice, and Ending at the sixth Turn with that of Intimate Secretary"; On the seventh or last round, he is led to the Altar, where the Thrice Illustrious speaks as follows. "Respectable Master, with great Joy, I am going to recompense your zeal and attachment for the Master of Masters, and to appoint you Prevost and Judge over all the workmen of this Lodge; As we are convinced of your discretion, so without any hesitation, we will confide in you the most important secret; Do your duty in the degree in which you will be Elevated, as you have done in the preceeding Degrees: I trust you with the key of the place where it is kept, the body of our Respectable Master Hiram Abiff, and Assure us you will never discover the place, where he is intered; kneel therefore and pronounce to me the following Obligation on the holy Bible. "I. N.N. do promise and swear before the Grand Architect of the Universe, and these

[34]

Illustrious Brethren here present, never to reveal any matter which Concerns the degree of a Prevost and Judge, directly or Indirectly to any person whomsoever, below this degree, and that I will regulate justly and impartially all matters between brethren; That I will be just and Equitable to all the world as I am constituted by this Lodge to render Justice; That I will pay just and due Obedience to the mandates and Commands of the Grand Council of Princes of Jerusalem, and regulate myself by their Recommendation; All this I promise under the penalties of my preceeding Obligations so God maintain me in Equity and Justice. Amen! Amen! Amen!" After this Obligation, The Thrice Illustrious orders the Candidate to arise and come to him; he then gives him a stroke with the scepter on each shoulder, and says, "By the power given me and with which I am invested, I Constitute you Prevost and Judge over all the work and workmen of the Temple: I decorate you in this Quality with

JEWEL} a Golden Key, suspended to this red Ribbon which you are to wear in the form of a Collar;
APRON} This Apron is lined with the same Colour; the red signifies the Ardor of the Master, and the pockett in the Center of the Apron, is to keep the Keys of the Plans.
SIGN} The sign is to bring the two first fingers of the right hand to the Nose; the Answer is to put the 2 first fingers of the right hand to the Nose and the Thumb under your Chin forming a square.
TOKEN} The Token is Interlacing of the little fingers of the right hand, and strike seven times in the palms of each others hand with the middle finger.

[35]

PASS WORD} The pass word is *Tito*.
WORDS The Words are seven fold; – Civi; Ky; Jua; Hiram; Stolkin; Geometras; Architect; and Xinxe.
GRAND WORDS} The Grand Word is *Jachinia*.
NB. There must be a key painted on the flap of the Apron.

THE LECTURE.

Q:–1st Are you a prevost and Judge?
A: – I render Justice to all the workmen without Exception.
Q:–2d How was you introduced into this Lodge?
A: – By four distinct knocks; and one separate.
Q:–3 What signifies the 4 and one separate numbers?
A: – The 4 signifies the 4 sides of the Temple, and the 1 the Temple itself, in which we ought to pay our devotions to God.
Q:–4 Who did you meet with, at the Entrance of the Lodge?
A: – A Warden, who conducted me to the west.
Q:–5 What was done afterwards?
A: – The Senior Warden made me kneel on my right knee and pronounce the word, Civi!
Q:–6 What did the thrice Illustrious Answer?

A: – After a little pause he said Ky!

Q:–7 What signify those words?

A: – *Civi* is to kneel; and Ky to arise.

Q:–8 What did the thrice Illustrious after that?

A: – From the Opinion which he had of my Zeal, he constituted me Prevost and Judge.

Q:–9 What did he deliver to you?

A: – A Golden Key, to distinguish this Degree; and then he gave me the sign; Token and Words.

Q:–10 What is the use of the key?

A: – To open a small Ebony box, where all the plans are kept, necessary for the Construction of the Temple.

[36]

Q:–11th What does all this signify?

A: – It signifies that only the Prevost and Judge knew where the heart of our Respectable Master Hiram Abiff is deposited.

Q:–12 What is the Word?

A: – *Tito.*

Q:–13 What signifies the Word?

A: – It is the name of the Past Grand Warden Harodim the Eldest Prevost and Judge who had the Inspection over the 300 Master Architects of the Temple.

Q:–14 What did you perceive in the Lodge?

A: – A Curtain; within which was suspended, a small Ebony Box enriched with Jewels.

Q:–15. What was in that Box?

A: – All the Designs which were necessary, for the Construction of the Temple.

Q:–16. Did you see any thing else?

A: – I saw a Triangle or a Deltha △ in the Center of the Lodge in which was the Letter *A*.

Q:–17. What signify them?

A: – That God was the Grand Architect of the Temple; and that he had inspired David with the Design and Solomon with the Execution thereof.

Q:–18. What was there more?

A: – A Balance.

Q:–19. What signifies the Balance?

A: – The Exactitude which we ought to Imitate, as our particular duty, being constituted and appointed in this Degree to decide all matters and differences that may arise among the workmen.

Q:–20. Where doth repose the heart of Hiram Abiff?

[37]

A: – In an Urn of Gold, on the Top of the Obelisk.
Q:–21st. What signifies the two letters *X* and *I*?
A: – Xinxe and Jackania: Xinxe the seat of the soul which is to pass; and Jackania, is the name of God; to whom the soul of man is to pass in hopes of mercy.
Q:–22d What signifies the Letters I.H.S. with the sprig of Cassia?
A: – The *I.* signifies Jua; the *H.* means Hiram and the *S.* Stolkin; the last is the name of him who found the body of Hiram Abiff under the sprig of Cassia which was put on the Grave, and was the means of finding him.
Q:–23 In what place was you received?
A: – In the middle Chamber.
Q:–24 Have you ever worked on any thing remarkable in quality of Prevost and Judge?
A: – I was put to perfect the Tomb of Hiram Abiff.
Q:–25 What did the Thrice Illustrious present you with when he invested you Prevost and Judge?
A: – A white Apron lined with red of a fiery Colour, on which was a pockett and a red and white rose.
Q:–26 What is the use of the pockett?
A: – To keep the plans secure for the Eldest Prevost and Judge, in carrying them to the Temple to communicate them to the Masters, and to take the proportions of the Threshings of the floor.
Q:–27 What means the Red and the white Rose?
A: – The *Red* repesents the blood of Hiram Abiff and the *white* the Candour of the Master.
Q:–28 What was Solomon's Intention in creating this Degree?
A: – It was necessary to create Order among such a number of the Brethren; Joabert was honored with

[38]

the Intimate Confidence of this Monarch, and received a new mark of distinction; Solomon first created *Tito*, prince Harodim; Adoniram and his father Prevost and Judges, and gave orders to them to Initiate Joabert his favorite into the most secret mystery, and to give him the key of all the plans of the Buildings, which were inclosed in a small Ebony Box, suspended in the Sanctum Sanctorum under a Rich Canopy: When

Joabert was admitted in that sacred place, he was seized with great Admiration and falling on his knees he pronounced "*Civi*"! Solomon seeing him prostrate said to him "*Ky*"! and gave him a Balance as a Badge of his Office, and his knowledge was Augmented thereby.

To Close.

Q: – What Age are you?
A – Four times Sixteen.
Q: – From whence came you?
A: – I came and am going every where.
Q: – What is it O Clock?
A: – Break of Day;—Eight, two and Seven.
Q: – How so?
A: – Because a Prevost and Judge must be ready at any hour to administer Justice.

Then the Thrice Illustrious close the Lodge by four and one as in the Opening.

Jewell A Golden key with a Triangle in the wards, and an A in the Triangle. It is to be suspended by a fiery red Ribbon in the form of a Collar, round the neck.

[39]

Intendant of the Buildings or Master in Israel

(many French Lodges call it Scots Master of three times 9.)

This lodge ought to be decorated with red hangings, and Lighted by Twenty seven Candles, distributed by 3 times 9; and also Five other great lights on the Altar before the Thrice Puissant Master who represents Solomon: The first Warden who is called "Inspector," represents the Thrice Illustrious Brother Tito, prince Harodim;—The second Warden represents Adoniram the Son of Abda; All the rest are ranged regularly. —The Thrice Puissant and all the Brethren are decorated, with a large red ribbon from the right shoulder to the left hip, to which is suspended a Triangle hung to a green Ribbon; on one side of the Triangle must be the three Hebrew Words, "Benchorim;" "Achard," and "Jackania," which signifies "Free Mason;"

Jewel} One God! "Oh! You Eternal! And of the other side in Hebrew "Judea;" "Ky;" "Jea"! meaning God! Puissant; God! God!

Apron A white Apron lined with Red; bordered with Green, in the Center is a star with nine points, and above it, is a Balance: On the flap is painted a Triangle, with one of the three Letters B.A.I. in each Angle. The Thrice Puissiant in the East;—The Right Worshipful Brother Tito, in the West, And Adoniram the Introductor in the Angle ready to receive the Orders from the Right Worshipful Brother Tito the Inspector.

To Open.

The Thrice Puissant with a Scepter in his hand says "Brother Tito are we Tiled? A: Thrice Puissant we are all Tiled.

[40]

Q: What is it O Clock?
A: Break of Day.

Then the Thrice Puissant strikes 5 times with his scepter on the Altar, which is repeated by Tito and Adoniram: When the Thrice Puissant says, "As it is break of Day my dear brethren 'tis time to begin the work. The Lodge is now Open."

After which all the brethren clap 5 times together, and make the signs of surprise and Admiration; that of surprize is the right hand to the forehead, extended from the Thumb, as if to prevent the glaring of the Light; that of Admiration is to extend both Arms and hands, looking up, the head reclined on the Right shoulder.

Form of Reception.

The Candidate is to be barefooted: The Thrice Puissant speaks to brother Tito, as follows, "Brother Tito can we repair the Loss of our dear Chief Hiram Abiff? You know he had in Charge the Ornaments of the secret Chamber, which contained the Holy Ark, that was Given to the Isralites to Assure them of the presence and protection of the most Holy God; He is now taken from us by the most <horrible> crime, and we are by that means deprived of that respectable Chief: See my Illustrious brother if you are able to give one Advice in this great Matter."—When in reply Tito says, "I feel in myself a very great difficulty to advise, what ought to be done in this Case; I however think the only remedy is to create one of the Chiefs from each of the Orders of Architecture in Order to Assist us all, in our Capacities and

[41]

Endeavours to finish the work of the secret chamber of the third Story": Then the Thrice Puissant says, "Your Counsel my Dear brother is too Good not to be observed, and to prove that I am willing to follow it, I establish you brother Tito, brother Adoniram and brother Abda Inspectors, and Conductors of this Work, and see in the middle Chambers if you can meet with 5 Chiefs of the 5 Orders of Architecture: Excellent brother Adoniram go into the middle Chamber and make a trial among the workmen to that Effect"; Adoniram (as Introductor) then goes into the middle Chamber, where he finds Joabert and others, And he then says, "Brethren," are here any of the Chiefs of the five Orders of Architecture," to which Joabert answers, "I am one," The Introductor says to him, "My Dear Brother, have you the zeal to apply yourself with attention to all the work which the Thrice Puissant will commit to your Care"; In reply to which Joabert answers, "I shall regard and consider it as the greatest happiness and advantage which can happen to me, to comply always in every manner the Thrice Puissant may be pleased to entrust to my Charge, and to raise the Edifice to his Honor and Glory;"—Then Adoniram demands the signs, Token and words of the three first degrees; which is given; After which the Introductor strikes 3, five and 7 at the door; A demand is then made from within, what he wants; He replies, "there is one who is to be employed, in the works of the middle Chamber;" When the door

[42]

is opened; Then the Introductor takes him by the Masters Gripe, and Introduces him before the Altar and lays him down on his back—Tito stands behind him and gives him a branch of Cassia in his right hand, and in this position he takes the following Obligation; "I. N.N. do promise in the presence of the Grand Architect of the Universe and before the Thrice Illustrious brethren here present, to keep eternally secret the Mysteries of this degree, which shall at this time, or at any other time hereafter be revealed unto me, and that I will pay due reference and submit to all decrees and regulations which shall be transmitted to me by the Grand Council of Princes of Jerusalem; Under the penalty of all my former Obligations and to have my Body severed in two and my bowels torn from thence, So God maintain me in Equity and Justice, Amen!"—The moment the Candidate pronounces the last word of this Obligation, brother Tito covers his body with a red viel, and relieves him by raising him by the masters Gripe, with the left hand to the Elbow; thus raised, he sets him on a Stool: And the thrice Puissant says to him as follows, "My Dear and Worshipfull brother; Solomon being willing to carry the highest perfection the work already begun, he was obliged to employ the 5 Chiefs of the 5 orders of Architecture and gave the Command over them to Tito, Adoniram and Abda his father, As Solomon was convinced of their zeal and Capacity in exerting all their power to the rendering perfect such a glorious Work; We flatter ourselves my brother that you will contribute all you can to attain the

[43]

same end:—The situation of Death in which you have been placed, shews, that you can imitate our Respectable Master Hiram Abiff in this work, only by the same firmness in despising Death, rather than deliver up the mysteries of our Orders; We have no doubt but you will do the same; I am going to relieve you in the same manner as he was raised from under the sprig of Casia," On which the Candidate is raised, and then the Thrice Excellent brother Tito gives him the following Signs, Token and Words.

SIGN 1st: The first is of surprize, by putting the Thumb of both hands, to the

Temples of the head; – the hands forming a Square, going 2 steps backwards and then coming up immediately with 2 steps forwards; then they bring the hands over the Eye brows and says "Benchorim"!

SIGN 2d. The second is by Interlacing the fingers of both hands, with the palms of the hands turned downwards as low as the Waist, and looking up to heaven each brother says "Achard."

SIGN 3d. The third sign is of Grief, figurative to the fellow Crafts sign, with the left hand on the hip, and balances with the knees 3 times; Then one says "Ky!" and the other says "Jea!" which is God.

TOKEN. The Token is to Clasp each others heart with the right hand; after which pass the right hand to each others middle arm, and which the left hand take hold of the Elbow; pass it three times; the one says, "Jackania," and the other answers "Judea."

THE LECTURE.

Q: 1st Are you an Intendant of the Buildings?

A: – I have made the 5 Steps of Exactitude, I have penetrated into the inmost part of the Temple;

[44]

I have seen a great Light, in the middle of which I have also seen three Mysterious Letters *I.I.I.* in hebrew Characters without knowing what they meant.

Q:–2d How was you received?

A: – By acknowledging my Ignorance.

Q:–3 Why was you received?

A: – To disipate darkness and procure me a true light to rule my heart and Enlighten my Understanding.

Q:–4. Where was you introduced?

A: – In a marvellous place full of Charms where reside Truth and sovereign Wisdom.

Q:–5. What is your Duty?

A: – To encourage all our brethren by Example to the practice of Virtue and to Correct the works.

Q:–6. How came they thus to desire of you, a proof of your being a fellow Craft and Master before you was received?

A: – To shew by graduation, that I am able to come to perfection.

Q:–7. What does the 3 first Degrees teach you?

A: – The Apprentice Moral Virtue; the fellow Craft political Virtue, and the Master Heroic Virtue.

Q:–8. How came they to make you advance in the steps of this Degree backwards and forward?

A: – To Demonstrate by graduation that we ought to sett in opposition Humility to pride, which is natural to us, and that we are to Advance in Virtue, and make it a Rule to form our Actions by, and never to do any thing, but what is decent.

Q:–9th Do you know how to Explain the Mysteries of your Lodge?

[45]

A: I will endeavour as much as possible.

Q: 10: What signifies the 3 Mysterious letters in the angles of your Jewell?

A: Jackinia, Jua and Jeva, those words signifies Divine Beauty, Divine Wisdom and the Initial of the Innamable word.

Q: 11: What signifies the circles in the Triangles?

A: To mark the Immensity of God, which has neither beginning nor End.

Q: 12: What Signifies the 4 Letters in the Circle J:A:I:N?

A: Oh you Eternal possessing all divine attributes.

Q: 13: What are the principle attributes of the Divinity?

A: Beauty 6. Wisdom 7. Boundless Mercy 14. Omniscience 11. Eternity 8. Perfect^{n}. 10 – Justice 7. Tenderness 10. Creation 8. 81.

Q: 14: Explain to me the Square which you saw in the triple Triangle?

A: Nine virtuous Attributes.

to the 3 first	9	9	9	9	27	form the square of 9 which
to the 3 second	9	9	9	9	27	added together makes 81
to the 3 third	9	9	9	9	27	

Q: 15th: How came they to place Solomon in the Temple?

A: To shew that he was the first that Consecrated a Temple to the true God.

Q: 16: How came they to put a Brazen Sea in the Temple?

A: To advertize that the Temple of God is holy which you cannot Enter without being purified of all uncleanness.

Q: 17: What signifies that left side of the Temple?

A: Masonic order under the Law of Types & Ceremonies.

Q: 18: What signifies the right side of the Temple?

A: True masonry under the Law of Grace and Truth.

Q: 19: What signifies the Tomb which is on the pavement

[46]

by the door of the Sanctuary in the Degree of Prevost and Judge?

A: It teacheth, that after being purified by Death, we can be introduced in the presence of the divinity.

Q: 20: What signifies the Candlestick with 7 branches?
A: The presence of the holy Spirit in the heart of every true observer of the Laws of God.
Q: 21st: What was the reason of your being bare footed at your Reception?
A: As I entered on some holy matters, and because Moses was the same when he entered the holy Land.
Q: 22^{d}: What did you hear before you entered?
A: Five great knocks.
Q: 23: What do they denote?
A: The 5 points of Felicity.
Q: 24: What did they produce?
A: A Warden.
Q: 25: What did they do with you?
A: He led me 5 times round the Temple and sustaint'd me.
Q: 26: How so?
A: to admire the Beauty of it.
Q: 27: What did those 5 Steps imprint in you?
A: Great surprize, Admiration and grief.
Q: 28: Why so?
A: On account of what I saw inclosed in the blazing Star.
Q: 29: What was Inclosed therein?
A: The holy name of the Grand Architect of the Universe.
Q: 30th: What is the reason that, Star, had only 5 Rays?
A: In allusion to several things 1st: the 5 Orders of Architecture which was used in the Construction of the Temple 2^{d}: the 5 points of felicity and 3^{d}: the 5 fences of nature without which a man cannot be perfect 4th: the 5 lights of masonry and 5th: the 5 Zones of the world Inhabited by Masons.
Q: 31st: What are the 5 points of felicity?
A: To go; to Interceed; to pray; to Love and help your Brother.
Q: 32^{d}: How came you to be seized with Admiration and Grief?
A: On seeing the Beauty of the Temple and all its Ornaments.

[47]

Q: 33^{d}: Did you see all its Beauties?
A: I saw only a part.
Q: 34: What was the reason of your not seeing the whole?
A: A think viel which Covered the rest prevented me but my zeal to arrive to the perfection of the Royal art will I hope one day disclose to my Eyes <what is hid by> the present Obstacles.
Q: 35: How came you to Grieve?

A: Because these Ornaments brought to my mind our dear brother and Master Hiram Abiff, Inhumanly sacrificed.

Q: 36: Was you Struck with grief?

A: No. I should have been so if I had not been sustained and held by some, whom I afterwards knew to be brothers.

Q: 37th: How did you know them to be brothers?

A: By the Grand Ineffable name which they invoked after they had pronounced *Jackinai* which is the sacred name that I saw in the Center of the blazing Star.

Q: 38: Have you promised to keep secret all those things which you saw?

A: Yes I have Illustrious Master.

Q: 39th: What did you impose on yourself in case of failure?

A: To have my body severed in two and my bowels torn from thence.

Q: 40: How have you marched?

A: By 5 grave steps which I made in Advanceing to the Illustrious when I went to pronounce my Obligation.

Q: 41: How came you to appear as a dead man and covered with a red Viel?

A: To Understand that all brethren must be dead to the world and all its Vices.

Q: 42^{d}: What Signifies the ballance given to you?

A: A ballance is an Attribute of Justice which was given me to Exercise Justice Indifferently among Masons and to rectify my Conduct Justly. If I am willing to deserve the title and name given me when I received the Degree of Prevost and Judge of the build^{ings}

[48]

Q: 43: Have you seen your Illustrious Master this day?

A: Yes I have seen him.

Q: 44: Where was he placed?

A: In the East under a Celestial Canopy spread with brilliant Stars.

Q: 45: How was he clothed?

A: In blue with Gold.

Q: 46: Why in this dress?

A: Because god appeared in blue and gold to Moses on Mount Sinai when he gave him the Tables of the Law.

Q: 47: Did you continue in darkness?

A: The Morn^{g} is light by me and the mysterious Star is my Guide.

Q: 48: Where have you been Conducted?

A: I cannot tell.

Q: 49: What <age> are you?

A: Twenty Seven.

Q: 50: What numbers have you marked?

A: 5, 7 and 15.

Q: 51st: Where have you attained those numbers?

A: In the manner as they placed the Lights.

Q: 52: What do they signifie?

A: I have already explained the two first, the last represents the 15 Masters who found the Body of H:A. under the Sprig of Cassia.

Q: 53: What is the Reason of the green Colour on y^{r} Apron?

A: That I am to expect to arrive by my Virtue to the most Sublime knowledge by my zeal and Study in masonry.

Q: 54: What signifies your Jewell?

A: The Triple Essence of the Divinity?

Q: 55: What is the hour?

[49]

A: Seven at Night.

To Close

My dear Brethren as you practice the 5 points of felicity it is high time to refresh and repose ourselves. Then the thrice Illustrious knocks 5 which is repeated by the Wardens and repeated by all the brethren by 5, 7 and 15 and Closed.

[49]

Elected Knights

The thrice puissant in the East, a Table before him Covered with black. In this Chapter there is only one Warden who goes by the name of *Stolkin* placed in the west with 7 other Brethren round him.

Here must be one Light in the East and 8 in the West.

To Open

Q: Are you an Elected knight?
A: One Cavern received me, One Lamp lighted me and a Spring refreshed me.
Q: Whats the Clock?
A: Break of day.

On which the thrice puissant knocks 8 quick and one Slow which

[50]

is first answered by Stolkin and then by all the Brethren with their hands, when the thrice Powerfull says "the Chapter is open."

Preparation

There must be a little place very Dark, the representation of a Cavern, in which must be a Lamp a fountain running into a Bason, a little Table, on which must be a poinard and a head bloody with hair on it, a large Stone to sit on by the Table, under the lamp must be wrote in large letters *vengeance*. The Candidate who represents Joabert must be in another room at some distance from the Cavern where he stays, untill sent for. N:B: the Chapter must be hung with black. All the brethren in the Chapter when a Reception is made, must be in black, their hats flapt sitting with their right legs over their left knee, leaning with their heads on their right hand, their Aprons bordered with black. A Broad black Order from their left shoulder to their right hip, a poinard hanging thereto. A nine fold Rose,

4 on each side and 1 at the bottom made of pink ribbon. One of the brethren who Officiates as master of Ceremonies goes out to the Candidate and knocks 9 times as aforesaid. When the thrice powerfull gives orders to let him in, (All the brethren in their proper Attitudes) he is led behind Stolkin, where he stays all the while. When the thrice Puissant asks him—

Q: What do you want?
A: To be admitted to the degree of Knight elected.
Q: Have you Courage enough to revenge the death of your Master[?]
A: I have.

Then the thrice Puissant says "if you have, I must acquaint you, with the place where one of the Murderers is had, which I had of a Stranger, and if you have Resolution enough

[51]

<as> you say to Revenge the death of your master, follow the Stranger." On which his Eyes are bound and he is carried to the Cavern and <set> down upon the Stone by the head of the Traitor. the Master of the Ceremonies tells him—"After I am gone, you may take off the bandage from your eyes—do not be afraid, but take Courage. I will not stay long from you. I will return and succor you—drink from the Cup you will find near you." N:B: generally a little of the spirit of Vitrol is put with <the water> to make it taste sour. Then he is left alone, and the door shut upon him for about 2 or 3 minutes. After which the master of the Ceremonies goes into him and tells him to take the head in his left hand and the poinard in his right he then Conducts <him> to the door of the Chapter and strikes 8 and 1 with his foot very hard, when the master of the Ceremonies who has given him his Lesson and is come into the Lodge (Opens the door and asks him what he wants) The Candidate answers "An Intendant of the Building demands to enter the Chapter" (Master of Ceremonies says) "Have you finished your time and have you satisfied your Master"—Answer "I have done a great honor for the service of the Craft, an Action which I have done to deserve this degree I now require." Of which Stolkin makes a report (being informed thereof) to the Thrice Powerfull who orders the Candidate to be introduced and is ordered to make 8 steps quick and one slow, in his proper posture, Holding the head by the hair, in his left and the poinard in the right hand

[52]

as if ready to Strike, brings him to the Pedestal when he falls on his knees. When the Thrice Powerfull sees him thus arrayed he says "Oh! Dismal what have you done, Do you know that you have deprived me of the oppertunity of punishing the Villian myself! Therefore Stolkin put him to death." On which all the brethren fall on their knees and Stolkin and all Assure the thrice Powerfull that what he had done was through zeal and not with an Intention to wrest the power from his hands. The King then Orders Stolkin to stop and tells Joabert that he forgives <him> this second time, but to take care how he Offends him the third time. After which Stolkin takes the head from him and lays it at the foot of the Pedestal and the Poinard on the top, when the Candidate being still on his knees takes the following Obligation. "I, N.N. do promise and solemnly swear, before the Grand Architect of the Universe and this Illustrious, Assembly, which composes this Chapter, never to reveal the secrets of the knight Elected which is going to be revealed unto me but only to a brother known to be such on the penalty of this and all my former Obligations I promise to revenge the most Execrable murder which has been Committed, and <on> all Villians who shall betray or discover the secrets of this degree like those old Ruffians, and to help an protect the order with all my might, and Brethren with all my Credit and power when Occasion shall require it I Promise to pay due regard and Obedience to all the decrees, sent me by the Grand Council of

[53]

Princes of Jerusalem and if I fail in this my Obligation I consent to be struck with the terrible Vindictive hand of Vengeance which is now presented to me, my head to be severed from my body and Stuck on the highest pinnacle in the East of the world as a token of my Villiany. *So God* maintain and recompence me, for my zeal fervor and Constancy. Amen, Amen, Amen, Amen"

N:B: while he takes the above Obligation all the brethren stands ready to strike. After which the Thrice Puissant raises him and relates as follows.

The History.

It was on a Certain time after the Death of Hiram Abiff that Solomon had not been able to discover the Traitors who had murdered him that there was an Assembly of a great number of masters who sat in Consultation, how to discover the Villians that had murdered him (who is the constant subject of regret and tears of all the knights and Princes of masonry,) when their Conversation was disturbed by a Captain of he Guards, who announced that there was a stranger who demanded to speak with the King in private and declared that he knew where the Traitor *Jubilum Akirop* one of the Assassins of Hiram Abiff had retired, and offered himself as a conductor to those the King would be pleased to appoint to go with him. On which all the brethren desired to go, in order that they might wreak their Vengeance on the Villian so justly due to him. Solomon put a stop to their zeal, and said there should be only 9 to undertake the task, and that he might not give offence to any, he ordered all their names to be wrote and put into an Urn, and the first 9 that should be drawn from thence should be the persons

[54]

that were to accompany the stranger, to seize the Traitor, and when taken to bring him into his presence in order that he might be made a memorable Example of. In short Joabert, Stolkin, and 7 other brethren departed at break of day with the stranger and travelled through many difficult and terrible roads, when the stranger acquainted Joabert that the Cavern that held this detestable wretch, was situate close to the sea side, on the Coast of Joppa, on which Joabert increased his pace with Zeal, and being before his Companions, he discovered the Traitor asleep in the Cavern by the light of a Lamp, and a poinard at his feet, which he took and stabbed the traitor with, on the head and heart, who had only time to pronounce the word *Necum* or *Nikah*, (which signifies vengeance is done) and died directly after. Joabert having done this perceived a Spring of water, of which he drank and being fatigued he slept untill the other brethren came and awoke him. When they perceived the head of the Traitor, covered with blood they all repeated *Necum* (which is, vengeance is done) When Joabert acquainted them with what had happened, they all envied him the glory of having alone revenged the death of their venerable Chief Hiram Abiff, and having refreshed themselves at the fountain *Joabert* cut off the head of the Traitor, and divided the body into 4 Quarters, which they burnt, and the ashes thrown in the Air, that it might be transported to the 4 quarters of the world. After which Joabert took the head in his left hand and the poinard in the right saying, *Ven*geance, they proceeded to Jerusalem, where they arrived

[55]

on the evening, and when Solomon saw Joabert with the head of the Traitor in one hand and the poinard in the other he was Wrothfull, on being deprived of giving the Exemplary punishment he designed the Villian, and having the power wrested from him, he gave Orders to Stolkin to put Joabert to death for his presumption. But the brethren being convinced that it was his Zeal that prompted him to the Action, and not any Intention of offending the King, fell on their knees and begged his life, which was granted to him the 2 time, having forfeited <it> before as is mentioned in the Intimate secretary. Solomon ordered the head of the traitor to be fixed on a long pole, and to be put on the East pinnacle of the Temple, untill they should find the other 2 Accomplices of his. Afterwards Solomon ever honored Joabert, with his most Intimate Confidence, and gave him with the other 8 brethren the Title of Elected Knights, and gave them the following Signs, Tokens and words.

SIGNS The sign is double, first, one raises the poinard and strikes the other on the forehead, and then the heart, he answers by Clapping his hand first on his forehead and then on the heart.

TOKEN The Token. Take a brothers thumb of his right hand in the middle of your hand, clinch all the fingers, and put your thumb up which signifies the 9 Elect^{d} 8 close and 1 by himself.

PASS WORDS} The Pass words, are the one says *Necum* the other answers *Joabert*, then the first says *Abiram* (that is Traitor) the other Answers *Akirop* (which is Assassin) The Grand word is *Bagulkal* (Chief of the Tabernacles or faithfull Guardian of the secret place of the sacred Ark where is deposited the most precious Treasure of Masonry.)

LECTURE.

Q: 1st: Are you an Elected Knight?
A – One Cavern I know and came to it by accident.

[56]

Q: 2^{d} What have you seen in the Cavern?
A – A Light, a Spring, a Poinard and the traitor Akirop.
Q: 3. What use were they to you?
A – A Light to enlighten me, the poinard to revenge the death of our respectable Master, and the spring to refresh <me>.
Q: 4 Where was you received an Elected Knight?
A – In Solomons audience chamber.
Q: 5 How many Intendants were chosen or Elected?
A – Nine including myself.
Q: 6 From what number were the nine Elected?
A – The number besides them were 90.
Q: 7 What was your reason and Intention to be received?
A – To revenge the death of Hiram Abiff and exterminate the Assassin, the Traitor *Jubulum Akirop*.
Q: 8 Where did you find the Assassin?
A – In the bottom of a Cavern, situated near a burning bush or rainbow on a Clift near the sea on the Coast of Joppa.
Q: 9 Who Conducted you there?
A – A Stranger.
Q: 10 Where did you travel to come to the Cavern?

A – A dark and intricate road.
Q: 11: What did you do when you came to the Cavern?
A – I seized a poinard which I found at the entrance and struck a blow so Violent, on the head and heart of the Traitor Jubulem Akirop which killed him in a moment.
Q: 12 Did he say anything before he Expired?
A – He only said one word.
Q: 13 What was that word?
A – N:E:C:U:M: (he letters it)
Q: 14 What signifies those letters?
A – Necum (which is Vengeance)
Q: 15 In what manner was you Election Consummated?

[57]

A – By Vengeance, Disobedience, Mercy and by 8 and 1.
Q: 16 Explain all this?
A – By Vengeance I destroyed the Villian, by disobedience in neglecting the Kings order, by Mercy in Obtaining my pardon by solicitations of my brethren and by 8 and 1 because the number of the Elected were 9.
Q: 17 What did you do after killing the Traitor?
A – I Cut off his head and refreshed myself at the spring that was at the bottom of the Cavern, and being much fatigued I fell asleep, untill my brethren arrived and awoke me, because on their Entering and seeing the head bloody they all cried out Vengeance.
Q:–18 How did Solomon receive you after presenting him with the head of the Traitor?
A – With Indignation, because he had reserved to himself the mode of Punishment, in order to make himself a publick Example, but forgave me on account of my Zeal.
Q:–19 What represents the mourning Chamber into which you was conducted before your Admission?
A – The Cavern of the Traitor.
Q: 20: How came you to be left there blind–folded?
A – To put me in mind of the sleep of the Traitor and ~~and~~ to represent to me how often Villians think themselves Secure after committing crimes, when they are most in Danger.
Q: 21: Why do the brethren lean their heads on their right hands in this Chamber?
A – Darkness obliged them to put their hands before their eyes to prevent being hurt, for the same reason as the difficulty of the roads, obliged

them to Cross their legs one over the other, so the Elected in a Chapter have their legs crossed.

Q: 22 What <is> represented <by> the dog which you see on the road in the Draft?

[58]

A – The stranger who Conducted the Elected Knights.

Q: 23 What is represented by the naked arm with a poinard?

A – That Vengeance is always ready to strike the guilty.

Q: 24 What is the signification of the black ribbon with the poinard at the bottom which you wear?

A – Grief to us, who had the sad misfortune to lose our dear master Hiram Abiff and more so, on account of his being murdered by Masons.

Q: 25 Can you Explain the number of the 9 Elected?

A – The first, by the 9 red roses on the ribbon at the bottom of which hangs the poinard—secondly by the 9 lights, thirdly by the 9 knocks, all these represent the 9 Elected and the blood that was Spilt is represented by the 9 Red roses.

Q: 26 How do you wear your Ribbon?

A – From the left shoulder to the right hip.

Q: 27. Of what Color is your Apron?

A – A white skin lined and bordered with black, speckled with red. On the flap a bloody arm with a poinard and on the front of the Apron a bloody arm holding a bloody head by the hair.

Q: 28 What Color is the Chapter Cloathed with?

A – Red and white, the red with white flames, the white with red flames, the red was the blood spilt and the white the order and purity of the Elected.

Q: 29 Why is there but 1 Warden?

A – Because the chapter was kept by Solomon and he had only his favorite with him.

Q: 30 What is now to be done?

A – Nothing, because everything is accomplished and

[59]

Hiram Abiff is revenged.

Q: 31 Give me the pass word?

A – *Necum* or *Nikah*.

Q: 32 What is the word?

A – *Bagulkal*, chief of the Tabernacle or favorite Guardian or friend.

Q: 33 Have you any other pass?
A – I have two more.
Q: 34 What are they?
A – *Joabert* and *Stolkin*.
Q: 35 What time went the Elected to search for the Traitor?
A – Evening.
Q: 36 When did they return?
A – Break of day.
Q: 37 What age are you?
A – 8 by 1 Accomplished.

To Close

Q: What is the Clock?

A: tis Evening. After which the thrice Puissant knocks 8 and 1 which is answered by Stolkin and then by all the brethren. Then the thrice puissant makes the sign with the poinard as Striking on the head and heart which is answered by all the Brethren by clapping their hands on their heads and heart, then he says *Necum* they all answer *Vengeance*, when the Chapter is Closed. The Order, of the 9 Elected is, a broad black ribbon with a poinard at the bottom, on the ribbon 9 red roses 8:8:8:8:0 } The Apron is to be of white leather bordered and lined with black. On the flap painted a hand suspended with a poinard. On the Apron a bloody arm suspended holding a bloody head by the Hair.

The End of 9

[60]

Grand Master Elect^{d} of 15

This lodge is decorated as the 9 Elected with the same colours and represents Solomons Apartment, has 2 Wardens the 1st is Called Inspector.

To Open.

The thrice Puissant knocks 3 times 5 which is answered by all the brethren, then he says the Lodge is open.

The Preparation

There is only to be 15 in this Lodge, when a reception is to be made, and if more they are to be in the Anti Chamber with the Candidate, who is to be introduced by the Junior Warden, who knocks 3 times 5. The Senr Warden goes to the door, opens it a little and demands who is there. The Junior Warden answers an Elected Knight of 9, who desires to know the fate of the other 2 Assassins of our Master Hiram Abiff, and to come to the Degree of the 15. On which the Senior Warden shuts the

[61]

door, and makes a report to the thrice Puissant who orders him to be admitted. Then the senior Warden makes the Candidate walk 15 Steps in a triangular manner which brings him to the Altar, having 2 heads 1 in each hand (all the brethren armed with poinards as if ready to strike) they stand about a minute in silence, and then let fall their poinards, and Interlacing their hands before their foreheads, the backs close to the flesh the palms out, and beg <the> pardon of the Candidate (the Thrice puissant says) Why do ye ask pardon for him (they answer) because he is not blameable (T:P:) Why do ye ask pardon is he <not> Guilty (they Answer) the grace we ask for him is to be admitted to the degree of Grand Master Elected (T:P:) is he qualified (all the brethren Answer) Yes (T:P:) if he is so, tell him to kneel. (When the thrice Puissant says to him) The Grand masters Elected here present request me to admit you to the degree of Grand master elected in order that you may become equal with them, do you find yourself able to keep the secrets of this degree, and will you take a solemn Obligation (he answers) Yes. The Wardens then divest him of the heads, and placing his hands on the Bible, and kneeling down, Takes the following Obligation — I, N:N: do promise and swear on the holy bible, never to reveal where I have been received in this degree nor never to tell who Assisted at my reception, and promise never to receive any person in this degree without a permission and full power from my superiors, nor to Assist at any reception unless in a regular Lodge of this degree, to keep exactly in my heart all the secrets that shall be revealed unto me, and in failure of this Obligation I consent to have my body opened perpendicularly and to be exposed 8 hours in the open Air for the

[62]

venemous flies to feel on my Entrails, my head to be cutt off and put on the highest pinnacle of the world and always to be ready to Inflict the same punishment on those who shall disclose this Degree and break their Obligation. So God maintain me Amen. After which the Candidate rises and the Thrice Puissant gives him the following Signs, Tokens and Words. The Sign is double one takes the poinard and touches his Chin (with the fingers) as if he would cut open his own belly. On which another answers with the sign of Entered Apprentice (with his fingers clinched) The token is to do the first sign against each others body with fingers clinched, the thumb raised upwards as if you would cut each others belly open. The words are, one says *Zerbal* the other answers *Eleham*, the Order is the same with that of the 9 Elect, with the poinard at the bottom, with 3 heads on spikes to be painted on the breast.

The History

Six months after the death of Hiram Abiff, Bengabee one of the Intendants of Solomon made enquiry in the Country of Cheth which was tributary to Solomon whether any persons had lately taken refuge there for Crimes done at Jerusalem, he also caused a description of their persons to be published, when he received an account of two persons that lately had retired there believing themselves protected and had proceeded to work, Upon Solomons hearing of this he wrote without loss of time to *Moacha* King of *Cheth* to

[63]

deliver to the persons he had sent, the bodies of the two Assasins, in order to bring them to Jerusalem, and there to receive the punishment due them for the Crime they had been guilty of. In Consequence of which Solomon Elected 15 Masters, the most zealous and trusty among whom were some of them who had been in the Cavern of *Akirop* and furnished them with troops sufficient to escort them. Upon their arrival they searched 5 days when Zerbal (who carried Solomons letter to king Moacha) and Joabert found the two Ruffians cutting of Stone in the Quarry of *Bendaca* they immediately seized on them and fixed them in Chains made in the form of a Rule Square and Mallet, on which was Engraved the Punishment they were to suffer, having at the same time the Crimes before their Eyes which they had committed and their approaching death. When they arrived at Jerusalem they were committed in the Town of *Achizas* untill the day arrived that Solomon had appointed for their Execution, which was to be by the most Excru<ti>ating Death, that was proportional to their crimes. On the morning at 10 O Clock the said Villians named *Jubula Gibs* and *Jubelo Gravilot* was tied to 2 posts by the neck and the middle, with their arms Extended, in the most publick manner, the Executioner then cut their bellies open Length and Crossways, and left them in that Condition untill 6 in the Evening, in order that the flies should glut themselves with their blood and Entrails, when their heads were Cutt off

[64]

and fixed with that of Akirop on the East, South and West pinnacles of the Temple, where they had Executed the horrible deed of Assasinating the respectable Hiram Abiff.

A Short Lecture

Q: 1st Are you a Grand Master Elected?
A – My zeal and my works has procured me this secret Degree.
Q: 2^{d} Where have you been received?
A – By Solomon himself in his Apartment.
Q: 3 Where did he receive you and upon what occasion?
A – When he sent me with my Companions to find out the other two Assasins, *Jubelo Gibs* and *Jubelo Gravilot.*
Q: 4 How came they discovered?
A – By the diligence of Bengabee Solomons Intendant in the Country of Cheth.
Q: 5 Who carried Solomons Letter to the King Moacha?
A – *Zerbal.*
Q: 6 How many Elected did Solomon send on this Occasion?
A – Fifteen in all.
Q: 7 Give me the Sign?
A – There are two Signs (and he gives them).

Q: 8 What is the token?
A – (by giving them)
Q: 9 What signifies those signs and tokens?
A – That I am always ready to inflict the same punishment on any person who breaks this degree as I have desired to be inflicted on myself in my Obligation.
Q: 10 Give me the word?
A – One says *Zerbal* and the other *Eleham*.
Q: 11 At what time did the 2 Accomplices expire?

[65]

A – Their Execution began at 10 O Clock in the morning and at 6 in the evening vengeance was Accomplished.

Then the Thrice Puissant says, may every traitor meet with the same fate. He then knocks 3 times 5 which is Answered by all the brethren and the Lodge is Closed. The Order is a broad black Ribbon as the 9 Elected and a poinard at the bottom, but there must be 3 heads on pikes painted on that part of the black Order that comes on the breast, The same Apron as the 9 Elected but there must be 3 heads painted on pikes on the flap.

[65]

Illustrious Knights

This lodge is called grand chapter. Where Solomon presides. A Grand Inspector and a Grand Master of Ceremonies in the room of Wardens.

To Open.

The thrice Puissant knocks 12 at equal distances and is only answered by the Grand Inspector, when the thrice puissant says, Tis now time to Improve our labors, by the Influence of the greatest Light. The Chapter is open.

Form of Reception

The Grand Master of Ceremonies goes out to the Candidate and knocks 12 at the door which is answered by the thrice Puissant and then by the

[66]

Grand Inspector, when the last goes to the door and asks who is there. The Grand Master of Ceremonies answers, there is a Grand Master Elect of 15 demands to penetrate into the Chapter of Illustrious Knights Upon which the thrice puissant gives orders to Introduce him with his Jewells &c of his last degree and to be carried to the Grand Inspector, Who Examines the Candidate in all his other Degrees. Then the thrice Puissant asks the Inspector, What does the Grand Master of 15 want?

A – To be admitted to the Degree of Illustrious Knights and to have the recompence of his works and travels.

<the> Thrice Puissant says to the Candidate. I suppose my Brother you Travel alone in view of Interest? The Candidate answers. My first view is to do my duty and as I have done it at my own Expence, and to punish all Traitors, I now ask for this honor as a recompence for my labors, the Thrice Puissant then says, Come and contract your Obligation (which is the same as in the last degree with the following addition) to be Charitable and to have my body cut into Quarters

and my memory lost as an Imposter. (he is then instructed in the sign Token and Word as in the Lecture).

The History.

After that Vengeance was fulfilled on the 3 Assasins Solomon in order to recompence the zeal fervor and Constancy of the 15 Grand Elected and to give a higher degree; in order to raise some other worthy Brethren

[67]

from lower Degrees to that of Grand Master Elected. He created 12 of the 15 Illustrious Knights by ballot so that none might be offended; And with the first 12 which should be drawn from the Urn, he was to form a Grand Chapter and gave them the Command of the 12 Tribes and summoned them by the name, of Excellent *Emerh*, a hebrew word signifying a true man on all Occasions, and shewed them all the precious things in the Tabernacle, and where they saw the Tables of the Law, which were wrote by God and Given to Moses near the B:B: on mount Sinai. He decorated them with a large black Ribbon, with an Inflamed heart thereon (instead of the 3 heads) over and against their heart, and in the room of a Poinard he gave them a sword of Justice, and shewed them many other favors; The name of the 12 Commanders are as follows.

1st Joabert Inspector General of the Tribe of Judah
2d Stolkin .... d° of....................... Benjamin
3 Tiercy. .... d° of......................... Simeon
4 Morphy.................. d° of.........................Ephraim
5 Alquebar. .... d° of...................... Manassah
6 Durson.................. d° of.........................Zebulon
7 Vicrem .... d° of............................... Dan
8 Birthomer............. d° of............................ Asher
9 Tito......................... d° of........................ Napthali
10 Zerbal. .... d° of............................ Ruben
11 Benecard. .... d° of..........................Issachar
12 Tabar. .... d° of................................ Gad

The 12 Illustrious Knights gave an Account to Solomon of all the work that was done every day in the Temple by their respective Tribes and these Chiefs received the pay of their Tribes.

[68]

The Lecture.

Q: 1st Are you an Illustrious Knight?
A: – My name will inform you.
Q: 2 What is your name?
A: – Emerh, is my name and profession.
Q: 3 How many Illustrious Knights are there in your Chapter?
A: – There can be no more than 12 who are the 12 Commanders of the 12 Tribes of Israel.
Q: 4 Give me the Sign?
A: – The Sign is, to Cross both your arms close to your breast, with your fingers clinched, and the thumbs raised.
Q: 5 Give me the Token?
A: – The Token is to take each others Thumb, reciprocally turn and says as in the Intimate secretary *Birit, Neder, Selemoth.*
Q: 6 What signifies your Sign?
A: – That my faith is Immoveable and my Trust in *God.*
Q: 7 Give me the word?
A: – *Emerh.*
Q: 8 What signifies that word?
A: – Adonai.

To Close

The thrice Puissant says, As you have received this days pay for the workmen, who have worked well, And as ye are worthy of your name, by your punctuality, in cementing peace and harmony, and Stiring the laborers up to proceed to their work Chearfully; I shall Close this Chapter, he then Strikes 12 times, which is answered by the Grand Inspector, and the Grand Chapter is Closed. N:B: In all Chapters and Lodges &c where Solomon presides, he uses as scepter instead

[69]

of a mallet or Hiram. The Apron is the same as the Elected of 15. The Order is the same Colour as that of the Elected of 15, but there must be an Inflamed heart painted thereon instead of the 3 heads, which comes on the breast, and a Sword of Justice must be appended thereto instead of a Poinard.

[69]

or Grand Master Architect

This chapter, is painted white, with red flames, the 5 Orders of Architecture, and the North Star; with 7 Stars round the Chapter, Solomon presides therein. N:B: Every Grand Master Architect ought to have a Case of Mathematical Instruments.

To Open.

The thrice Puissant knocks 1 and then 2. The Grand Master answers the same.

Q: – Are you well Tyled Grand Warden?
A – We are all well Tyled thrice Puissant. I have seen the doors and windows well secured, so that no Cowan can either hear or see Us.
Q: – Are you a Grand Architect?
A – I know the name and use of every Instrument relative to the mathematicks.
Q: – What are they?
A – A Square, A simple Compass, A Compass with 4 points, A Rule, A Line, A Compass of proportion, A Quadrant of 90 degrees, A Level and a Plumb.
Q: – Where was you received?

[70]

A – In a white place painted with red flames.
Q: – What Signifies that place?
A – The white signifies the purity of the heart; and the flames the zeal, which every Master Architect ought to possess.
Q: – What signifies the Star in the North which you see in this Chapter?
A – Virtue; which every man ought to be led by, as the North Star is a guide to Mariners in their Navigation.
Q: – O Clock is it?
A – A Star appeareth which announces the break of Day.

Q: – If it is so, Let us to work?
A – Let us to work. This Chapter is Open.

The Form of Reception

The Candidate must have some Instructions and then he is introduced by one and then 2 knocks, he is them Conducted once round the Chapter, (he is made to stop a little to Examine the Star in the north, and from thence proceeds to the thrice Puissiant by three square steps, and then kneels and takes the Obligation, which is to be the same as in the preceeding Degree of Illustrious Knights. After which he returns by 3 Steps backward and is brought to the 2 Wardens, when the Senior warden gives him the following Sign, Token and Word.

Sign. The Sign is, as if you are drawing a plan with your right hand in the palm of your Left.

Token The Token is to Interlace the 3 last fingers of your right hand with that of a brother, in a Square form and Clap each others right shoulder, with the left hand.

Word. The Word is *Rabucim* (that is) I am a Grand Master Architect.

The Lecture.

[71]

Gr^{d} M^{r} Do you work?
A – I do.
Gr^{d} Mr Let us see it?
A – Command me Thrice Puissant Grand Master Architect.
Gr^{d} Mr Open the Case of Instruments?

The Candidate opens the Case of Instruments and takes them all out and arranges them on the Table 3 by 3.

Gr^{d} Mr Thats well done my brother. Let us now work in another manner?
A – I Consent Grand Master Architect. (they then take up all the Instruments and return them into their Case)
Gr^{d} Mr Give me the word?
A – *Rabucim.*
Gr^{d} Mr What signifies that word?
A – It signifies that I am a Grand Master Architect.

The History.

(The thrice Puissant then says) Solomon being willing to form a School of Architecture for the Instruction of the workmen of the Temple, and to Encourage the perfection of the Royal Art. This King being always full of Justice and foresight, was willing to recompence the Talents and virtue of the sublime Emerhs in order to make them perfect and fit to approach the throne of the Grand Architect of the Universe; He cast his Eyes on the Chiefs of the 12 Tribes to fulfill the promise that was made to *Enoch* to *Moses* and *David* with great ardor to penetrate the bowels of the Earth. I recompence you with this Degree that the attachment that you will shew in the study of Geometry into which you are now Introduced will procure you such knowledge as will take from you the Viel which is now before your Eyes, and discover unto you the truth of perfection in Masonry.

To Close.

Grd Mr Give me the word?

A – Ask me for it in a Regular manner.

Grd Mr Make yourself known. I am a grand Master Architect?

[72]

A – *Rabucim.*

Grd Mr What signifies that word?

A – Grand Master Architect which you and I am.

Grd Mr Give me the Sign?

A – There it is (he then draws in his hand)

Grd Mr Do you know any thing Else?

A – I know another.

Grd Mr Work?

A – We work. (then all the brethren take their Instruments out and lay them in a regular manner 3 by 3 and then says every thing is in readiness.

Grd Mr Begin?

A – We have begun. (Then the Grand Master Architect makes a Triangle with the Compass of Proportion, the Square, and the rule, and then puts the Instruments into the Case again and then he says My Brethren finish?

A – We finish.

Grd Mr What O Clock is it?

A – Break of Day. Then the Thrice Puissant Grand Master, Strikes 1 and then 2 which is answerd by the Grand Inspector, and then by all the Brethren, after which they all salute the Thrice Puissant and the Chapter is Closed.

JEWEL. The Jewel is a gold medal with 5 Orders of Architecture on both sides, suspended by a dark blue water Ribbon, from the left shoulder to the Right hip.

APRON. The Apron to be Lined and bordered with black, with a Compass, square and Rule forming a Triangle painted thereon.

[73]

The 13th Degree,

or Royal Arch

This lodge ought to be kept in a secret place Vaulted, and without any door or window and if possible under ground, with a small hole on the Top, Big enough to let a brother pass through. N:B: to form a Vault, may be done with a large Screen set and closed round; In the Center of the Vault must be a pedestal of the triangular form, made hollow, and a white Cloth to go round the three sides the top to be hollow also, on which there must be fixed a Triangular Cube, in the top of which and on ea[ch] side is the letters יהוה and a light must be placed on the inside to shew the Characters. Not less than 5 Brothers can form a Lodge 1st the thrice Puissant Grand Master Solomon in the East, under a rich Canopy, with a Crown on his head a Scepter in his hand and Sitting in a Chair of State, dressed in a Royal robe of yellow and a Vestment reaching to his Elbows, with a border of blue sattin, a Grand purple Ribband from his right shoulder to his left hip with a Gold Triangle appended thereto, 2^{d}, The Grand Warden representing Hiram King of Tyre sitts at his left hand as a Stranger with the same Jewell and Ribbon; his hat on, and a Scepter in hand, Clothed with a purple robe and a yellow Vestment, 3^{d} A Grand Inspector representing *Gibulum* in the west, with the same Ribbon and Jewell as the Kings, a naked sword in his hand and his hat on. 4th A Grand Treasurer representing *Joabert* in the North, with the same Ribbon and Jewel as the others, his hat on and a Golden key hanging on the 5th button, appended to a white ribbon with these <4> letters engraved thereon, I: V: I: L: 5th The Grand Secretary representing *Stolkin* in the south, with the same

[74]

Ribbon and Jewell as all the others, and his hat on the last 3 officers are to be clothed in Robes of blue without any Vestments.

The Opening

Q: – Brother Grand Warden what place are we in?

A: – Thrice Puissant we are in the Center of the most sacred place of the Earth.

Q: – How comes it, that you are paced in this most sacred placed?

A: – By an Effect of Providence.

Q: – Explain this point to me?

A: – I dug in the Antient ruins of Enoch; I penetrated the 9 Arches under ground, and in the end found the Divine △ or Deltha, which God had promised to the holy Patriarchs.

Q: – What is this Deltha?

A: – A Gold Triangle with a great Light on it; on which was engraved by Enoch, the great and mysterious name of the Grand Architect of the Universe.

Q: – Who are you?

A: – I am that I am, my name is Gebelum.

Q: – Do you know the true Pronunciation of the name of the Grand Architect of the Universe?

A: – It is a sacred word only known to the Grand Elect Perfect and sublime Masters.

Q: – What is your quality?

A: – A Knight of the Royal Arch.

Q: – How was you received in that Quality?

A: – Solomon in Company with Hiram of Tyre, to recompence my Zeal and Constancy, created me to this Degree in Company with Joabert and Stolkin.

[75]

Q: – Give me the signs Token and word?

A: – The <1st> sign is that of Admiration, which is to extend your arms, with open hands, your head leaning on the left shoulder, then fall on your left k[n]ee, your right hand behind your back, your left hand on the Ground. The second and third signs, are to help to raise each other, by the Token which is to put the left hand on the others right Elbow, their right hands in each other. The Word is Hamalachet Gibulum.

Q: – What signifies that word?

A: – That Gibulum is a Good man, we must help and recompence him.

Q: – Have you anything further to desire here?

A: – The Degree of Perfection, known only to the sublime Masters.

Q: or Reply. God will permit you perhaps, one day to have your wishes accomplished, and to recompence you as you shall deserve.

A: – Amen, Amen, Amen.

A Prayer at Reception.

O! Most holy and gracious God: Supreme director of the Universe; We who are now Assembled before thee, most humbly, and solemnly pray: that thou wilt be pleased to receive this our petition; and grant us thy support in this laudable undertaking: Enable us O, good Lord, to pursue good, and to shun Evil; Enable us to practice virtue, and to shun all the paths which may lead to Vice: And furthermore we beseech thee, that, these our brethren, who are before thee, may be cleansed from all Corruption, and that their hearts and minds from this time and ever after, may remain pure, and Undefiled: Incline their hearts to truth, Charity and Benevolence; Grant O! God, thou Grand Architect of the Universe, that their actions may be such, as to merit thy ever kind protection; Enable them O! God, to make full

[76]

discovery of the inestimable treasure, they are now in search of; and Incline their hearts to secrecy; Bless them with the means and Inclination to serve their fellow Creatures and especially such Brethren as stand in need and are deserving; Incline their hearts to Industry; Incline our hearts to vie with each other in the practice of all virtues, and may we be linked together in the bands of Eternal friendship, through thy bountiful and ever mercifull Goodness. Amen.

The Reception.

No more than 3 persons can be made at a time and they must first pass regularly all their former Degrees.

The 3 Candidates must be in a room, above the supposed vault, and having knocked as Grand Master Architects, he'll ask to be received Knight of the Royal Arch: The Grand warden answers that he is a going to inform the Most Powerfull of their demand. The Brother Conductor having the Consent of the sovereign, Introduces the Candidate and leads him into the middle Chamber which Covers the vault he is then asked if he will go down by a rope to seek some treasure, If he Consents to it, he is accordingly secured and let down, when he is about halfway, there is a parcel of rubbish thrown over him, and the Taper blown out, which he must have in his hand—when on a sudden the pedestal is unveiled, and on the Candidates beholding of it he falls on his knees and pay due respect

[77]

thereat. The Candidate continues in that posture untill the 2 other are Introduced in like form, When the Grand inspector acquaints them, as follows. The Grand Architect of the Universe hath done you the greatest favor, it is him who hath chosen you to discover the most precious and the most sacred treasure of

Masons, you are his Elected; And I give you Joy of it, Come to me to Contract the most solemn Obligation, And I will reward you for your hard labor.

The Obligation.

I: N:N: Do promise and vow in the most solemn and inviolable manner, on the Holy Bible, and in the presence of the Great and most holy, Puissant Terrible, Just and most merciful Grand Architect of the Universe, that I will redouble my zeal in love and friendship for my Brothers, which have arrived to this Royal degree: I promise never to receive any brother to this Degree, nor Consent any to be received; Unless by permission under the hand and seal of the founder of this Royal Lodge, or the consent of him given to this Lodge for such purpose; according to the Laws established in this Lodge by the founder: I promise never to give the word or words, to any number less than 3 and those being first Examined; Unless authorized for that purpose by a proper patent, and then in Case of necessity to raise a Lodge of Royal Arches: And that I never will Assist nor Consent to the Erecting any such Royal Arch Lodge, unless properly Constituted and Established

[78]

I promise never to receive or Consent to be received, any brother to this Royal Degree, who has not regularly past the other degrees and has been a member of a Regular Lodge and has been an Officer of the same, and having demonstrated his zeal, fervor and Constancy, in Masonry and Charity and Benevolence for his Brothers: I furthermore promise to observe and keep all the Laws rules and Regulations, that shall appear and be approved of, by this Royal Lodge, and will also keep inviolably secret every transaction of this Lodge, with the bye Laws: I further promise that I will never lay with my brothers wife, nor dishonor his Mother, sister or any female of his family, knowing them to be such; and Consent in failure of this my Obligation to suffer all my former Penalties, and to receive in this place, their whole Tenor, with my further Consent, that my body shall be exposed to the wild beasts of the forrest for their food: So God maintain me in this my Present Obligation with Equity, Uprightness and Justice. Amen, A^{n}: A^{n}: A^{n}: A^{n}:.

The Discourse

My worthy Brethren; to Continue the history of masonry as far as you have now received the Elements; It will be necessary to recount to you things past: Enoch the son of Jared, was the 6th Generation from Adam; he lived in the fear and Love of God. God appeared to him in a Dream, and spoke to him by Inspiration he also Communicated to him as follows:—As thou art desirous of knowing my name, follow me; and I will Communicate to, and teach thee my name; on this, a mountain seemed to rise to the heaven and *Enoch,* was carried there; when God shewed him a gold

[79]

Triangular plate, Enlightened Brilliantly with Characters and on which was marked יהוה his ever blessed name; he gave him strict directions, never to pronounce it: After which Enoch seemed to be carried under Ground perpendicularly through Nine arches and in the 9th or deepest Arch he saw the same Gold brilliant plate, with the flaming light around it, which he had afore seen: Enoch being full of spirit of the most Puissant Great God; Built a Temple on the very spot; dedicated it to the living God, and Accompanied the same with 9 Arches, one above the other, in the exact form of what he had seen in his Reverie or Dream. Methusalah his son was the Architect of that Structure or Building, at the same time, not knowing, the reason why it was built: This Edifice was Erected in the Land of Canaan, which had since been called the Land of promise, and afterwards Jerusalem the holy Land: Enoch made a Gold plate of a Triangular form, a Cubit long each way, and enriched the same with the most precious stones; he Incrusted this plate in a Stone of Agate, of the same figure; and afterwards transported it to the 9th Arch, and engraved thereon the same Characters that God had shewn him, and he put the whole on a pedestal of white marble, of a Triangular form: After Enoch had finished the Temple under Ground; God appeared to him again and informed him of the making of a trap door on the 1st Arch, which must be laid down and a ring of Iron to be fixed thereon; for the purpose of opening it Occasionally; because that the Almighty would, be obliged, from the wickedness of mankind to Exterminate every living Creature on the Earth:

[80]

The 9 Arches being finished and exactly closed up; no person could penetrate therein as they knew it not; and to Enoch alone was known the precious treasure those Arches contained; and only himself living, knew the right pronounciation of the Great name of יהוה: The wickedness of mankind Increased every day and God threateaned the world with Universal destruction; Enoch foreseeing that the knowledge of the arts would be lost by the Universal Deluge that was then to happen; and being desirous of preserving the principles of the Liberal arts and particularly of Masonry: Methusalah was the father of Lamech who was the father of Noah, who was pious and always loving and serveing God; his virtues gained him the Love of God; who thus spoke to him: I will direct you to Construct an Ark, to contain yourself and family; with apartments for a pair of every living Creature; for those only will I save from the Punishment. I am now about to inflict on all flesh: He then gave unto Noah, the plan upon which the Ark was Constructed: Noah was 100 years in building the Ark, and he was 600 years of age and his son Shem 99 when the flood came upon the earth, it was but a little time before that his father Lamech died Aged 777 years; There was not one of the patriarchs since Adam, alive save Methusalah the Grand father of Noah, who was about 969 years, and as we have never had any accounts of him since the Deluge, there is no doubt but that he perished therein: God directed Noah with his family, and a pair of every kind of Animals to retire into the Ark, which he had built: The deluge

[81]

happened in the year of the world 1656, and every thing (but what was in the Ark) perished thereby; the most superb monuments were destroyed, with the marble Column which Enoch had raised; but by the divine permission of God, the Column of brass resisted the force of the water; by which all the liberal arts, has been Communicated to us and masonry takes from thence its Antient rise. The history of the Bible teaches us the succession of the times, and the Doctrine of the holy men instructs us, that the people of Jerusalem, were slaves to the Egyptians, and redeemed from thence under the Conduct of Moses their leader: We learn from the Annals deposited in the Archives of Scotland, and only to be reviewed by us, that in a certain Battle the Ark of Alliance was lost in a forest, and that the same was found by the roaring of a Lyon who ceased to roar, and Couched on the approach of the Isralites; which Lyon before had by Instinct devoured a number of Egyptians, who attempted to carry away the Ark: he also kept secure in his mouth the key thereof; but on the Approach of the High Priest he dropped the same, and retired at a distance couchant and tame, without offering any violence to the Chosen people of God: The history of the Bible instructs us, that Moses was well loved and Cherished by God; That he spoke to him on Mount Sinai in the Burning Bush and communicated to him his Divine Laws, which written on 2 Tables of Stone and many promises renewed his Alliance with him and gave a true pronounciation of his holy name; by which

[82]

he always would be invoked: It was at this time that Moses replied, who art thou? And God said יהוה is my true name, which is, I am a strong and Jealous God; Most Mighty and puissant: The Pronounciation of that word was Corrupted in after times, by the different Traditions; Because God had directed Moses and his descendants never to pronounce it, but promised in fulness of time, some of his descendants should find it Engraved on a gold plate. The same history informs us of the different movements of the Isralites to the time of their having possession of the holy Land or Land of Promise, and in the beginning of the City of Jerusalem we observe that David never would begin the Temple of God; which honor was reserved for his Son Solomon the wisest of Kings: Solomon remembering the promise that God had made to Moses, of finding his holy name in the fulness of time; His wisdom inspired him that the same could not be found untill he should consecrate a Temple to the Infinite God; in which he could deposit the precious Treasure already set aside for his worship: He followed the plan that David his father had Communicated to him on the model of the Ark of Alliance, and began to build the Temple in the 4th year of his Reign, and laid the foundation on the most healthy and beautiful plain in all Jerusalem:—The found in diging for foundation an Antient Edifice, with a very great Quantity of Riches, such as Vases of gold, and Silver Urns; Marble, Porphyry, Jasper and

[83]

Agate Columns; with a number of Precious stones which were all carried to Solomon: The virtuous King presuming that before the Deluge; there had been a Temple erected on that spot to some false God, and least that Intended to the true Deity might be prophaned, he resolved not to build on that place but made Choice of another spot in the plain Arunia, therefore abandoning those ruins they found no more precious things: The Temple of Solomon was built as we are instructed by masons and as we know of it by the event of the melancholy death of Hiram Abiff: Solomon having given direction to build a cavern under Ground like unto a Cave, gave it the name of the secret Vault; in which was Erected a large pillar of white marble to support the Sanctum Sanctorum, and by Inspiration called it the Pillar of Beauty; from the beautiful Arch which it was bound to support, and the sacred Treasure Providence had designed to be intrusted therein: To arrive at the secret Vault you was obliged to pass through a long narrow, close Entry or passage of 9 Arches following each other by a Communication under ground, from the Palace of Solomon to that place: Solomon was Accustomed to enter therein in Company with Hiram King of Tyre and Hiram Abiff, privately, and secretly, to contemplate on holy Mysteries: The loss of Hiram Abiff deprived them of this satisfaction; as the number of two was not sufficient to enter therein: they were therefore at

[84]

a Loss who they should Choose to compleat their number: Some Masters Intendants, Sublime Elect and Grand Masters Architects, were Informed that the King of Tyre was at Jerusalem and they were not Ignorant that when Hiram Abiff was alive, Solomon had a particular place under ground, which was a secret vault, and only known to the deceased and the Two Kings; These Masters came and intreated, that some of them might be Introduced into the Secret Vault; just at the time when Solomon and Hiram of Tyre were renewing their Alliance together: When Solomon answered them with open hands and head reclined, as follows; "You cannot expect it, God will perhaps permit ye one day to come to the knowledge of what you now Intreat": Some days after Solomon send for the 3 masters Architects—*Joabert, Stolkin,* and *Gibulum*; and gave them Orders to go and search once more in the Antient ruins, where they had already found many treasures, in hopes of finding many more: They departed in order to fulfill the Kings order; one of them by name Gibulum, in working with a pick Ax, met with a large Iron ring; which he remarked to his Companions: They conceived that this must be something Extraordinary deposited there: Upon which they fell too and labored with Ardor and zeal with their Shovel, Crow and pick ax to clear away the Earth that Covered the Ring, and when finished they found it was fixed to a perfect square stone, and

[85]

with great pains and trouble they lifted it up and found that it covered a most dismal deep Cell: Gibulum proposed to them to descend and for that purpose fixed a rope round his Body to let him down by, and told him that he shook the Rope they should draw him up quick. His two Companions strictly observed his directions; Gibulum after he had descended, found himself in a Vault arched; on the pavement of which he found another opening, into which he descended, and found again an opening, into which he also descended and found yet another opening; but being afraid to pursue his search he shook the rope; on which his Companions drew him up: Upon which he acquainted them with what he had seen, and Observed; he them proposed, that they should descend by Turns, but they refusing he again descended, telling them that through every Arch he descended, he would slightly shake the rope and when he wanted to be drawn up, he would greatly shake the Rope; On being let down he passed through 3 other Arches, and when he came to the 6th Arch, he shook the rope greatly and was drawn up; he then informed them, that he had passed through 6 Arches, and that there was still an opening to descend further, and again proposed to one of them to descend, for that he had labored much, and was afraid to descend again; this affrighted them so much, that they refused to go down; on which he took Courage and with a lighted

[86]

flambau in his Hand told them he would descend again, under the same precaution as afore, He accordingly descended and went through 3 Arches more, and when he entered the 9th Arch a parcell of stones and Mortar fell suddenly down from above and struck out the light of his flambau; Upon which he saw the rays of the sun penetrating very lively on a Golden Triangular plate adorned richly round with precious stones: The Brightness thereof so affected Gibulum, that it almost deprived him of sight; on which he made a sign of Admiration, which was the same that Solomon and Hiram King of Tyre made to him when he came first with his 2 Companions and asked to be admitted into the sublime Degree:—Gibulum fell prostrate on his knees, with his right hand before his Eyes, his left hand behind his back shaking the Rope 3 times; When Joabert and Stolkin drew him up, and he recounted to them all that had happened, and the amazing things he had seen in the 9th Arch: They then proposed and did descend by a ladder of Ropes, which they fixed on the Occasion; when they arrived in the 9th Arch, they did as Gibulum had done, and prostrated themselves in the like manner, as did Gibulum with them: When Joabert and Stolkin had recovered themselves, they stood up and seeing Gibulum still prostrate, they went and raised him up and said *Hamalaheck Gibulum*, which signifies Gibulum is a good mason, we must help and recompence him: They then Examined the Golden plate and perceived on it some

[87]

Characters of which they were Ignorant; the plate was Incrusted on the Top of an Agate stone of the same Cubic form; they admired the plate with respect and conceived the characters to mean יהוה which was only known by Solomon Hiram of Tyre and Hiram Abiff the Architect; and then it seemed to them by suspicions and other Occurrences, that since the Death of Hiram Abiff the two Kings were not a sufficient number to bestow this Degree on them that aspired thereto, and which they now hoped to received from the Circumstances of Solomons sending them to search, and their having found this precious Treasure: They determined among themselves to raise the Cubic stone, on which was fixed the Golden plate, and carry it up to Solomon when in his Apartment with the King of Tyre: It was at the break of day when they arrived at the apartment of Solomon; and when the two Kings saw the Precious Treasure, they were struck with amazement and Admiration, and made naturally the same sign of Admiration to the three Masters, as what they had made in the 9th Arch, and fell down on their knees: Solomon got up first from his surprize and seeing the King of Tyre still on his knees, ran to him in an Extasy, raised him up and said *Hamalaheck Gibulum*; he examined Immediately the Characters which were Impressed on the Gold plate and knew them to be יהוה but could not explain any part thereof to the 3 Masters Elected: Solomon told them that the Grand Architect of the Universe, had bestowed on them the most signal of all his favors, that he

[88]

had chosen them to discover the most precious Treasures of Masonry, that they were his Elect and that he wished them great Joy; and to recompence their Zeal, Constancy, fervency, and fidelity, he created them Knights of the 9th Arch as it was them alone that discovered the same and by which discovery that Arch was called the Royal Arch, he also promised to give them an Interpretation of the sacred and Mysterious characters which they saw engraved on the Gold plate, after that they had in Company fixed it in the place destined for it, and would discover to them, the most high and sublime degree of Masonry. The 3 Masters elected observed to Solomon that the first word he and Hiram King of Tyre spoke to them, was the same they had naturally pronounced in the 9th Arch, on finding the Treasure; they also recounted every thing that they had seen and done precisely; by which they found Instantly the Sign, Token and Word of this degree, since known by the Title of Knights of the Royal Arch. "Solomon explained afterwards that the promise which God had made to Noah, Moses and David his father was accomplished, which was, that one day the true name of him, by which he was to be invoked should be discovered on a Golden plate—and that the same he would now extend to them, with Liberty only to letter it, for their Consolation; but

[89]

never to pronounce or speak it, and that in lettering it they must do <it> with great Circumspection: Solomon in Continuation said to them that, during the Construction of the Temple the Masters word was in true knowledge, untill the Tragic scene of Hiram Abiff our Grand Master when it was lost, and never came to us but by Tradition untill now, and that corrupted successively but never the true one. We are now very happy my Dear Brethren to have at this present moment the true Characters, which we will very soon give you the Interpretation and pronounciation of: We have nothing at this Instant to do, but to recompence you with Justice, the merit due to your works; you are now stampt by the divine hand with his signal favor." The two Kings and the three Knights then took the precious things, and went to the secret vault, by the private way through the 9 Arches, which none but themselves knew; they arrived at the pillar of Beauty and worked together thereat, to invest the plate on the Pedestal thereof. The two Kings seemed Gloriously rejoiced to work with the Trowel (having their arms bare) on the things God had destined to be done by their hands only. After having finished their work, all five prostrated themselves, to adore the Grand Architect of the Universe, paying him homage, thanks and praise for his gracious decrees in their favor: the brilli-

[90]

-ancy of the plate; the splendor of the Rubies and Diamonds placed one on the other was sufficient Light for this place, there was no other artificial light, but to mark the principal and different ages of Masonry which was 3, 5, 7 and 9 which when multiplied by the Calculation we know, makes 81.—and which will be explained fully in the General Instructions of our Doctrine.

It was the very moment after this work was finished, that the two Kings changed the name of the Secret to that of the Sacred Vault, only known by the Grand Elect perfect and Sublime Masters: It was now time to recompence the virtue of the three Elected Masters and Knights of the Royal Arch Joabert, Stolkin and Gibulum; the two Kings gave the Degree of Grand Elect, Perfect and Sublime Masters. Explaining the sacred word engraved on the Golden plate, that which was, and is the name of the most sacred Omnipotent—and that he would be always Invoked by that name; A pronounciation which had suffered much—and had been greatly Corrupted and this is the method of pronouncing it, and always remark the number of Letters, and Characters which compose the words, in whatever degree they are broke, are some mysterious numbers in Masonry, of which you will have

[91]

an Explanation when you arrive to the sublime Degree of Perfection. The name of the syllables which Compose the Mysterious name are as follows.

3 Jub . . . . All puissant.
3 Jeo . . . . Divine Light.
3 *Jua* . . . . *Striking Light.*

5 Hayah . . . . it is, it was, it will be
5 Gotha . . . . God himself alone
5 *Jeeva* . . . . *God Eternal.*

7 Adonai . . . . O you that is Eternal.
7 Jakinai . . . . Sustain us Oh God,
by your Gr^{d} force, that we may aid and assist each other.
7 *Jehovah* . . . . *Brilliant God.*

9 Heleneham . . . . Mercy of God
9 Jahabulum . . . . In God is my faith
9 J∴∴∴ . . . . The Lord Almighty

The last is the appellation among us, which you will know, when you are Initiated into the sublime Degree of perfection: This is very certain from the different variations of which the *Moors* have taken *Juba* and the *Latins* their *Jupiter;* The true pronounciation is not a little lost, of the greatest of names; Moses himself having been taught by the Grand Architect himself relative to the efficacy of this Great name, he having provided in Egypt against the drought hunger

[92]

and Sickness; They could see the sacred name in the Temple in the time of S^{t}. Jerom it was wrote in the Antient Samaritan Characters, unknown to strangers, which was the reason the word could never come truly to them, neither could it serve them in their Necromancies or Magic—for they would have been well pleased to have Employed it, as the Roman pagans had done already, for they were well persuaded of the great power thereof. Thus you will see the true pronunciation only rested in the heart of the sublime Master Masons. This Mysterious word is covered by 3 pass words and 6 Covered words and by 3 Touches preceeding the figurative signs to the Incidents that had happened at different times. The 3 new Elected Brothers *Joabert, Stolkin* and *Gibulum* took their Obligation before God and the two Kings never to pronounce fully, that word, and never to admit any Mason into this sublime Degree before he had given long proofs of his zeal for the Craft and to use the same Ceremony to commemorate the mysterious History of the Divine *Deltha* near the burning bush, where God made the Patriarch Moses promise the same. The number of the Grand Elected began by 3 that is Solomon, Hiram King of Tyre and Hiram Abiff, they were afterwards augmented to 5 by what had happened and they remained a long while at that number, that is Solomon, Hiram King of Tyre, Joabert, Stolkin and Gibulum. When the Temple of

[93]

Solomon was finished and he had dedicated it he recompensed with the Degree of perfection the 12 Masters who had commanded the 12 Tribes since the death of Hiram Abiff and 9 other Masters Elected, who were distinguished by their Virtue; there were chosen sand formed in the sublime Royal Arch, and in a short time to the Degree of perfection, to be admitted to the sacred vault: The 9 Knights were obliged to Tyle the doors of the 9 Arches—which led from thence to the palace of Solomon; The most Antient was placed at the door of the vault, and the others by degrees to the 9th Arch, which was the door near the apartment of Solomon—never permitting Entrance to any but the Grand Elect and perfect Masters and them giving the Sign Token and word, of each Arch: The Reason they Knights take their Quality, is because, from the sacred vault—you have an Entrance to the Royal palace. The pass words of each are—1st, Jub—2^{d}, Jeo—3^{d}, Jua—4th, Hayah—5th, Gotha—6th, Adonai—7th, Jackinai—8th, Heleneham and the 9th, Jehabulum.

The Brother that gives on the inside the sacred word, was obliged to give another pass word beside which is Shiboleth 3 times with an aspiration. The number of the Antient master Masons were 27 being the Number 3 times Nine, to wit

[94]

2	Kings, Solomon and Hiram of Tyre	2	in all 27
3	Knights of the Royal Arch	3	
12	Antient Commanders of the 12 Tribes	12	
9	Elected Antient Masters	9	
1	Antient Grand Master Architect	1	

There was now 3568 Antient Masters who had served in the Construction of the Temple and who became very Jealous, on seeing a preference given to the 25 Brethren, whom we have already mentioned, for they saw them very of ten in the apartment of the King, and which was shut to them; at which they received such Shagreen—that they sent deputies to Solomon to desire that he would hear thier complaints. Solomon having <heard> them, with great sweetness of Temper said, That the 25 Masters deserved such preferment, by a Zeal in working the most hard, that he loved and cherished them particularly but that their time was not as yet expired:—Go said he, God will perhaps permit that you shall one day be recompensed as you deserve. One of the Deputies being transported with passion left him; and not being contented with the soft and sweet reply of King Solomon, said, we have not any business for higher Degrees, we know how the word has been changed; we can travel as Masters and received the pay as such: Solomon was struck with this reply, but as he was always full of Goodness and Wisdom, would not rebuke

[95]

him, but by Inspiration spoke to him in this manner. "The Antients deserves this degree of perfection, as they have been in the Antient ruins and penetrated into the bowels of the Earth, which frightened them, and from thence took Immense treasure to Embellish and decorate the Temple of the Living God! Go in peace and do as they have done; work to adorn the Temple of the most Almighty God, and you shall be recompensed as you deserve." These Masters being proud and vain made a Report of their Embassy—and not having received a reprimand: Ambition being mixed with Jealousy, prompted them to go Altogether to the Antient Ruins, to search underground They departed for that purpose the next morning at break of day, and as they arrived there, they discovered the Ring to lift up the Square Stone; which having done, by a ladder of ropes, entered the Cell with flambeaus. God having a design to punish the Masters for their ambition and give a clear proof of his Justice and providence, pronounced their doom; insomuch that when the last of them was Entered, the 9 Arches fell upon them successively one after the other with all its Appurtenances, so that they were no more seen; the Antient word that was Corrupted, was lost with them and no person knew it since in any wise, as it was only kept by those Masters of which you have

[96]

heard this History. It was not long before Solomon, heard what had happened; he sent Joabert, Stolkin and Gibulum to Enquire and inform him particularly of all that had happened: They departed at the break of day according to the Kings Orders, and when they arrived at the place, where the disaster happened, they found such strange things, that they were amazed and were at a loss to find the pristine state of the Arches, neither could they perceive any of the presumptious Masters who had gone in search of the Treasure; they therefore Imagined that they were all Enveloped in the ruins, that they saw had fallen. They Examined the place with attention, and found nothing but a few pieces of Marble on which were some Characters in Hyroglyphicks, which they took and carried to Solomon and informed him of every thing they had seen: Solomon placed the pieces of marble together, and send for one of the Brethren (named *Abdemon*) who could decypher and Explain those Hyroglyphicks by which they learnt, that the ruins they had seen and which had destroyed the Masters, was the Temple *Enoch* had built and consecrated to the true *God* which was built before, and destroyed by the Deluge, which swept away every thing but the 9 Arches, where was deposited the △ or Treasure so often spoken of to Moses and David by the Almighty; from which History of the Antient Masters is taken this true and Interesting History of Masonry, of

[97]

which the Bible speaks so little of and which cannot be Illustrated upon. Solomon caused all the Marble stone to be put together, and ordered them to be kept in the sacred vault.

I exhort you my Dear Brethren to meditate on the Grandeur of our Mysteries, you are not yet come to the ultimate Knowledge of what you wish to be acquainted with, but you may expect it by your zeal, fervor and Constancy.

The Lecture

The thrice Puissant asks the Grand Inspector

Q: – Where are you?

A: – We are in the Center of the most holy place in the Earth.

Q: – How came you introduced into this place?
A: – By the Effects of the divine providence.
Q: – Explain that point to me?
A: – I dug in the Antient Ruins of Enoch; I penetrated the 9 Arches under ground, and in the end found the del△tha which was promised to the Patriarchs.
Q: – What is the del△tha?
A: – A Golden Triangular plate, replenished with a great Light, on which was Engraved by Enoch the great and mysterious name of the Grand Architect of the Universe.
Q: – What are you?
A: – I am that I am—my name is Gibulum.
Q: – Do you know the name of the Grand Architect of the Universe?
A: – It is a sacred word, only known by the Grand

[98]

Elect, Perfect and Sublime Masons.
Q: – What is your Quality?
A: – Knight of the Royal Arch.
Q: – How was you received in that Quality?
A: – Solomon in Company with Hiram King of Tyre to recompence my zeal and Constancy created me to this degree in Company with Joabert and Stolkin.
Q: – Give me the Sign, Token and Word?
A: – The 1st is of Admiration—which is to Extend your Arms—the hands open—your head resting on the left shoulder—The 2d is to fall on your left knee and hand, your right hand on your back—The 3d is to raise and help a Brother with both hands the right hands in each other and the left on the right Elbow of each other—The Word is *Hamalachet* Gibulum.
Q: – What signifies that word?
A: – That Gibulum is a good man, we must help and recompence him.

To Close

Q: – What remains for you to desire, respectable Brother and Inspector?
A: – Perfection here, and Eternal happiness hereafter.
T:P: God will perhaps, permit you one day to have your wishes accomplished.
Q: – What is the Clock brother Grand Inspector?
A: – It is Evening.
T:P: Acquaint the Brethren that I am going to close this Royal Lodge by the most perfect and myste-

[99]

-rious Numbers.

Gr^d In^r Take notice Respectable brethren That the thrice Puissant Grand Master, is a going to Close this Royal Lodge by the most perfect and mysterious Numbers.

Solomon then Knocks .... 3 times 3.
Hiram of Tyre.............................. 3 times 3.
The Grand Inspector .... 3 times 3
The Grand Treasurer....................... 3 times 3
The Grand Secretary .... 3 times 3
} in all 45

After which the Grand Inspector says to order Brethren.—When the 2 Kings and all the Lodge fall on their knees and make the sign of admiration, all the brethren repeat the same, and before they get up they give the sign with their right hands before their backs, after which they help each other to rise; The 2 Kings begin and so the others go on, all make their obedience to the 2 Kings, when Solomon says—This Royal Lodge is close with all its honors.

The Initials of the following Motto is to be engraved on the Edge of a Golden medal, to hang on the Breast of the brethren of the Royal Arch

"Regnante Sapientissimo, Solomonis.
"Gibulum, Joabert, and Stolkin.
"Inveneriunt Preciossissimum
"Aurum, Artificium, Jubeor
"Ruines Enoch Ann° 2995.

On the same side of this medal must be engraved, a square Trap door on an Arch

[100]

Two Brothers above with their heads against each other, letting a third brother down by a Rope; and in the Reverse side of the Medal must be Ingraved Rays, like those of the Sun, in the Center of which is the △.

[101]

The 14th Degree,

or Perfection.

Form of the Lodge

The lodge of grand elect perfect Master and Sublime masons, represents a subteraneous Vault of a red Colour, with Columns without number painted, of a fiery red colour; behind the Master must be a transparent Light or sun, which gives Light to all the Lodge, and shines through a Deltha or △ with the Hebraic Characters [blank space]* therein: The Lodge must have some artificial Lights to shew the different Degrees of Masonry and their numbers are 3, 5, 7 and 9; At the head of the Venerable Junior Grand Warden 3; at the head of the Venerable Senior Grand Warden 5; in the South 7 and behind the Master 9: these Lights are used when the Grand Light cannot be had. The thrice Puissant Grand Master is placed in the East under the △ and close to it must be painted some ruins, and before him a pedestal as if it was broken.

The two Grand Wardens are placed in the west, and on the Thrice Puissants right hand sits the Grand Treasurer with a Table of perfumes before him and on his left hand the Grand Secretary with a Table of shew bread before him To go to the sacred Vault, you must go through a narrow passage lighted with a lamp and Oil; on

[102]

the Entrance must be a brother with a Sword in his hand, another brother in the middle and a third at the door of the Entrance to the sacred vault: When a Grand Elect wishes to penetrate, he must give the following words to the Guards; to the first *Mahabin*, to the second *Heleneham*, and to the third *Shibboleth*, 3 times with an Aspiration: The thrice Puissant must be decorated with a large flame Coloured ribbon, which must hang Triangular on his breast, to which the Jewell must be appended, which is a Compass crowned, the points extended and fixed in a Circle of 90 degrees; A sun in the middle, and on the other side a brilliant stone with a

* The blank should be filled in with the Hebrew letters הוהי, Yahweh. —*Ed.*

Deltha in the middle △. The Apron is, a white skin bordered and flowered with red and a blue Ribbon round the Edge and the Jewell painted on the flap.

The Thrice Puissant with the Crown and Scepter on the pedestal, and a Hiram in his hand, to Call to order: The Grand Wardens with the like Hirams. The thrice Puissant must be in the robes of *State*: The Grand Wardens and Brethren with the same Jewell, Apron and Ribbon; dressed in black, with swords in their hands, to use Occassionally. There must be on the Table of perfumes, a small silver hod with a little trowel, and on the table of shew bread

[103]

must be 7 or 12 loaves of bread, with a Cup of red wine for a Libation; A Gold ring for each Candidate, with this Inscription on the inside, "Virtue unites, what death cannot seperate," And all the Jewells &^{ca} necessary for a Candidate. The Lodge being well prepared and well Clothed, the thrice Puissant makes the following demands.

To Open.

Q: – Thrice respectable Wardens, is every thing well prepared and Tyled in the Sacred Vault?

A: – Thrice Respectable Puissant, we are well tyled and in security.

G^{d} M^{r}:– If we are well tyled and in security let us pray. The Grand Warden repeats the same.

The Prayer.

"Sovereign Architect of this vast Universe, who by thy great Divinity doth penetrate into the most secret thoughts of Mortals; Purify our hearts by the sacred fire of thy Love: Guide and direct us, in the path of Virtue; cast from thy adorable sanctuary all Impiety, and perverseness; We pray the to Intirely Occupy us in the Grand works of our perfection, which will be a sufficient price of our Travel, and that peace and Charity may closely link us in the Bonds of Union; And that this Lodge may be a

[104]

faint. Resemblance of what the Elected will enjoy in thy heavenly Kingdom: Give us a spirit of holy discernment, to distinguish the good and refuse the Evil; And that we may not be deceived by those, who are to be marked with the formidable zeal of Perfection; and finally that we may have no other design, but thy Glory and an Advancement in good works in the reign of true masonry; Amen; Amen; Amen."

God bless us, and our works. When this prayer is finished, profound Silence should be observed for a minute, and then the Trice Puissant asks the following Questions.

Q: – Venerable Brother Senior Grand Warden who conducted you hither?
A: – Thrice Respectable and Puissant, the Love of Masonry, my Obligation and a desire I have to the perfection of Masonry.
Q: – What have you brought here?
A: – A heart zealous for friendship and a love of Virtue.
Q: – What are the proper qualities for the acquiring this?
A: – The two first conducts us immediately to the third, when they are properly attained, they lead as to the happiness of perfection.
Q: – What is the true disposition of an Elected perfect Mason?
A: – To divest his heart of Iniquity, Vindictiveness and Jealousy; to be always ready to do good and

[105]

never to employ his tongue to Calumniate; lie or detract against, or from his brother.
Q: – How are you to behave in this place?
A: – With a profound respect.
Q: – How comes it, that the rich and poor; Prince and Subject; are here always, equal friends and brothers?
A: – Because there is something in that Triangle, repeated on the pedestal and firmament, which is greater than you.
Q: – Why is the △ the subject of your respect?
A: – It contains the sacred name of the Divinity known, revealed and Exalted in heaven and on Earth, by the name of the Grand Architect of the Universe.
Q: – How old are you?
A: – Three times three, the perfect number of 81, if it is often repeated by our mysteries Calculation.
Q: – How so my Brother, can you demonstrate this?
A: – I am a perfect sublime and Elect mason, my trials are finished, and it is now time for me to reap the fruits of my labor.
Q: – What did you Contract when you was made Grand, Elect, Sublime and perfect Master?
A: – I contracted an Alliance with virtue and the virtuous.
Q: – What mark have you to show for it?
A: – This Gold ring a symbol of Purity.

[106]

Q: – What is the Clock?
A: – It is high Twelve.
Q: – What do you understand by high 12?
A: – Because the Sun darts its Rays perpendicularly into this Lodge, for us to work Efficaciously the end of our perfection; which is the time to profit by its Generosity.
Q: – Where will you find materials?
A: – In the Treasury of, and Virtue of perfect masons in regularly composing my Actions in my heart by the square and Compass of the Divine Wisdom.
Q: – Where will you find this Divine Wisdom?
A: – In the heart of every Brother that Composes this respectable Lodge of which you are the supporter.
G[d]: M[r]: It is to you my most respectable Brethren, that I am going to impart my designs; to this Effect my venerable Brother Grand Senior Warden, Announce that I am going to open the Lodge of Grand Elect perfect and sublime masters, by the mysterious numbers of 3, 5, 7 and 9.

The Senior Warden having announced the same. The Junior Warden strikes 3 times, the Senior Warden 5 and the Thrice Puissant 7 times; After which a profound silence must reign for a minute then the thrice Puissant says—To Order brethren he then strikes 3 slow; On which the brethren make the first sign, he then strikes 3 more, on which the brethren make the second sign, the Thrice Puissant strikes 3 more; on which the

[107]

Brethren gives the third sign. He then says Venerable Grand Warden the Lodge of perfection is opened, which the Senior Wardens repeats to all the brethren; After which the thrice Puissant makes the sign of Admiration which is repeated first by the Wardens and then by all the brethren, after which the thrice Puissant salutes the Lodge by the first sign which is answered by them all, then they cover their heads and take their places, When the Minutes of the Last Lodge night must be read by the Grand secretary.

Form of Reception

The Candidate must be in a Chamber, near the narrow passage, with all the Ornaments of the former degrees; The Grand Master of the Ceremonies must inform the Candidate to strike 3, 5 and 7 on the first door of the passage, and also must give him the first pass word which he is to give to the Brother that keeps the door, and which is *Shibboleth* 3 times repeated with an Aspiration, on which the Brother a the door says pass; in the middle he meets the second Brother, who demands the pass word, when he gives *Mahabin*, the brother says pass which he does, and comes to the door of the sacred Vault, where he gives *Heleneham*, to the brother who guards the door, The Master of Ceremonies directs the Candidate to strike 3, 5, 7 and 9 on the door, which is answered within by the Junior

[108]

Grand Warden, Senior Grand Warden and by the thrice Puissant, who says go and see brother Junior Grand Warden who knocks at the door in the manner of a Grand Elect and perfect Master: the Junior Warden goes to the door, opens it a little and demands who is there; The Master of Ceremonies answers and says, A Sublime Knight of the Royal Arch, who demands perfection in being Introduced to the sacred Vault: The Junior Grand Warden shuts the door, and reports the same to the thrice Puissant, who gives Orders to introduce the Candidate in proper Order: The Junior Grand Warden on the inside, when the Candidate approaches, presents a naked sword to his breast and the Master of Ceremonies does the same and leads him between the two wardens, when he is there the Master of Ceremonies whispers him to make the sign of Admiration, when a general Silence is to be observed for about a minute And then the thrice Puissant Examines him as follows.

Q: – What do you want here my Brother?
A: – Thrice Respectable and perfect Grand Master I ask the perfection of Masonry.
Gr[d]: M[r]: Do you consent respectable Brethren that this our brother Knights of the Royal Arch should be passed to the Degree of Perfection?

[109]

All the brethren give their Consent by holding up their right hands.

The thrice Puissant then says to the Candidate Before I initiate you my dear brother into the secrets of our Mysteries of Perfection, you must answer the Questions, I am now going to demand, otherwise you must be sent back.

Q: – Are you a Mason?
A: – My brethren know me to be such.
Q: – Are you an Entered Apprentice?
A: – I am.
Q: – Can you give the Sign, Token and Word to the Grand Junior Warden?

A: – I can. (and gives them)
Q: – Are you a fellow Craft?
A: – I have seen the letter G and know the pass word.
Q: – Can you give the <pass word> Sign, Token and word to the Grand Senior Warden?
A: – I can, (and gives them).
Q: – Are you a Master Mason?
A: – I know the Sepulcher, and every thing at Consumates.
Q: – Can you give the pass word, Sign, Token and Word to the Grand Junior Warden?
A: – I can (and gives them) Just as he gives the word, all the brethren presents their swords to him and the thrice Puissant says, "What have you said, you affright us my brother, in speaking this word so loud; We are always ready to

[110]

punish the Indiscretion of the person who pronounces this word aloud, least some prophane person might hear it; but as you intended no harm, we forgive you.
Q: – Are you a Secret Master?
A: – I have passed from the Square to the Compass I have seen the Tomb of the respectable Hiram Abiff and have shed my tears thereat.
Q: – Can you give the sign Token and Words to the Grand Senior Warden?
A: – I can, (and gives them)
Q: – Are you a Perfect Master?
A: – I have seen the three Circles and the three perfect squares, put on the two Columns across.
Q: – Can you give the sign Token and Word to the Grand Junior Warden?
A: – Yes—(and gives them) Just as he gives the word *Jeva*, all the brethren present their swords to him and the brethren present their swords to him and thrice Puissant says "What have you said you affright us my brother, when we hear this word given, we are always ready to put to any man to death who dare to pronounce the least Syllable of the sacred and mysterious name of the great Architect if the Universe: Let is pass to the 6th degree.
Q: – Are you an Intimate Secretary?
A: – My Curiousity is satisfied which had almost cost me my Life.
Q: – Can you give the Sign, Token and Words to the Venerable Senior Grand Warden?
A: – Yes. (and gives them)
Q: – Are you a Prevost and Judge?
A: – I render Justice to all the workmen without

[111]

distinction or partiality.

Q: – Can you give the Sign, Token and Words to the Venerable Junior Grand Warden?

A: – Yes (and give them)

Q: – Are you an Intendant of the Buildings?

A: – I have made the five Steps of Exactitude, I have penetrated into the inermost parts of the Temple, I have seen the Effect of the great light in the middle of which I perceived the hebrew Characters [BLANK SPACE] which is unknown to me.

Q: – Can you give the sign Token and Words to the Venerable Senior Grand Warden?

A: – Yes (and gives them)

Q: – Are you an Elected Knight?

A: – One Cavern received me, one lamp lighted me and one fountain refreshed me.

Q: – Can you give the Sign Token and Words to the Venerable Junior Grand Warden?

A: – Yes (and gives them)

Q: – Are you a Grand Master Elected?

A: – My zeal and labor has procured me the favor of receiving this degree.

Q: – Where was you received in this degree?

A: – By Solomon himself in his Study.

Q: – When was you received and on what Occasion?

A: – When he sent me with my Companions to search for the two other Ruffians who destroyed our Grand Master Hiram Abiff.

Q: – How came they to be discovered?

A: – By the Industry of *Bengabee*, Solomons

[112]

Intendant in the Country of Cheth.

Q: – Can you given the Sign Token and Word to the venerable Senior Grand Warden?

A: – Yes. (and gives them)

Q: – Are you a Sublime Illustrious Knight?

A: – My name will inform you.

Q: – What is your name?

A: – *Emerh* is my true name.

Q: – Can you give the Sign, Token and Word to the Venerable Junior Grand Warden?

A: – Yes. (and gives them)

Q: – Are you a Grand Master Architect?
A: – I possess all the Sciences of the Mathematicks and I know all the Attributes.
Q: – Can you give the Sign, Token and Word to the Venerable Senior Grand Warden?
A: – Yes. (and gives them)
Q: – Which is the most Sublime Degree that you have received in Masonry?
A: – The 13th Which I received by an Effect of providence
Q: – Can you Explain that my Brother?
A: – Yes; I searched in the Antient ruins of the old patriarchs, *Gibulum* at last found the divine Deltha △.
Q: – What do you understand by this Deltha?
A: – It is a Triangular Gold plate, filled with rays on which was Engraved by *Enoch*, the sacred name of the Almighty God.

[113]

Q: – I suppose you know that mysterious word my Brother?
A: – I do not know it yet; as my time is not Expired. That sacred name is only known by the Grand Elect, Perfect and Sublime Masons, All my hopes is in God, and I expect to have a knowledge of it, in the fulness of time.
Q: – What is your Quality?
A: – A Knight of the Royal Arch.
Q: – What is your name?
A: – Gebulum.
Q: – Can you give the Sign, Token and Word to the Venerable Junior Grand Warden?
A: – Yes. (and gives them)
Q: – What do you now desire my Brother?
A: – The sublime Degree of Grand Elect, Perfect and sublime Master.

The thrice Puissant then answers him with the sign of Admiration; and says, "brother retire; God will permit you to receive this day what you so much crave."

The Grand Master, Orders the Master of Ceremonies to take him away untill he is wanted. Then the thrice Puissant says, "My dear brethren do you consent at last, for this Knight of the Royal Arch to be passed to the degree of Perfection." On which all the brethren hold up their right hands, as a sign of their Consent.

The thrice Puissant then says, "Let us applaud

[114]

it by 9, 7, 5 and 3. After which the Candidate is ordered to return; when the door is opened and he is Introduced by the Grand Master of Ceremonies between the two Wardens. The thrice Puissant then demands of him as follows

Q – Do you know in your Conscience my dear brother of any thing since you have been a Mason of any falsity to your brother, or hurting him in his Character or family; your Religion or King;—Answer me: Answer me?
A: – Never: Never.
Q: – Have you communicated, or let Escape from you, any of our Mysteries to Cowans: What would you have done to the Assassins of our respectable Master *Hiram Abiff*, had you lived in those days; would you have revenged his death: be sincere; Answer me? and do not hesitate.
A: – I would have done as *Joabert* did.
Q: – Have you been always mindful of the Obligations which you have contracted in the presence of the Grand Architect of the Universe, Answer me?
A: – I have.
Q: – Did you ever find any thing in your Obligations which was Contrary, and against your Religion, The State, yourself or any thing that might hurt your delicacy; Do Answer me?
A: – Never.

After which the thrice Puissant speaks further and says, "Remember now my Brother: If you approach Cool, and Indifferent to our sacred

[115]

Mysteries, you will be more blamable after receiving this Degree of Grand Elect and sublime Master, than you could have been heretofore, and you will have more to answer for, at the great and awful day of Judgment, where the secrets of all hearts shall be disclosed: This Degree my Brother is the end, and full measure of Masonry, to which you are now going to be attached; particularly by some Indispensible which is, as yet unknown to you: So I hope you will fix them in your heart, when communicated and demonstrated to you. Your goodness by a pursuit of virtue and close united love, for all your brethren particularly for us, who are your fellows and superiors, will be the only means to Exemplify your attachment to this Sublime Degree."

Q: – Do you desire to be contracted to those new Engagements, my Brother?
A: – I do most Cordially.

The thrice Puissant then says, "If you do, then go my Brother and wash your hands in the brazen Sea, to prove your Innocence, and that you have not violated any Engagement that you have solemnly made; remember that our fore fathers used the same Ceremony, when they were accused of Crimes, and by that means proved themselves guiltless." Then the Master of Ceremonies, shews the Candidate the brazen sea, to which he goes and washes his hands—he then returns between the Two Wardens and the

[116]

thrice Puissant proceeds, "You are now introduced my dear Brother into the most sacred place of masonry; the most sacred mysteries of which are now going to be revealed to you:

The Rampart of this Degree has been properly guarded by the strictest care of the Grand Elect against every vile discoverer, when the 3 first Degrees has been laid open to the publick eyes of the world: We are now going to Confirm you in our grand secrets, as we are certain of your discretion; and have no doubt among us concerning you. Come then my dear Brother and add to our Tranquility , by Swearing inviolable fidelity to us." Then the Candidate is ordered by the Grand Master of Ceremonies and is led with 8 quick steps and 1 slow up to the thrice Puissant, with the Sign of Elected Master on him; where he kneels and takes the following Obligation.

Obli^{n}: – "I A.B. do swear on the holy Bible, and in the presence of the Grand Architect of the Universe, and before this respectable Lodge of Grand Elect perfect and sublime Masters; to be Eternally faithfull in my holy religion: I promise never to take up arms against my King, nor to enter directly or indirectly into any Conspiracy against my King or Country or to know of any doing the same without makeing it known. I further promise never to reveal to the Grand Masters Architect or Knights of the Royal Arch, or to any person whatsoever to whom it doth not belong, the mysteries of this our

[117]

most high Degree; or any other matter that shall occur in our Lodge, or any of our laws or Regulations, under every penalty of the different Obligations by me taken. I promise to have an equal regard for my Brethren of this Royal Degree, without the distinction of Riches, Poverty Noble or Ignoble Birth or Parentage, and of making no other distinction but that of excelling in Virtue: And that I never will refuse acknowledging a Brother who is a good man, in whatever state or Condition he may be in, and to support him in Indigence, provided he is virtuous and on makeing it appear sufficient. I promise if possible to meet my Lodge at least once a year; and that on the 27th day of December or 24th of June, and to meet the Lodge further as often as my Affairs will permit. I promise to visit my Brother in sickness, and to help and assist him with my Council, my purse and with my Arm; whether in affliction or pain and in Case of the Accidents of Life and death to give him all the Consolation and Assistance in my power. I promise never to give my voice for the Admission of a Candidate in these our Mysteries without being very scrupilously circumspect and having a sufficient knowledge of his life and conversation as near as I possibly can. I promise that I never will lay with a Brothers wife, nor dishonor his daughter, sister or any of his family knowing them to be such: And that I never will break the present Engagement that I am now

[118]

Contracting. I promise that I never will make or Assist in making by my presence, any person whomsoever to be a Grand Elect Perfect and sublime Master, who is not, or has not been an Officer of a regular and Legitimate Constituted Lodge: And I promise never to receive or cause or Consent to be received any person in this Degree, but on the following Conditions, (to wit,) By the permission and Consent of all the Grand Elect perfect and sublime Masters that Compose this respectable Lodge and are members thereof, or by their permission in writing, or by patent or power vested in me, for that purpose; And in failure of this my Obligation, I condemn myself to undergo all the penalties of my former Obligations, and with this addition, to have my belly cut open, by bowels torn from thence, and distributed to the Voracity of the Vultures, So help me God and maintain me in Veracity and Equity, Amen, Amen, Amen.

The Candidate remains on his knees, and the Grand Master of Ceremonies, brings the hod and trowel, and then the thrice Puissant Annoints his Eyes, his lips and heart, and says, "By the power committed unto me, and which I have acquired by my Assiduous labor, Constancy and integrity; I make sacred your Eyes; your lips; and your heart, with the holy Oil that Annointed the pious Aaron; the penitent David and the wise Solomon: I stamp you with the r[e]doubtable zeal of the Grand Architect of the Universe, to the end that you might always live in his

[119]

adorable presence, and that he may always be in your mind, and in your heart; That a fervent zeal and Constancy, might by always the rule to your Action." Then raising the Candidate the thrice Puissant presents him with the bread and wine, in a gold Cup, and says, "Eat with me this bread and drink this wine, in the same

Cup with me, and learn therefrom to succor each other mutually and graciously." The Candidate Eats and drinks. Then the thrice Puissant gives him the Gold ring saying, "Receive this ring as a token of Alliance, and to shew that you have made a Contract with Virtue and with the Virtuous: Do promise me my dear Brother never to part with this Ring, untill death, and that you never will give it to any, but your wife, your Eldest son or your nearest friend."

The thrice Puissant then gives him the Ring. After this Ceremony the Brethren all, eat of the Bread and drink of the wine, and make a Libation according to the Antient Custom that was practiced at the Sacrifices. This being finished; The thrice Puissant decorates the Candidate with the Ornaments of the Degree and says, "I now salute you my dear Brother, and give you the Title of Grand Elect perfect and sublime Master, and with inexpressable pleasure I ornament you with the symbols thereof. Receive this Ribbon of the Order, the

[120]

triangle appended thereto, represents the Deltha on which was Engraved by *Enoch*, the holy name which is the principal Object of our Mystery, and which was Accomplished by the utmost labor, trouble and danger without our having a knowledge then of what it was. The red Colour represents to you two things; first the rays that encompassed the burning Bush, when Moses received the first time the sacred name; and secondly the preeminence of the Grand Elect perfect and sublime Masters over all the other Brethren of Inferior Degrees. The Jewel that hangs round your neck, gives us a great deal of useful Information: First the Crown designs the Royal Origin of Masonry; Second the Compass and Circle of 90 Degrees represents the Operation of the most important things which the Grand Elect perfect and Sublime Masters profitt by, and thirdly the Sun designs the superiority of their rank, and the triangle represents the sacred name of the Divinity or *Deltha* which was found by the Knights of the Royal Arch: All of which is suspended on your breast, to the end that you may continually see the Ornaments of our Dignity, so that we should never fail in the Duties imposed on us by the Instruction of an History which we are about to reveal to you in the Study of Masonry.

There are 3 Signs, 3 Tokens, 3 Covered words 3 pass

[121]

words and 1 Grand word.

SIGN 1st. The first Sign Is made by bringing your right hand from the left side of your belly to the right.

TOKEN 1st. The first Token, Is to take each others right hand as in the Intimate secretary and say *Berith* the other answers *Neder*, the first says *Selemoth*.

Cov^{d} W^{d} 1st. The first Covered word Is *Gebulum* (which Signifies friend Chosen; Elected favorite, and zealous brother.

PASS W^{d} 1st. The first pass word is Shibboleth, 3 times repeated (which signifies plenty)

SIGN 2^{d} The Second sign, Is to bring your right hand upright with the back part towards your left cheek and support your right Elbow with the left hand, and so Vica versa. This represents the Impression that the burning Bush made on Moses, which Caused him to shelter his Eyes from the brilliancy thereof, as that light was too powerful for his Eyes to bear.

TOKEN 2^{d} The second Token is the same as the Masters, and you then ask, "can you go farther," then slip your hands first, above the wrist, to the middle of the lower part of the arm and then to the Elbow, place your left hand on each others right shoulder, then pass or ballance your hands 3 times in the same manner as in the secret Master you do 7.

Cov^{d} W^{d} 2^{d} The second Covered word Is *Mahabin* (which signifies silence and respect.)

PASS W^{d} 2^{d} The second pass word is *Heleneham* (which signifies

[122]

mercy of God.

SIGN 3^{d} The 3 Sign is double, first the sign of Admiration by Extending your Arms and looking up, after that the second is to put the 3 fore fingers of your right hand upon your lips.

TOKEN 3^{d} The third Token is to seize each others left Elbow at the same time your right hands on each others Neck as if you would raise each other up.

Cov^{d} W^{d} 3^{d} The third Covered word is *Adonai,* (which signifies God Eternal.)

PASS W^{d} 3 The third pass word is *Mahac–Maharabac* (which signifies God be praised we have found it.

GR^{d} W^{d} The Grand Word Is [BLANK SPACE]

After which the new Initiated Brother has a plan of the Lodge laid before him, for his Inspection while the following History if read to him.

THE HISTORY.

Your Good conduct my Brother, your zeal and discretion, have been the Cause of our determining to give you in the end, the true knowledge of perfection. You have now received the name of Grand Elect perfect and sublime Mason: We are also happy my Venerable Brother in having a Circumspection in giving you this knowledge, without which we should be liable to the same fatality that the three first degrees has been subject to; You know my Brother when the Temple at Jerusalem was finished, the Masons had atchieved [*sic*] great honor, their society was Established into an Order and the Extreme niceness of the brethren

[123]

<in> their choice of fit Objects rendered them respectable for Merit, and Merit only, proved as yours have been; procured them this Advantage. The Grand Elect perfect and sublime Masons were not by any means to be seduced to determine in favor of Candidates who were unworthy, but received those (if at the utmost hazard to themselves) who appeared deserving of that honor. The principal members of the Grand Elect perfect and Sublime Masons, being able workmen, passed from Jerusalem after the dedication of the Temple, and dispersed themselves among the neighboring nations, to Instruct them in the truth of the Royal Craft, but with the precaution of only Initiating the Males, and those of a free and Eminent Understanding. Notwithstanding this resolve, Masons in the lower Degrees multiplied over the face of the Earth; their numbers encreased beyond measure, by which means their secrets were disclosed; their knowledge was made common, and they were held in no Esteem. The Grand Elect perfect and sublime Masons only, had the precaution to conceal the higher Mysteries, by coming to a Resolution not to raise any higher than a Master, and if such were not circumspect in their words and actions and lives, to give them no further knowledge; As it was through the Imprudence of some of the brethren in the three lower Degrees, that Cowans frequently obtained their signs and Tokens. These disorders Chagrined the perfect Masons, (who luckily at that time

[124]

were but few in number,) they took great pains to stop the Contagion but all their Endeavors were in vain; the Craft degenerated Insensibly. Receptions were obtained too easily, the intervals between the Degrees were broken into too hastily and were scarce seperated at all: In the end they were not prefered by merit, but prefering amusement to Instruction, Innovations encreased and new doctrines arose, which destroyed the old, (that they ought to have adhered to.) These differences occasioned disputes, quarrels, heart burnings, and dissentions, which in the end produced a total discovery of our works: for which we grieve, and by which, Masonry suffered in the three first Degrees. Happy it is for us who have the Consolation of knowing the secret of the Grand Elect perfect and Sublime Masons; let us endeavour to render it impossible for this Degree to share the same fate as the three lower; let us be animated with zeal to procure that Antient perfection: We travel to obtain their science and to follow their direction, in order to get a

full knowledge of their noble Occupation: The study and Imitation of the Grand Architect of the Universe were always their principal Object, and his holy name was the Ancient Masters word. Solomon Chose that word expressly in Order to fill the principal workmen with due veneration for the great God, to whom the Temple was dedicated, and also to excite them never to neglect the Execution and Duties of their Office; so that the Masters uniformly followed their Occup–

[125]

tion with this their Grand secret. The Sign token and words of which make a part of those of this degree. The sage King knew all the force of this holy name; he knew that the Grand Architect of the Universe appeared to Moses in the burning Bush, (near which our Lodge is kept,) and declared to him that this was his name, and that he was the only one of the patriarchs that knew it; and further that he would be invoked by no other name in the Temple, which he would order to be built in the Land of promise, upon the plan and design of the Tabernacle; giving him at the same time, the Tables of the Law to be deposited therein. This his holy name having so great a report in, and to, the Construction of the Temple, was the reason of its being made the Masters word. When Hiram Abiff was killed, we being convinced of his Courage and discretion in never disclosing this secret: It was resolved never to intrust a matter of this Importance in future to a single person; therefore the Masters Sign, Token and Word were changed as it is before related, and no other than the Antient Masters knew it, untill it was taken by the Knights of the Royal Arch from the △ in the ruins of Enoch, where was wrote the true name that was made the principal object of the Perfection of Masonry. Solomon and Hiram King of Tyre being satisfied in having placed in safety the precious deposit of the Grand Elect perfect and sublime Masons under

[126]

the Sanctum Sanctorum, he named this place the sacred Vault, a denomination truly just; because there was nothing on the Pedestal, save the Divine △, and this Column was the third that supported the Temple of which you know every thing but Indifferently, and have always been, Ignorant of the true situation of the hebrew name thereof, which is that of the Grand Architect of the universe, and which is called the pillar of Perfection and sustains wonderfully the most beautiful place in the Universe. The Curious Cowans have not been able to discover the place where this sacred word was deposited, as it was always kept a secret from all Masons, but those of the Royal Arch and of this Degree. A strict guard was ever kept at the door, to prevent admittance to any but the Grand Elect, who repaired there to Contemplate the Mystery of the sacred word, and there was one substituted in its place for the Inferior Degrees; so that it was not possible for any greater precaution to be taken by this wise Prince, to preserve this great name from all prophane persons, and which rule has always been observed by the Grand Elect who lived after him, and were possessed of his zeal, and which has been handed down to each other: Then Commenced the Unity of the fraternity, which was sworn by the Grand Elect, to which this word was a seal. The Temple was finished in the year of the world 3000, being Six Months and Six days from Solomons

[127]

laying the first stone, and finished with the utmost Pomp, Brilliancy and Magnificence: This Ceremony being over, Solomon gave audience for three days successively to all the brethren; the first day was to the Elected Masters who were Introduced into the sacred Vault; the Knights of the Royal Arch took care of the Arches of the vault and guarded the Entrance thereto, at the same time the Grand Masters Architects were in the Kings Apartment. He qualified with the Degree of perfection, the most virtuous among the two Orders, and made them promise solemnly, to live by themselves in peace, Union and Concord, to Exercise the works of Charity and Benevolence in Intimation of their deceased Chief, and that the basis of their Actions might like him, be that of Wisdom, Justice and Equity, and to keep a profound silence relative to their Mysteries, and never to reveal them, to any one who did not deserve this signal favor by their zeal, fervor, and Constancy, and to assist mutually each other by their works, and to punish severely treason, perfidy and Injustice: On which he gave them this blessing, and discovered to them the Ark of Alliance open, from which the Grand Architect of the Universe used to deliver his Oracles: He ordered many sacrifices and admitted them to a holy Libation; he embraced them, and gave to each a gold ring, as a proof of the Alliance they had Contracted with virtue, and the virtuous: He gave them many presents, with a permission to stay or retire

[128]

as they should Choose. The second day Solomon gave Admittance to the Masters and Knights Elected in the heart of the Temple, and made them promise as the others had done, that they never would depart from the principles of virtue, of which their Antient Chief was a model; to live always united, and to help each other in their works; he bestowed on them the Degree of Grand Master Architect, and decorated them with all the honors relative thereto; he made them promise that they would be faithful Guardians of their Mysteries and never to communicate them to any who did not merit them: He bestowed on them many favors and permitted them to stay or retire at their discretion. The third day Solomon gave audience to the fellow Crafts and Apprentices in the Eastern part of the Temple, he gratified the fellow Crafts who appeared to him to be virtuous, with the Degree of Master, and the Apprentices with that of fellow Craft; he introduced them into the porch of the Temple, and made them of both Degrees, promise never to depart from the principles of virtue, of which their Antient Chief was their pattern, and to be always United, Assisting each other mutually, and to keep secret among them, the Sign, Token and Word of each Degree, and never to communicate them to any but those who should merit it, by their goodness, and were known to be virtuous: he loaded them with presents, and permitted them to

[129]

stay or go where they pleased, he also gave Orders to his Intendants to defray their Expenses untill they should arrive at their own Countries and homes. King Solomon so wise and so just, in all that he had heretofore done; become in his latter days deaf to the Voice of the Lord, proud of knowing himself to be the greatest Monarch on Earth, and having built a temple so large, that the structure and magnificence of it was the Admiration of the Universe: Soon did this King forget the goodness of God, and gave himself up to Licentiousness and Idolatry; his shameful and excessive Complacency to his wives, led him into their Vices, and that means destroyed the piety of his former life, and drew upon him the displeasure of the Almighty; he also prophaned the holy Temple by offering the Incense to the Idol Moloch, which should have been burnt in the Sanctum Sanctorum: This conduct of the King was soon imitated by a great part of the nation; And was viewed with a great deal of Concern, Anxiously and detestation by all the good men and Masons, who brought up their Children in the paths of virtue, and according to the Tenets they had received by the holy and respectable Union that subsisted among them: They also endeavored by their Counsel and good Example to deter and dissuade their fellow Citizens from that Impiety and Sacriledge, which they was so guilty of; but despairing of being able to succeed,

[130]

they remembered in the bitterness of their hearts the vengeance that God had taken on their forefathers, for their disobedience; they Imagined that Lightning would fall on their heads, and that the superb Temple would be laid low, that Jerusalem would be destroyed, and that their Children would suffer for the Iniquities of the nation, by a dreadfull slavery: These Expectations, determined the greatest part of the good Masons to banish themselves voluntarily out of Judea, so that they might not be spectators, and sharers in the expected horror and destruction, whenever it should happen. The crimes of the nation having arrived at their utmost pitch, and the time come, when God had resolved to deliver them into the hands of their Enemies: Nebuchadnezer King of Babylon, be means of Nebuzaradan his General, laid siege to Jerusalem which he took, and having mastered all Judea, he razed the walls and destroyed to the foundation the Temple of the living God; took the Inhabitants with their King Zedekiah Captive into Babylon, exporting with him all the Riches of the Temple: This Event happened According to Josephus 470 years 6 Months and 10 days after its dedication. The Grand Elect who was left at Jerusalem, defended it with Intrepidity, but could not resist the force and Vivacity of the Conqueror, they were not under any Concern about the Riches of the place, nor had they any Inquietude concerning the Treasure thereof, but only, least the sacred vault should

[**Pages 131–2 are missing.** *The following text is from a similar copy of the ritual in the Archives of the Supreme Council, 33°.*]†

[be discovered and Randsacked these apprehensions remaind lively in the bitterness of their Hearts they viewed the Temple ruined and Destroyed and with eagerness exposed themselves to the fury of the soldiers, who guarded the Door, until they penetrated into the Ruins of the sanctuary and searched into the sacred vault till they found the Golden Plate on the Cubical Triangular Stone, and found there also the Body of *Galahad*, the son of *Sophoris*, a Considerable Man among the Perfect Masons, and Chief of the Levites.

This *Galahad* was guardian of the sacred vault, to take care of the Burning Lamp and to adore and contemplate on the ineffable Word, he was a Man equal to *H.A.* who 400 years before lost his Life rather than discover the secrets of the Master. *Galahad* preferred being burried in the Ruins of the temple, rather then discover by his coming out, the Treasures undefiled by the Hands of the barbarians. Then they Cried out

Mahac Maharabac

which signifies God be praised we have found it, and this is the third and most necessary Pass Word to be known, to be the guardians of the Sacred Vault or Treasury. It is difficult to express the Demonstration of Joy with which they were filled at that time, they immediately sat to work to efface this mysterious and sacred Word that it never should be legible, not run any Risque of its being discovered by the impious. On which they melted down the Cubic Stone as they found it impossible to Carry it off, oversetting the Pedestal on which was the sacred name Deposited. They took from *Galahad* the Robes of the Chief of the Levites, which consisted of a Tiara & a vestment of fine Linen, and retired well satisfied.

† The pre-1800 manuscript, which reads nearly verbatim with the Jamaica Manuscript, is simply titled "Perfection."

Resolving never to trust in future to any thing but their memory of Carrying down to their Posterity by Tradition. From this comes the Custom of spelling by Letter by Letter the most high name of names, without Joining a syllable, a usage afterwards observed when the Temple was rebuilt by Cyrus, and has been particularly observed by us.

The High Priest in the middle of a Number of Perfection Brethren who formed a Circle like a chain, and used to spell it once a Year in the Temple, giving orders to the People to make a great noise least they should be heard, by their having se great Circumspection, they lost the habit of Writing or Pronouncing it, they were uncertain of the number of Letters which]

[133]

composed it, and by stopping and giving the syllables, the true pronounciation, which had securely rested to this time with the Grand Elect perfect and sublime Masons only: As God permitted the Antient Masters, who were not Elected, and who had the knowledge of this word, before the death of Hiram Abiff, and who had treated Solomon so ill, to form the blameable project of penetrating into the Antient ruins of *Enoch*, by which means they were all destroyed. The Grand Elect and Perfect Masons who had penetrated into the ruins of the Temple at Jerusalem for the purpose of securing this inestimable treasure, and who had so happily succeeded; Left Judea and travelled into strange Lands and new Countries, into Egypt, syria and Scythia, even to the desarts of Thebais, others passed the Seas and took shelter in the southern Climes, principally in England, Scotland and Ireland, where they continued faithfull in virtue, Assisting each other, and knowing no superiority among them, but only of those who excelled in virtue and good works; by this means they became the Admiration of the people among whom they had taken refuge, and excited them to the practice of their Virtues, which determined many to enter the society of good masons, beseeching them to be initiated into their Mysteries: The good Brethren chose among them the most Eminent, and acquainted them

[134]

with their History, and exhorted them to deplore the uncertainty of human Affairs, of which King Solomon was a remarkable Example; to Shun Vice and practice Virtue, in Imitation of their Master Hiram Abiff, and to crown their zeal and constancy, by imitating them in their Mysteries. Some of the few who preserved themselves from the general Corruption, having with a regret of heart seen some of their Brethren depart from the road of virtue, took a resolution of keeping and preserving their secrets, and remembering certain Signs, which the folly of their brethren made them forget; they seperated themselves from them as if they were not Countrymen. The time arrived when the Christian princes combined together for Conquering the holy Land, and delivering Jerusalem out of the hands of the Turks, who had it in possession: The Good and virtuous Masons worthy of the heritage of those who built the Temple, voluntarily contributed to the Execution of so holy and Enterprize and offered their service to the Confederate princes on these Conditions, that they should have no other Chief but one of their own Choosing; The princes accepted their offer and they hoisted their own Standard and departed: In the tumult and disorder of the war they still retained the principles of Virtue of which their fathers had given them the Model; they lived perfectly united, lodgeing together in the same tents without any distinction of rank; they

[135]

never knew any General, but in the time of battle, retiring on an Equality and giving mutual Assistance to each other, and extending their Charity to the Indigent, and even to their Enemies: In all their Actions they sustained and gave proof of their great valor, and frequently resisted the whole force of the enemies troops; the Confederates themselves could not withstand the violent impetuously of the Turks, But the Brethren reestablished the Combat and gained the Victory: A Memorable Example of their Courage and Intrepidity; On signal given they would all Attack, Open, Close, Rally, and fall on the Enemy with such Impetuously and firmness, that nothing could resist them: These Prodigies of Valor succeeded Alternately, The South wing did not destroy so fast, as did the Masons, on every Occasion; Their Order, their Intrepidity in all dangers, joined to the wisdom, the Union, the Charity and the disinterestedness of the Brethren in refusing to partake of the Spoils of the field, awakened the Attention, principally of the Knights of Jerusalem, who when they came to have a knowledge of the heroes, and saw them, Entreated their Alliance. What a moving spectacle was it to see those Illustrious Knights, such worthy defenders of religion, throwing themselves into the arms of those Masonic heroes, calling them their fathers, and Offering them the tribute of a grateful acknowledgment: The generous Masons replied that tribute was only due to the Grand Architect of the

[136]

Universe: That they took up arms to defend the common Cause; that Judea was their Antient Country, and that their fathers had been Obliged to abandon it for many years, the particular Circumstances of which, when they reflected on, brought tears from their Eyes. The princes were surprized to meet with so great virtue among the Brethren, and requested to be admitted into their Society, and to be particularly Initiated into their Mysteries: The Masons replied that Wisdom, Justice and probity; peace, good manners and Equality; friendship and Union, were the Principal laws which charmed them, and their zeal and fervor were recompensed, by partaking of the mysteries of which they had become worthy by their constancy: The Knights of Saint John of Jerusalem readily assented to what the Masons had laid down to them, and were Initiated into all their Mysteries, Instructed in the history, and learnt of them the Grand Mysteries of Universal religion and benevolence, and by the Instructions of the Antient Masons, Masonry in General has been gloriously perpetuated from age to Age in all Europe and part of America: And although there has been many revolutions in the form of Empires and Kingdoms, yet have they never affected our glorious profession, which has ever handed down to us my Dear Brethren in all its primitive purity: Let us therefore offer us our prayers at the footstool of the Grand Architect of the Universe, that we may never

[137]

be divided, and that Masonry may Continue throughout all Ages! Amen! Amen! Amen!

The Lecture

Q: 1st Who are you?
A: – I am what I am, and more, I am a Grand Elect perfect Master and sublime Mason, and nothing is unknown to me, relative to this Degree.
Q: –2d Where was you received a Grand Elect and perfect Mason?
A: – In a place where the rays of the Sun or Moon was not needed.
Q: –3. Where is that marvellous place situate?
A: – Under the Sanctum Sanctorum of the Grand Architect of the Universe in a holy and sacred place called the sacred Vault.
Q: –4th Who Introduced you into this sacred place?
A: – The most wise and Puissant of all Kings in Company with his Ally.
Q: –5. Which way did you enter that place?
A: – Through a long entrance composed of 9 Arches.
Q: –6. How was you Introduced into the holy Vault?
A: – By 3 knocks.
Q: –7. What signifies the 3 knocks?
A: – The Age of an Apprentice and the number of Knights Elected, who penetrated into the bowels of the earth and took from thence the precious treasure of the Grand Elect perfect and sublime Mason
Q: –8. What did you procure by these 3 knocks?
A: – 5 other knocks, which distinguish the Age of the fellow Craft and also the numbers of the 5 who were compleat when Gebulum, Joabert and Stolkin

[138]

arrived loaded with the precious treasure which they brought to the two kings Solomon and Hiram to be deposited in the place which providence had destined for it, and to be done by the 5 Brothers.

Q: –9th What answer was made to the 5 knocks?

A: – 7 other knocks, which signifies 3 things, 1st the age of the master, 2d that there was Chosen 7 Expert brethren to replace one, 3d that Solomon was employed 7 years in the Construction of the Temple.

Q: –10th What answer was made to the 7 knocks?

A: – 9 great knocks, which marks the age of a perfect Master, and when often repeated makes the number 81, revered by the Grand Elect perfect and sublime Masons.

Q: –11. What did you derive from these great knocks?

A: – It opened to me the 9th Vault of the Earth, and I penetrated into the most holy and sacred place pronouncing 3 times with an Aspiration, Shibboleth!

Q: –12. What signifies this pass word?

A: – Abundance, or floods of water.

Q: –13. What did you perceive on entering this holy place?

A: – The most Brilliant Light, which dazzled my Eyes and struck me with Amazement.

Q: –14 What was that Brilliant Light?

A: – It was the brilliant or the Triangular golden plate deposited by the Antient patriarch and found by the Grand Elect, on which was engraved the holy name of the Almighty; placed on a pedestal in the

[139]

sacred subterraneous vault.

Q: –15. What do you call this pedestal?

A: – The Pillar of Beauty.

Q: –16 How came this to us?

A: – By the laborious search of the Antient Knights of the Royal Arch, who took this treasure from the ruins of the patriarch Enoch and was found after the Deluge 1345 years.

Q: –17. Give me the word?

A: – I cannot.

Q: –18. How will you make me sensible that you know it?

A: – Mahabin was substituted in the place of it, The Grand pass word is Mahac–Maharabac or 3 times 5.

Q: –19th To whom did God first Communicate this word?

A: – To Enoch before the flood, and by the care of that holy patriarch it is come to us, 2dly when God shewed himself to Moses in the burning Bush on Mount Sinai, and approveing his merit 3dly The Grand Elect and Perfect who found it.

Q: –20. What became of the word afterwards?

A: – It was Intirely Effaced and the golden plate was melted down by pious masons on the destruction of the Temple by Nebuchadnezer, they being afraid that if the divine △ fell into hands of the impious the sacred name would be prophaned.

[140]

Q: –21st What have you perceived in the Degree of Illustrious Knights?

A: – 12 great Lights.

Q: –22^{d} What do they signifie?

A: – The 12 Masters that were Elected by Solomon for carrying on the works of the Temple, after the death of Hiram Abiff, and who commanded the 12 Tribes of Israel.

Q: –23. What were the names of these 12?

A: – 1st Joabert 2^{d} Stolkin 3^{d} Tiercy 4th Morphy 5th Durson 6th Kerim 7th Berthemer 8th Tito 9th Alqueber (these were the 9 that were Elected to be sent for the Traitor, *Jubela Abiram Akirop* the Assassin of Hiram Abiff) 10th Zerbal 11th Benechred and 12th Tabor, these are the other 3 Masters that Solomon Elected to make up the 12.

Q: –24. How were the Masters divided in the Temple to have the proper Cognizance of the work?

A: – Joabert over the Tribe of Judah, Stolkin over Benjamin Tiercy over Simon, Morphy over Ephraim, Durson over Manassah, Kerim over Zebulon, Berthemer over Dan Tito over Ashar, Alquebert over Napthali, Zerbal over Ruben, Benechard over Isachar and Tabor over Gad these names as well as their Governments are fictitious as observed in the 11th Degree, the true names and their Governments you will find in the 1st Kings Chapter 4th verse 8th to 19th—These 12 Masters rendered a daily account of the work that was done in the Temple and received the wages due to their different divisions.

Q: –25th What signifies the Ivory key of the secret Master?

A: – It serves us to remember that the Grand Elect and perfect Masons, were the only depositories of Antient Ma-

[141]

-sonry, which ought to be locked up in their hearts and are always to rule their conduct in such manner as never to render themselves unworthy of that great trust.

Q: –26th What means the Tomb placed at the (*West*) door of the Temple?

A: – It ought to be the East door, as there was no Door in the west beyond the Sanctum Sanctorum, It is the place under which is deposited the body of our Respectable Master Hiram Abiff, which Solomon caused to be placed there as a lasting mark to the Brethren of the great Esteem they had for their grand Master Architect.

Q: –27. What signifies the ballance?

A: – It teaches us to be Just and Equitable.

Q: –28. What signifies the sword which the Grand Master of Ceremonies carried naked in his hand at your Entrance in the Lodge.

A: – It is employed to defend our Grand Master and to destroy those who shall depart from Virtue and those who shall be so perfidious as to reveal the secrets Committed to them or to their Charge.

Q: –29th What reward or recompence received the 12 Masters from Solomon?

A: – He gave them the name of favorites and Initiated them sublime Knights, decorating them with a large black ribbon, on which was an Enflamed heart painted opposite their hearts, and did not permit them to travel without this mark of distinction, and Instead of the poinard gave them a sword of Justice, and said to them, as you have been the Conductors of the Buildings of the Temple you are to defend it with this sword.

[142]

Q: –30th What signifies the flaming heart?

A: – The Ardent Charity we ought to have one towards the other.

Q: –31st What signifies your word in Quality of Knight Elected?

A: – *Balgulkal* is the word of the Knights Elected, which signifies, Chief of the Tabernacle or faithfull Guardian; there are 3 pass words proper to be known first Nekum or Nekah which signifies Vengeance Second Stolkin the name of him who took the Corps of Hiram Abiff from under the Sprig of Cassia, third Joabert who cutt off the head of the Villian Abiram Akirop and brought it to Solomon in Company with his 8 Brethren.

Q: –32d What signifies the 8 lights together an 1 seperate?

A: – The 9 Elected who were sent in search of Jubilum Akirop

Q: –33d Have you received any distinction since you have been a Knight Elected?

A: – Solomon being willing to recompence the trouble of the Elected, Advanced them to the degree of Sublime Knights and Joined to their

Chapter 3 zealous brothers, being willing it should consist of 12 members: he shewed them all the Riches of the Tabernacle and gave to each a Golden key and to be among the rest of the brethren, he gave them the name of Excellent *Emerh*, a word signifying a true Mason on all Occasions; and gave them the Command of the 12 Tribes.

Q: –34th Have you penetrated any further?

A: – Solomon soon after (being full of Justice) Initiated me into the Degree of Grand Master Architect being

[143]

willing to recompence me for my zeal fervor and constancy, and in the end to lead me to the Celestial Throne.

Q: –35th What was the name of the unknown person who acquainted Solomon with the place where the Traitor had secreted himself?

A: – His name was Perignan, he was a squarer and polisher of marble in the quarry of Gibulum near Joppa between the sprig of Cassia and the sea, where was found the Body of Hiram Abiff, beyond the Cavern of the Traitor; This Perignan was not enrolled among the workmen of the Temple, but for this piece of service Solomon recompensed him by enrolling him and changed his name to Gibulum because he continued to work in the Quarry so called.

Q: –36th What signifies the 3 lights placed at the 3 doors of the Elected Masters?

A: – The 3 fellow Crafts who Assassinated our Respectable Master Hiram Abiff, and as their heads are placed in the same manner.

Q: –37th What was their names and of what Tribe and Parentage?

A: – They were from the Tribe of Dan, sons of the same parents, and were called Vizt the 1st Jubelum Akirop by some he is called, Vizt the 1st Jubelm Akirop by some he is called Oben Akirop, the 2d Jubelo Gravilot, the 3d and youngest Jubelum Guibs or Kumwel.

Q: –38th What became of the two younger brothers of Akirop?

A: – They fled to the Country of Cheth.

[144]

Q: –39th How came they discovered in that Country?

A: – By the Assiduity of Bengabee, Solomons Intendant whom he appointed in the Country of Cheth.

Q: –40th What method did Solomon take to have them apprehended?

A: – He demanded them from Moacha King of Cheth to whom he wrote on that Occasion.

Q: –41st Who was the bearer of that letter to King Moacha?

A: – *Zerbal* Captain of the Guards.

Q: –42d Did the King of Cheth start any difficulties?

A: – No! On the Contrary he gave a Guard to Escort them and search with them.

Q: –43d Where were they found?

A: – In a Quarry called Bendaca.

Q: –44th Had not Solomon an Intendant by that name?

A: – He had one, who Intermarried with one of his daughters.

Q: –45th How came they to discover the two Assassins?

A: – By the Intelligence of a shepherd who shewed them the place of their Retreat.

Q: –46th Who were the persons that discovered them first?

A: – Zerbal and Eleham after 5 days search.

Q: –47th In what manner were they conducted to Jerusalem?

A: – In Chains, with their wrists tied behind their backs.

Q: –48th What were the form of their Chains?

A: – It was a rule, square and mallet, on which were engraved the kind of punishment they were to suffer at Jerusalem.

Q: –49th On what day did they arrive at Jerusalem?

A: – On the 15th of Nisan 3775 which answers to the month

[145]

of April.

Q: –50th What time was it before the Execution was done?

A: – One entire month.

Q: –51st How many masters did Solomon send on that search?

A: – There was 15 and I was of the number.

Q: –52d Was there not other numbers?

A:– Solomon gave troops to Escort us.

Q: –53d What was done to the 2 Assassins when they arrived at Jerusalem?

A: – They were presented to Solomon who reproached them, and after they had been close confined day and night in the Tower of Achizas in a dungeon, he ordered them to be executed.

Q: –54th What kind of punishment did they suffer?

A: – At the hour of 10 in the morning they were tied naked to 2 pieces of wood by the neck and middle, their arms and legs extended, in this Attitude their bodies were opened from their necks to their middle, and remained in that Condition in the heat of the sun for 8 hours, the flies and Insects feasting all the time on their blood and Entrails although alive. In order that they might experience the most Excruciating torments: their cries was so lamentable, that it drew tears from the Executioner who in Commisseration of their sufferings severed their heads from their bodies, which bodies were given to the voracious Birds for food. Solomon gave Orders to take the head of Akirop, which was before exposed on the East pinnacle of the Temple and to fix it on the East gate of the City, that of Gravelot on the

[146]

south and that of Guibs on the West pinnacles of the City Gates, in order to show an Example of their perfidious treatment of our Respectable Master Hiram Abiff.

Q: –55th What is the word of the Elect of 15?
A: – Zerbal and Eleham.
Q: –56th What hour was it when the 2 Ruffians Expired?
A: – At 6 in the Evening vengeance was Accomplished.
Q: –57. What signifies B: N: S: which you have perceived in the Triangle of the Intimate Secretary?
A: – The Alliance of Moses and Aaron, the same of Solomon with Hiram of Tyre and the promise which is made to the Grand Elect perfect and sublime Masters, and the result which is given to their enterprising Characters, by the words Alliance, Promise and Perfection.
Q: –58th What is the word of the Grand Master Architect?
A: – Rabucim, which signifies Grand Master Architect.
Q: –59th What recompence did Solomon honor you with after?
A: – Providence looking on us, with the divine promises made to Noah, Moses and to David, my ardour was recompensed by the Sovereign Creator, conducting my steps into the bowels of the Earth, and I took in the end the brilliant charged with the sacred name of the Almighty, when my eyes with those of my 2 Companions were dazzled with the splendor thereof: In recompence whereof Solomon gave me the Degree of Guardian of the narrow passage and Entrance which leads to the sacred Vault.
Q: –60th What quality did you receive on this Occasion?
A: – Knight of the Royal Arch.

[147]

Q: –61st How was you received?
A: – By Solomon and Hiram of Tyre, who to recompence my Labor, creat-

ed me in this Quality with my 2 Companions Joabert and Stolkin.
Q: –62^{d} What was your name then?
A: – Gibulum.
Q: –63^{d} What is the sign of the Royal Arch?
A: – Admiration.
Q: –64th What is the Token and word?
A: – Here is the token (gives it) the word is Hamalachet Gibulum.
Q: –65th Are you a Grand Elect perfect and sublime Mason?
A: – I have penetrated into the most sacred place of the Earth.
Q: –66th What is the name of that place?
A: – It is now the sacred, but was before the secret Vault.
Q: –67th Where does the Grand Elect perfect and sublime Mason work?
A: – Underground.
Q: –68th Where is this place situate?
A: – Under the Sanctum Sanctorum of the Temple at Jerusalem.
Q: –69th What is the work of the Perfect and sublime Masons?
A: – To keep in their hearts with respect, the sacred Mysteries of Masonry: To sanctify those that have been Initiated: To practice the most pure morality and to Assist and succour the Brethren.
Q: –70th Where do the perfect and sublime Masons travel?
A: – In all quarters of the Globe to spread their mysteries.

[148]

Q: –71st What does the sacred Vault contain?
A: – The precious treasure of the Grand Elect perfect and sublime Masons.
Q: –72^{d} What is the Treasure?
A: – The △ on which is engraved the sacred name of the Almighty.
Q: –73^{d} Where is the precious treasure deposited?
A: – On the pedestal which is called the pillar of Beauty and which was deposited in the most sacred and secret place of the Earth.
Q: –74th What is your name?
A: – Gibulum.
Q: –75th What doth that name signifie?
A: – Friend Elected, Chosen favorite, or zealous master.
Q: –76th How many figurative Signs has a grand Elect perfect and Sublime Master?
A: – Nine in all, but 3 are most necessary to be known.
Q: –77th Give me the 3 principal ones?
A: – The 1st is, as if cutting your belly across in Token of your Obligation, the 2^{d} is in respect to the burning Bush, and the 3^{d} is silence, the 3 fore

fingers on your lips.

Q: –78th Go on my Brother and give me the other 6 Signs?

A: – The 4th is that of Admiration, advancing the left foot on the toes thereof, lifting at the same time your hands and Eyes up to heaven, the 5th, is Interlacing all your fingers, with the hands raised over your head the palms upwards (this sign serves to call a brother on an Emergency or when in distress) the 6th is Admiration after which you answer the brother on the opposite side

[149]

by looking over each shoulder alternately, the 7th is <by> clapping your hand on your heart, then raising your hand to its extent, after which clap it on your right thigh, the 8th is by putting your hand clinched to your mouth, as if to pull out your tongue, then clap your hand to your heart briskly, the 9th is to raise your hand as if with a poinard in it to strike into your brothers forehead; then clap the palm of your hand briskly on your forehead; this is to show that vengeance is accomplished.

Q: –79th What are the Tokens?

A: – The principal ones are 3 in number, but there is 9 in all, the 1st is that of the Intimate secretary, by turning one anothers hand and saying, Berith, Neder and Selemoth, words which signify, Alliance, Promise and Perfection. The 2d is that of Silence or circumspection, which is by advanceing ~~the~~ reciprocally the right hand to the Elbow and saying one after the other let us advance, here I am, and pronounce Gibulum, the 3d is defiance, Resistance and remembrance, advancing reciprocally the right hand as in the 4th Degree drawing them to each other 3 times, then putting the left hand to your brothers back, then to his neck as if to raise him out of a hole or pitt.

Q: –80th How many pass words are there and what are they

A: – There are 3 principal ones, the 1st is Shibboleth, 3 times repeated with an Aspiration, which signifies Abundance or the running of waters, the 2d is Heleneham

[150]

or the mercy of God, the 3d and the most Essential is Mahac Maharabac which signifies God be praised we have found it.

Q: –81st What are the Covered words?

A: – There are 3, the 1st is Gibulum, which signifies favorite, zealous or elected master, the 2d is Mahabin which signifies it is him, he is dead or silent, this word was pronounced by Moabo a particular friend of Hiram Abiff and favorite of Solomon the 3d is Adonai, which is to say, O! thou alone Eternal.

Q: –82^{d} Give me the Grand word?

A: – Thrice Puissant I cannot—I am not able to pronounce it: Mahabon was instituted in its place.

Q: –83^{d} How did you enter the Lodge of Perfection?

A: – With firmness and Constancy in my heart, the ordinary characteristics of the virtuous.

Q: –84th Why do you always in a Lodge of perfection stand in a posture of Surprize?

A: – Because Moses was Obliged to stand in the same Attitude when he received the Law from God and the two Kings Solomon and Hiram were seized with the same surprize when Gibulum Stolkin and Joabert brought to them the divine gold plate, which struck them with holy respect.

Q: –85th What signifies the sign of cutting the belly?

A: – In remembrance of the wounds of our Respectable Grand Master, Hiram Abiff, and to Instruct us also that we ought to endeavour to subdue and destroy our shameful passions of which that place is the seat.

[151]

Q: –86th What are the tools of the Grand Elect perfect and Sublime Mason?

A: – A Shovel, a Crow, and a pick ax.

Q: –87th What use did they put them to?

A: – They served to discover and raise the Square stone or trap to the Arches of Enoch, which covered the precious treasure of the Grand Elect perfect and sublime masons, by the help of the Iron ring that was fixed at the Top of the stone, and afterwards served to break the pedestal, whereon the Treasure was deposited: Also on the destruction of the Temple by Nebuchadnezer, They served the Grand Elect to penetrate into the vault of the Temple to search for their Treasure, and when they found it, they broke the pedestal on which it was deposited, to the end that the Impious might not find the △ but be always Ignorant where the name of names was deposited, and that no risk might be run hereafter, they resolved to melt down the plate of gold, and never to write, Engrave or pronounce it, but to secrete it in the depths of their heart.

Q: –88th When the Grand Elect came to the vault, did they find any thing else but the pillar of Beauty?

A: – They found also the body of Galaad.

Q: –89th Who was Galaad?

A: – He was the son of Sophinia, a considerable man among the Perfect Masons, and the Chief of the Levites he was the Guardian of the sacred vault, to take

[152]

care of the Lamp that <there> burnt without ceasing, and to adore and contemplate on the Ineffable word. He was like unto Hiram Abiff who 470 years before had lost his life rather than disclose the secret of the Master, so Galaad chose rather to be buried under the ruins of the Temple, than to discover (by his coming out) the Treasure of the secret vault of which he was the keeper.

Q: –90th What did the Grand Elect do with the body of this worthy chief of the Levites?

A: – They were willing to Imitate the Example of Solomon in paying the last honors with a pomp the most brilliant, and to raise a monument to his memory in order to Eternize the generous sacrifice he had made of himself; but the distresses of the times were such as prevented their putting their laudable design in Execution, they only took away his habit of Chief of the Levites, Consisting of his Tiara and a robe of fine linen, which they burnt; and Interred his Body in the ruins of the sacred vault under the pillar of Beauty.

Q: –91st How did Solomon live after the dedication of Temple?

A: – This wise King so virtuous, this King whom God had Chosen, became deaf to the voice of God, being proud to see himself the most Puissant Monarch of the Earth, he gave himself up to all manner of Excesses, and his great Complaisance to <a> sex equally dangerous as amiable, made him give into their

[153]

vices, and abandon his duty to God, he even profaned the holy Temple in offering to the Idol Moloch the Incense that was sett aside for the use of the Sanctum Sanctorum. All these crimes penetrated the hearts of the good Masons, the Major part of whom determined to exile themselves voluntarily in order that they might not be spectators of the horrors they expected would fall on Jerusalem, they accordingly left Judea and went in search of new Countries amongst Strangers.

Q: –92d How many years did Solomon reign?

A: – He reigned 40 years, and died when he was 58 years old, and was buried at Jerusalem; his breaking of the Laws of God, was the Chief cause of all his misfortunes and of those which happened afterwards to good Masons.

Q: –93[d] Who was King of Israael after the death of Solomon?

A: – Rehoboam his Son.

Q: –94th What remarkable things happened in his Reign?

A: – The Division of the Kingdom of Israael, which God permitted to punish the Crimes of Solomon, as he had predicted to that prince in his life time by the prophet Ahijah.

Q: –95th How ended the Kingdom of Judah?

A: – The crimes of the Inhabitants being compleat God put it into the heart of Nebuchadnezer King of Babylon (by the prediction of the prophets) to send Neburazadan his general against Jerusalem

[154]

who made himself master of that City and all Judea after 2 years war, he put Jerusalem in flames, razed the walls, ransacked the Temple of the living God and carried the Inhabitants with their King Zedekiah Captives into Babylon taking also with them all the riches of the Temple 470 years 6 months and 10 days after its dedication. The Grand Elect and Perfect masons, who were at Jerusalem at that time, defended it with Intrepidity but were not able to resist the force and vivacity of the beseigers, they had no other uneasiness but for the treasure that was deposited in the sacred vault least it might be prophaned: This apprehension struck them to their hearts, and to see the Temple ruined and destroyed: they exposed themselves to the fury of the Soldiers who were stationed at the Gates and in the end, they penetrated into the ruins of the sanctuary and searched in the sacred vault where they found the Triangular plate on the Cubic stone, then they could not express the transport of Joy that seized them on the Occasion and they cried out with one voice Mahac Maharabac whis is [*sic*], God be praised we have found it. This is the 3[d] and most Essential pass word to make yourself known to be a guardian of the sacred vault.

Q: –96th What did the Grand Elect do after this discovery?

A: – They retired contented, resolving never more to trust this holy word, but in the most secret part of

[155]

their hearts, and that it should pass to their descendants, by Tradition; from whence arose the Custom of pronouncing the letter only, as was used when the Temple was rebuilt by Cyrus.

Q: –97th How long lasted the Captivity of the Israalites after the destruction of the Temple by Nebuchadnezer King of Babylon?

A: – That Captivity lasted 70 years and the 2 years of war makes 72 years as was foretold by the prophet Jeremiah.

Q: –98th How did the Israalites behave in Babylon during their Captivity?

A: – By the Example of the good masons who retired with them, they served god faithfully, under the spirited Conduct of the Grand Elect and also by the prophets that God sent to support them in their Captivity.

Q: –99th Who were those prophets?

A: – The most Celebrated were Ezekiel, Daniel, Habakuk, Zechariah, Haggai and Malachie.

Q: –100th Who was it that gave permission to the Israalites to return into their own Country?

A: – Cyrus King of Persia having made himself master of all the East gave permission to them to return to their Country and reestablish the City of Jerusalem, giving them for presents all the sacred vessels which belonged to the Temple

[156]

and had been left from the general ravage, under the Care of Mithridates the Grand Treasurer.

Q: –101st Where do the Grand Elect and perfect Masons work at this day?

A: – In a secret place to establish the Edifice ruined by the Traitors.

Q: –102d What is the wages of your success?

A: – Virtue, which is common to all the Brethren.

Q: –103d What Recompence do you expect?

A: – The destruction of vice and the love and knowledge of my Brethren.

Q: –104th What did you find in this place

A: – Some bones, some blood, and a burning lamp.

Q: –105th What did you do with the burning Lamp?

A: – I put it out.

Q: –106th Then you were in Obscurity and darkness?

A: – No thrice Puissant, I have no Occasion for Lamp or light, I am sufficiently enlightened with the most Brilliant of all lights the holy △

To Close.

Q: – From whence came you respectable Senior Grand Warden?

A: – From Judea I came.

Q: – What did you bring from thence?

A: – The Precious Treasure of the Grand Elect, which I have engraved on my heart, and now come to give it unto you. The thrice Puissant then says

[157]

"approach my Dear brother (at this Instant the Grand Senior warden approaches the thrice Puissant with the sign of Admiration on him) and delivers in his right ear the word letter by Letter Then the thrice Puissant orders the Chain and form a Circle (the hands above their heads) and delivers the word himself in the same manner which goes round untill it comes to him again. Then he says, "My dear brethren the word which was lost is found, Engrave it in the deepest part of your hearts—Let us enter into silence and purify our hearts from all uncleanness.

The Prayer.

Let us Pray! Direct our steps O! [BLANK SPACE] Supreme Master of the Universe: Grant that we may shun the pitt which our Enemies have made for us, and that by the brightness of thy divine spirit we may never fall into darkness: Give us the means to bestow on the poor, the precious Gifts of thy liberal providence: Grant that we may not be unprofitable in our labour: bless and sanctify our works to the end that we do not deny thy holy power and strength: May we always add to thy Glory in practising without Intermission, the virtue which masonry teacheth us. Amen, Amen, Amen.

When the prayer is finished, the brethren all take their places, and the thrice Puissant continues the following questions, to close the Lodge.

[158]

Q: – Venerable Senior Grand Warden what is the Clock?
A: – Thrice Puissant it is midnight.
Q: – Why do you say it is midnight?
A: – Because after labour comes rest.
Q: – Why do you close the Lodge at midnight?
A: – Because night is the time for the workers of Iniquity.
Q: – What motive brought you hither?
A: – The desire of practise in Common the Acts of virtue Justice and Charity.
Q: – What is it, that attracts you hither?
A: – The Brilliant Deltha or △.
Q: – How comes the △ so often mentioned here?
A: – To extol the grand Architect of the heaven and earth.
Q: – What do you carry from hence?
A: – A great desire of doing good.
Q: – What does a Grand Elect perfect and sublime mason desire more, when he is come to the sublime Degree of Masonry?

A: – The Eternal Beatitude for which he ought ever to sigh without ceasing, and which he must acquire by his good works?

Then the thrice Puissant says, "Venerable brothers Grand Wardens, acquaint the Brethren that I am going to close this Lodge by the mysterious numbers of 3, 5, 7 and 9, which is repeated by the Wardens, after which they give 3, 5 7 and 9 knocks and make the signs as at the opening of the Lodge, After which the Thrice Puissant says, "Venerable brother Wardens, Officers and Brethren of this Lodge of perfection

[159]

I exhort you to retire in peace, to practice virtue and to live always as if in the immediate presence of the Grand Architect of the Universe, Amen, Amen, Amen. God bless the King and our works.

All the brethren applaud the same by 3, 5, 7 and 9

The Lodge is then Closed and they all retire.

Apron. The Apron should be lined and bordered with red within the Edge a border of Green, and a Crowned Compass extended to 90 Degrees painted on the flap thereof.

Jewell. The Jewell is a Crowned Compass extended to 90 Degrees, to be of Silver gilt, suspended by a white Collar in the form of a Triangle, round the neck.

[160]

The 15th Degree,

Knight of the East (or the Sword)

There are no wardens in the Council yet their Function is nevertheless complied with.

To Open the Council

The Grand General of the Army, who is seated in the west, Opens the Council by saying, "Brother Knights, the Sovereign Assembles us to hold a Council; here he comes, let us therefore be attentive to what he proposes to us."

The Sovereign then enters, and passes in the manner herein after mentioned.

All the Knights form the Arch with their Swords or sabers unsheathed, and he passes through them to the Eastern side of the Council room, where he places himself under a Canopy on a Throne, dressed in his Royal robes of State, On which he salutes the Knights by putting his right hand on his heart, and bowing a little, with his hatt (or Crown) on his head. All the Knights return the salutation in the same manner, holding their hats in their left hands and putting the points of their Lances, (or swords) to their hearts, making an Obedience to the Sovereign at the same time; After which the Knights take their seats.

[161]

The Reception or Initiation of a Candidate

The Candidate stands at the out side of the door, covered with a large black crape from his head to his breast, and situates himself in such a manner that the Guards within can hear his sighs: As soon as the Inward Guard has heard him, he half opens the door, to observe from whence arises the Complaint, and finding that it proceeds from a man in mourning, he shuts the Door briskly, and directly approaches the Grand General of the Army, whom he makes acquainted with what he hath just heard and seen: The Grand General immediately arise from his feet, without uttering a word; goes to the

Candidate and asks him the following Questions, to which he answers, being prompted by the Guard without.

Gr^{d} Genl What do you want here? (to be pronounced with a serene air and solemn voice)
Cand^{e} I beg that you will permit me the honor of speaking to the King.
Gr^{d} Genl Who are you?
Cand^{e} I am a Jew by persuasion, and a prince by blood, descended from the race of David and the Tribe of Judah.
Gr^{d} Genl What is your name?
Cand^{e} Zerubabel.

[162]

Gr^{d} Genl What is your age?
Cand^{e} Eighty one years.
Gr^{d} Genl What motive brings you hither?
Cand^{e} The tears and distresses of my Brethren.
Gr^{d} Genl Wait a while and I will go and Interceed with the King for you:—

He then strikes the bottom of the door with his foot, which is opened by the Guard within, who recognising the Grand General gives him admittance: on which he goes to the foot of the Throne and relates to the sovereign the conversation which had past between Zerubabel and himself.

The sovereign then Orders Zerubabel to be ushered in, with his face vieled with a Crape. The Grand General makes a profound Obeisence to the commands of the King, and then going to Zerubabel says, "You have found Grace from the greatest King on the Earth; he suffers you to appear vieled in his presence": Then the Grand General of the army immediately gives one stroke at the door which is opened, and he Introduces the Candidate covered with a black Crape, (the Guard having taken previous care to examine him, and seen that he had concealed no arms by which the life of the sovereign might be attempted.) He is then introduced by the Grand General to the foot of the Throne, where he falls on his knees. The Minister of state or Grand Orator of the

[163]

Council advances to him, Unviels his face and asks him the following Questions; (the Answers to which are prompted) N:B: all stand up with swords drawn and hats on.

Minister of State} What brings you hither?
Cand^{e} I come to implore the Bounty and Justice of the King
Min^{r} of S^{e} On what Occasion?
Cand^{e} To ask a grace for my Brethren, Masons in Captivity these seventy two years.
Min^{r} of S^{e} Who are you?
Cand^{e} Zerubabel, a hebrew prince and one of the blood of David.
Min^{r} of S^{e} What is the grace you would ask?
Cand^{e} To sett my Brethren free; to suffer us to return to Judea, rebuild the Temple, and revive the laws of the God of Battles, and the Ordinances of Moses.

After this a signal is made to Zerubbabel to withdraw;—The Grand General conducts him to the door, out of which he goes escorted by the outer Guard and the door is shut by the Inner Guard.

The Sovereign then addresses the Knights in the following Terms; "Princes, I have a long time meditated to give the Captive Masons their liberty it troubles me to see those people in Chains;—Their God, whom they call the Mighty God, has appeared to me in a Vision, and lo! I thought this God threatned me, like a raging Lion, ready to

[164]

fall upon and devour me:—I thought I heard two words from his mouth which signifies in our Language, "Render my people their Liberty or thou shalt die." From you therefore beloved Princes, I expect Counsel which ought to done in regard to the people of Zerubbabel.

The King having ceased to speak, the whole Council observes a profound silence, and in the Interim the Minister of state, gathers the suffrages of the Knights and reports the same in the Kings right ear, who commands the General of the Army to introduce Zerubbabel; which is done, and his is decorated with a white rose, girded with a broad green Ribbon; In this state he is brought up to the Throne where falling upon his knees, the King says, "Rise. I grant your request; I consent that the Israalites may be sett at Liberty: Yea, that they may be permitted to return to their own Country, and remain in their own Dominions: Also that you may go and build a Temple to the mighty God! And that the Vases and other Ornaments of the old Temple, be all restored to you for the Ornaments of the New: I furthermore appoint you, the Chief of all the Jewish nation and I command that they obey you as such; And as an Authentic mark of my good will for you, I shall arm you with a terrible sword to combat against your Enemies, and make you formidable

[165]

to such of your Brethren, as may Cabal against you, and I command my Grand General Zatrabuzanes to instruct you in the art of war."—As soon as the King has armed Zerubbabel with a sword he is conducted to the Grand General of the Army who teaches him the method of making himself known, and asks him the following Questions; (The answers to which are prompted by Mithradates)

Gr^{d} Genl Where is your Country situated?

Cand^{e} Beyond the River Euphrates to the East of Syria its name is Judea.

Gr^{d} Genl What are those who are Captives?

Cand^{e} Israelites divided into Tribes, namely those of Benjamin and Judah.

After these Questions the Grand General says to the Candidate, "My dear Brother I rejoice at the favours which you have received from our Sovereign: By his Bounty you and your nation are become free;—He has armed you with a sword to defend you against your Enemies.

By the Authority he has given to me, I will decorate you with a Ribbon, to which you may suspend your *Jewel,* which is a Saber, and you must wear it from your right shoulder to your left hip. The *Sign,* is to carry your right hand to your right shoulder and then bring it downward to your left hip, where the sabre hangs, which you draw out of the scabbard and raise

[166]

it as if you was going to engage an Enemy. The other answers in the same manner. The *Token* is to clinch the fingers of the left hand with your Brothers left hand, as if your repulse your Enemy to obtain a free passage, putting the points of the Sabres reciprocally on each others Breast; One says, "*Judah,*" and the other answering, "Benjamin." The pass words are *Yahaveron Hamaim* meaning (as literally translated from the Hebrew Characters) "A liberty of passage." N.B. in order to make yourself known, you must give the Grand Word, which is *Raf Odom,* signifying "True Masters." The following is then tendered to the Candidate being his Obligation.

The Obligation.

I: A: B: do promise and engage, solemnly and sincerely in the presence of the Grand Architect of the Universe, and before all the Brethren Knights of the East (or Knights of the Sword,) at present here Assembled, and <on> the faith of an honest man and a true free mason, to be faithful to the Tenets and principles of my Religion and the Laws of the State, as far as in my power to comply with the same: I also solemnly promise never to reveal any of the mysteries of the Order of Knights of the East (or Knights of the Sword), which I am now receiving, or about to be Instructed in, to any

[167]

Brother or Brothers in any of the Inferior Degrees and that I will never receive or Initiate to this Eminent Degree, any Brother Mason, but conformable to the Antient Customs, Statutes and constitutions of the Order: And also I do most faithfully promise to Recognize in any part of the known world, the Sovereign Princes of Jerusalem as the Chiefs of Masonry, and to render to them in that distinguished Capacity, all the honors; homage and Advantages due to their Dignity and to do my best to merit and deserve that eminent Degree: All this I do most sincerely swear to observe, do, perform and keep under the pains of all my former penalties, with the addition of my being dishonored, and losing the Title of a freeman, and being for ever afterwards deprived of the Advantage, of entering into this Council, or any other Council Chapter or Lodge whatsoever. So help me God! And maintain me in uprightness and Justice. Amen. (He then kisses the holy Bible.)

Form of the Council.

The Hangings of the Council should be Green or water Coloured in remembrance of those events which happened at the River Euphrates (otherwise called Stabuzani) on the return of the Israelites whereof a particular account shall be hereafter given. These hangings ought to be Interspersed

[168]

with red, in memory of the Assyrian blood which stained the water of that River.

The Lights which Illuminate the Council should be seventy two, in memory of the Seventy two years Captivity of the Israelites (but may be represented figuratively by Seven large, and two small Candles) to wit, the two last years of Zedekiahs Reign, the time the siege lasted, and the seventy years Captivity, from the time that the Israalites were carried into Babylon by Neburazadan, under the reign of Nebuchadnezer who destroyed the Temple, unto the time of the Building it, In the reign of Satrabuzanes King of Persia; Secondly on Account of the Seventy two Letters that compose the words of the Knights of the East, and those of the Grand, perfect and sublime Masons, as may be seen in the following Example;

Words of the Knights of the East or the Sword.		Words of the Grand Elect perfect and Sublime Mason	
Yahaveron Hamaim	15	Berith.	6
Raf Odom.	7	Neder.	5
Benjamin & Judah.	13	Selemouth.	9
Jabahon.	7	Shibboleth.	10
Librittis.	7	Eleneham.	8
Ryat	9	Mahac, Maharaback.	15
Lebanus	4	Gabaon	6
Jachin.	7	Mahabin.	7
Boaz	4	Adonai.	6
	72		72

[169]

All the Knights are decorated with a large broad Green coloured water Ribbon, from the right shoulder to the left hip: A wooden Bridge painted in the middle of it, which comes on the right shoulder with the two Initial letters *Y* and *H* of a fiery Colour, ornamented with gold, meaning "Liberty or free passage," to free Masons; The ribbon must be interspersed with heads and limbs of Bodies newly slain—broken Crowns, Scepters and swords And the word Strabuznai, divided by single Letters, in two parts or rather on each side of the Bridge: On the bottom of the Ribbon must be appended a small eastern Sabre to a narrow pink Coloured ~~coloured~~ ribbon, tied to its Scabbard which must be of a scarlet Colour: In this Order, neither on the Apron or upon the Sash or Ribbon with which a Knight of the East (or of the Sword) is decorated, must <there be> any deaths heads, dry bones, black drawings or any other black Colours, such having an appearance of mourning. Whereas the Knights of this superior Degree should not seem by any external emblems to mourn; And Indeed why should they be represented to Grieve; When the most happy revolution recorded in the Annals of Masonry informs us that a most Triumphant victory was obtained in a Combat wherein but few were slain excepting those only who endeavoured to oppose the

[170]

passage of the Israelites contrary to the Orders of the greatest King of Persia. The Green water colours is the only proper Ribbon for the them to wear, as well on Account of the victory they obtained as being also the Colour of the water of the River on whose banks they triumphed: The Interspersion of heads, Limbs, and other trophies, displayed on this Ribbon is a natural representation of what happened on the Banks and the Bridge of the Euphrates, whose green water, at, and after the bloody Battle, was tingled with Assyrian Blood, and was covered with their limbs, heads and Bodies; The River is called by the Knights of the East Stabuznai, the name of the Chief of the Adversaries, who opposed the Rebuilding of the Temple, which in hebrew signifies Tra Drovoceur,* as we are taught in the Talmud, which wonderfully agrees with the Knight of the East, a name which in short is composed of nine Letters, and which being added to the other words of the Order, form the mysterious number of 81, as will be amply Explained hereafter. The Apron is a white skin lined with red and bordered with Green, a bloody head between two Swords in a Saint Andrews Cross either embroidered or painted and in the Æra of the apron should be represented 3 heaps of broken Triangular Chains.

Explanation of the Draft.

1st – At the upper end at the East, stands an Eagle

[171]

upright on his Legs, with his wings extended his head fiercely erected, stareing at the Sun on his right side, on his left side the moon; On the outer side of his right foot is a large letter or vowel I, and on the outer side of his left foot is the large letter B, and at an equal distance on either side of him the two Initials of the compound words of the Order Y and H.

2dly Immediately under the Eagle is a great oblong square representing the second Temple constructed according to the directions of King Cyrus.

3dly In the Eastern part of the Oblong square is represented the holy of holies, where the ark of the Covenant is, or was once deposited, covered by the wings of the two Cherubims, which sustains the Deltha on which is the name of the sacred Architect of the Universe, never to be pronounced without fear and trembling.

4thly The Curtain or viel by which the holy of holies was seperated from the other parts of the Temple.

5th In this sacred place is to be an Altar of the sacrifices on the middle of which is an Enflamed heart with these two Letters R.O. The Initials of two words Raf, Odom, which comprehends something very great in their meaning, and signifies "Free masons, or True masons, such as those who devote their heart to God, and the general good of the order: On this Altar are all the

* Read backwards, *ruecovord art*, i.e., "recovered art." —*Ed.*

[172]

several Tools and Implements of Masonry which were made use of at the Construction of the Temple.

6th At the west door is the Grand stair Case of 7 steps.

7th Beneath the Altar of the sacrifices is the Square of 9 which when 3 times multiplied make 27, and which last number multiplied by the same mysterious figure 3, make the favorite Masonic number of 81—whereof you have the first example referring however the Explanation to another occasion, which will be given to you hereafter, to shew why this selected number of 81, is so peculiarly dear to the perfect Masons; The Square which gives 3 times 27 Explains the Tripple Essence of Masonry, marked by the Tripple Triangle, whereof we shall give you hereafter the figure. Its explanation is 9 virtuous Attributes to the first of the 3 Triangles, and are Composed of 81 Letter.

Boundless Mercy......	Creation...............	Almighty...............
Justice..................	Omniscience...........	Perfection..............
Immensity.............	Beauty..................	Eternity................
3 virtues....................	3 virtues....................	3 virtues....................

which added together make...9
Applied to the Tripple Triangle 27
and in Letters...81

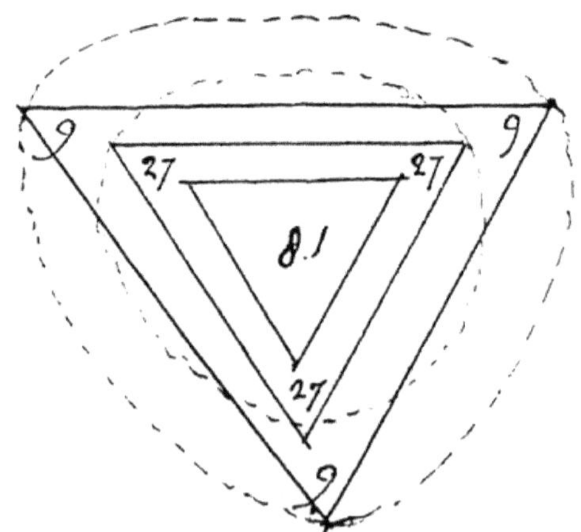

[173]

3 WORDS OF ENGAGEMENT

1st Berith. 6
2 Neder 5
3 Selemouth. 9

3 PASS WORDS

1st Shibboleth 10
2d Heleneham 9
3. Mahac Mak 15

3 COVERED WORDS

1st Gabazon 7
2 Mahabin 7
3 Adonai. 6
74

The Grd Word—Jehh. . 7
. . . . .81 Letters†

B	E	T	E	H	A	G	H	A
E	R	H	T	A	H	A	A	I
R	S	S	H	M	A	B	B	J
I	E	H	H	M	R	A	I	E
T	L	I	E	A	A	Z	N	H
H	E	B	L	H	B	O	A	O
N	M	B	E	A	A	N	D	V
E	O	O	N	C	C	M	O	A
D	U	L	E	M	H	A	N	H

EXPLANATION OF WORDS

1st Alliance
6d Promise
3d Perfection

3 PASS WORDS

1st Abundance or running of waters
2d Mercy of God
3d God be praised we have found it

3 COVERED WORDS

1st favorite or zealous and Elected Master
2d silence or respect
3 Oh thou who art Eternal

8th Without side of the Temple, on a line with the Arch below the Sun, stands Mount Horeb, known by all Masons and represented by the Initial of its name H. Under the Moon on the left side stands mound Gabazon, represented likewise by the Initial G. On this last mount were the sacrifices made before the Construction of the Temple.

9th At the South side is a hand, holding a trowel and 5 Steps, opposite this Gate is a hod for carrying of Morter, Underneath the 5 steps are a heap of Cubic stones fit for use, and a little further a heap of rough and common stones destined to fortifie the Building.

10th At the north Gate is a hand armed with a sword and 3 steps, underwhich is a trophy of arms for the use of the Builders in case of urgent necessity

[174]

11th Lower down are figured the vases, Urns, and other sacred Ornaments of the new Temple, the Molten sea, The table of the bread of proportion the Candlestick with 7 branches, the Altar of perfumes, placed immediately before the Steps and Invironed by the Instruments of the sacrifices.

† For purposes of readability, the above letter chart has been retypset. The original art appears on p. 143.

12th In the Center of the Draft beneath the 7 steps is the Bible, Square and Compass.

13th Still beneath on another line at the right hand are represented a Shovel, a Level, Perpendicular, Cube, Triangle and Quadrangle so disposed that they may occupy the whole Lodge from North to South on the same line.

14th Upon another line is placed Triangle wise, the Rule, Chissel and mallet and in the Center of the void, upon the bank of the River the word Adonai or the Initial letter I.

15th You see in the North the Square stone with the ring, and the Opening which it did Cover of Enochs Temple underground with the 9 Arches and the perspective of the South you see an Egyptinian Pyramid.

16th The Lodge towards the west end is traversed from North to South by the River Euphrates, called by the Knights of the East Stabuznai, in the middle of which is built a Wooden bridge for the passage of the free Masons to get into Judea, and on one side of the Bridge is seen the 2 Initials

[175]

Y.H. signifying free passage for free Masons.

17th The foresaid River displays and is strewed with heads, bodies, Limbs, broken Crowns and Scepters.

18th On the void and west side of this River opposite the Bridge, you see the word Syria, and at each extremity of the same side is represented heaps of Chains of triangular links and in the middle of those Chains the Seven fold Candlestick oversett.

19th On the right in the Mountains is a great letter *T* representing the Quarry of Tyre, from whence the stone was drawn for the Construction of the Temple, and on the left a Mountain with the letter *L* representing Mount Lebanus, from whence the timber was taken; below the letter *L* is a little oblong Square with a proportional little Triangle, in the Center the Tomb of Zedekiah the last King of the race of David.

20th In the Center are two Columns of Jachin and Boaz laid across each other and broken.

21st Intirely at the bottom of the Tiford‡ is represented the plan of the City of Babylon in Ruins.

22d Underneath the Quarry of Tyre is a heap of Triangular Chains broken, and paralel with the Tomb of Zedekiah Each article of the Tiford Includes a Mysterious Scene, a part of which shall be Explained in the Instructions which will be given you, the rest must remain as an Ænigma; untill the

‡ The Baylot FM4 reads, "tableau."

> moment when Truth shall be wholly unveiled—Happy moment when free Masons shall
>
> [176]
>
> be wholly attached to the first principles of Masonry, as that only can direct every amusement into a solid and permanent End of Everlasting happiness: but how minute are the number of those who are happy Enough to be Initiated therein and thrice happy those who can merit so to be.

All the Knights are stiled Princes by the Sovereign, and among themselves they have the title of Excellency. The Candidate represents Zerubabel the door of the Council must be guarded by the two Junior Knights, armed with their pikes one without and one within the door of the Council. All the Knights ought to be armed with Javelins, and when the Sovereign enters the Council, they form an Arch therewith for the Sovereign to pass through.

1st The Sovereign who represents either Cyrus, Darius, Artaxerxes or Longimanus, whose names he assumes, Indifferently, places himself in the East under a Canopy on a throne in his Royal robes.

2d Called Nehemias places himself on the right hand of the Sovereign, and should never leave his place, not even for a visitor Prince of Jerusalem, who is to take place at his right hand.

3d The Grand General called Satrabuzanes takes his seat at the west of the Council to the right side of the Sovereign.

[177]

4th The Grand Treasurer Mithridates his place is likewise to the West on the right side of the Grand General.

5th The Grand Orator or Minister of State named Esdras, places himself on the left side of the Sovereign. The other Brethren Princes place themselves indifferently on either side: It is not forbid the Council to nominate the 5 Grand Officers of the other brethren in Case of absence of either or all of the Grand Officers.

The Origin of the Knights of the East

The Knights of the East, drew their Origin from the Captives of Babylon, where the Israelites remained 70 years, after 2 years seige. They had their Liberty given them by King Cyrus of Persia by the Solicitation of Zerubabel a Prince of the Tribe of Judah, descended from the race of David; and Nehemias a holy man and of a distinguished family. Cyrus pemitted them to return to Jerusalem, and to restore the Temple: he caused all the vases, and Ornaments that had been carried away at the Destruction of Solomons Temple by Nebuzaradan, General of the Army of Nebuchadnezer in number 7420, to be restored to them. He Instructed the whole to Zerubabel, commanding that the new Temple should be 60 Cubits

[178]

high and as many broad: He Issued an Edict, enjoying all his Subjects, to let pass all the free Masons in his Dominions, without giving them the least molestation, under pain of death to such as should enfringe his commands

He ordered Satrabuzanes his General, to teach Zerubabel the Art of war: He armed him Knight and gave Zerubabel power to confer the same Degree on such of the Masons as he should Judge worthy. Zeruababel then assembled all the Israelites, the Number of whom he found to be 42,360. Exclusive of Slaves. He made choice of those free Masons that Escaped the fury of the Soldiers at the Destruction of the Temple and Assembled 7000 of them; he armed them all Knights and put them at the head of the people to fight against those that should oppose their passage on the road to Judea: The March of the Israelites was prosperous untill they reached the banks of the Euphrates or Stabuznai, which seperates Judea from Syria, when the Knights Masons who arrived there first, found armed Troops to hinder their passage on Account of the Treasure belonging to the Temple, which they carried along with them. Neither the Remonstrances of the Knights nor the Edict of Cyrus was able to restrain their Insolence, they fell upon the Knights, who on their side repulsed them with such Ardour that they were all to a man drowned

[179]

or cut to pieces, at the passing of the Bridge. After this Victory Zerubabel caused an Altar to be erected on the field of Battle, on which he offered an holocaust to the God of Armies who had fought for Israel and took Yahaveron Hamaim for a Pass word as it signifies Liberty of Passage.

After the Israelites passed the River they arrived at Jerusalem after 4 month march, on the 22[d] of June at 7 O Clock in the morning. After 7 days rest the 3 Architects with their Associates began to lay out the works of the new Temple: They divided the workmen into Classes, each of which had its Chief and two Assistants: Every degree of each Class was paid according to their rank in the work, and each had his respective word. The word of the first Class was Judah and were paid at the Column which stood at the Entrance of the Temple. The word of the second class was Benjamin and received their wages at the Portico. The 3[d] Class received theirs in the middle of the Temple after pronouncing their word which was Yahaveron Hamaim.

The same Order was observed in the construction of the new, as was practised in the building of the first Temple. The work was hardly begun before the Knights Masons were disturbed by false Brethren from Samaria; who being jealous of the Glory which the two tribes of Judah and

[180]

Benjamin were to acquire being now free; They therefore resolved to wage war against them and defeat their design of rebuilding their Temple; but Zerubabel having received Information of their design, ordered that all the workmen should be armed, with the trowel in one hand and a sword in the other, that while they worked with the one, they might defend themselves with the other, and be able to repulse the Enemy if they should present themselves. The Construction of the new Temple lasted 46 years. It was begun in the Reign of Cyrus and was finished in that of Artaxerxes: This temple was Consecrated in the same manner as the first had been by Solomon. The Decalogue and the Ordinances of Moses were observed anew and a Chief was appointed to Govern the nation he was Chosen from the Knights Masons called Knights of the East, because they were freed and created Knights by Cyrus King of Persia.

Their Second Temple having been destroyed by the Romans, the Knights Masons of the present age and descendants of them that Constructed it were Obliged under the Conduct of Zerubabel to raise a third to the Glory of the Grand Architect of the Universe.

The Doctrine of the Knights of the East

Q: 1st — Are you a Knight of the East?

[181]

A: – I have been received in that Character my name, my robes, my Sword, and my firmness will assure your thereof.
Q: – 2d — By what means did you arrive to this high Degree?
A: – By my humility, my Patience and frequent Solicitations.
Q: –3d — To whom did you apply?
A: – To a King.
Q: – 4th — What is your first name?
A: – Zerubabel.
Q: – 5th — What is your Origin?
A: – I am an Israelite of the Tribe of Judah.

Q: – 6th What is your Profession?
A – Masonry.
Q: – 7th What building did you erect?
A – Temples and Tabernacles.
Q: – 8 Where did you Construct them?
A – In my heart.
Q: – 9 What is the Sirname of the Knight of the East?
A – That of a most free, Mason.
Q: – 10 Why are you a most free, Mason?
A – Because the Masons who wrought in the temple of Solomon were qualified free, and of course they and their descendants were declared exempt from every charge or Duty, Even that of going to war, their families being called free by Excellence. But in process of time, having been subdued, and

[182]

only recovered their Rights through the County of King Cyrus, who confirmed it to them. It is therefrom that they are called, "most free."
Q: – 11th Why did Cyrus give the Israelites their liberty?
A – Because God appeared to him in a Dream and gave him a Charge to sett his people at Liberty that they should rebuild the Temple which had been demolished.
Q: – 12th What are the Duties of the Knights of the East?
A – To love God and adore him, to hold Tradition in Esteem, to succour our Brethren in necessity, to anticipate their wants, to receive with friendship strangers and brothers, to visit the sick and comfort them, to aid in the burial of the dead, to pray for them who are under persecution, to love mankind in General, to avoid the vicious, never to frequent places of debauchery, or women of Infamous lives, but to be religious in adoreing our Maker and to be exact observers of the laws of Princes and of states; In fine to follow the precepts of Masonry in all its points, rendering Justice and Honor to the Princes of Jerusalem and respect to all superior Degrees.

To Close the Council.

The Sovereign says, "Princes the Council is Closed." He then strikes the steps of the Throne 7 times with his Sword.

A: – The Knights says together, "Glory be to God, honor to our Sovereign and prosperity to the Knights of

[183]

the Order." The Sovereign is saluted by all putting their hands on their Hearts.

Feasts of Observance of the Knights of the East

The thrice Excellent Knights of the East shall celebrate the feast of the Reedification of the Temple of the Living God, the 22^d of March and 23^d of September at the Equinoxes or the renovation of the long and short days, in commemoration of the Temple being rebuilt twice by the Masons.

N:B. When a Knight of the East visits a Lodge of Perfection or Royal Arch, they are to be received with the honors of the Arch and if the Master of the said Lodge is not a Knight of the East, he offers the Hiram and his seat to the Knight, who may accept or refuse it. If he accepts it, he only seats himself for a little while and them returns it again, Seats himself at the right hand of the thrice Puissant, who offers him the Inspection of the minutes and Transactions of the said Lodge If more Knights visitors than one, they take their rank on the right and left side of the thrice Puissant, and he that had the superiority in Degrees, has always the honor of the Hiram and seat offered him.

B	E	T	E	H	a	G	H	a
E	R	H	T	a	H	a	a	I
R	S	S	H	M	a	B	B	J
I	E	H	H	m	R	a	I	E
T	L	I	E	a	a	Z	N	H
H	E	B	L	H	B	o	A	O
N	M	B	E	a	a	N	D	V
E	O	O	N	C	C	m	O	a
D	U	L	E	M	H	a	n	H

Original letter chart from p. 173 of the *Jamaica Manuscript.*

[184]

or Prince of Jerusalem

To Open the Council

The sovereign represents zerubabel and is stiled the Most Equitable. The Second Officer is stiled the most Enlightened. There is no other Salutation offered but that of a bow of the head, by the Grand Council who all stand.

The most Equitable knocks 5 times, and the most enlightened repeats it; When the most Equitable says, "Princes and most enlightened are we in security?"

A – By the most Enlightened, "We are."

Most Equitable – "Since we are in security give notice that the Sun has risen; The Indispensible Duty of our function calls us here; we must proceed to Business."

The most Enlightened Announces the same to all the Princes as follows, "The most Equitable declares that the sun is risen, and that it is time to commence the work." Then all the Princes make an Obesience to the most Equitable, by an Inclination of the head, and they all take their seats.

Another form of Opening.

The most Illustrious and Valorous prince Zerubabel says to the Wardens in the west, Thrice Illustrious Princes, How comes it that this place is divided into two parts, and that the East part is decorated with yellow, and the West with Red?

[185]

A – The Eastern part represents Jerusalem with a yellow or gold Coloured Hanging, and is the holy place where the first Temple dedicated to the service of the living God was Constructed; the Western part which is decorated with Red represents the Great City of Babylon: the red hangings are the Emblem of the blood that was spilt at the different Combats which were fought on the Road between Babylon and Jerusalem by the Knights Masons when they returned from their Captivity.

Q: – Who presides in this our Grand Council?

A: – The Prince Zerubabel under the title of Equitable.

Q: – Who are the Grand Wardens?

A – Two of the Princes under the Title of most profound, or most Enlightened.

Q: – If that is so, Thrice Excellent Brothers princes most Enlightened Grand Wardens, acquaint the Thrice Valorous Brethren here present that I am going to open the Grand Council.

A – Most Excellent Brothers, most Valorous and most Illustrious Princes, the Sovereign of the Sovereigns hereby acquaint you, that the Grand Council is opened, And you will therefore be attentive to what he proposes.

Q: – What is the O Clock?

A: – It is the hour of five in the Evening.

The Sovereign strikes 5, one by itself and

[186]

four quick on the steps of the Throne, and says, "Most Valiant princes, the Council is opened," which is repeated by the Grand Wardens, as also the 5 knocks.

Form of the Council

1st The Council must be divided into two parts with an Arch in the middle—the first part in the West must be decorated with red, representing the City of Babylon where the most Illustrious and most Valorous King Darius sits on a Throne under a Red Canopy, a small square table before him on which is a naked sword, a ballance and a hand of Justice with a Roll of paper, and a Scepter in the Kings Hand.

2d The part in the East must be decorated with yellow, and represents Jerusalem: The Sovereign places himself on a Throne under a yellow Canopy, a small Triangular table before him on which must be a naked sword, a ballance a shield, a scepter, and a Candlestick with 5 branches, and a broad yellow ribbon on from his left shoulder to right hi

3d The two Grand Wardens represent the General of the army and the Grand Treasurer: They are seated under a small Canopy in the Western part of the room, on the right side of the Arch in the same manner as the Sovereign, except the Crown.

The Grand keeper of seals is called Nehemias

[187]

and sitts on the Right hand of the Sovereign.

The Minister of State is called Esdras and is seated on the left hand of the Sovereign.

4th The other princes are placed to the Right and left by Gradation and the door of the Grand Council must be always Guarded by the two youngest princes, who receive their Orders from the General of the Army, and they must be armed with a spear instead of a sword: All the princes who are in Office ought to be armed with a sheild and Lance.

5th The Council must be lighted by 125 lights distributed by fives, representing the Embassy which was composed of 5, and the second room or apartment of the Council must be lighted by several Lights placed without Order, to represent the feudejoy which was made at the City of Jerusalem on the Return of the Embassy; In one Corner of the apartment must be a Cabinet, where King Darius worked with his Satrap.

Form of the Reception

The Candidate must be in the Anti Chamber where, after he had remained for some time, the Master of Ceremonies goes to him, blindfolds him and Conducts him to the door, and announces him by 5 knocks, when the door is opened, he Introduces and carries him to the East to Zerubabel

[188]

who demands for what purpose he comes before him. He answers, that he comes on an Embassy to the Great King Darius to Complain against the Samaritans. Zerubabel answers that the Great King Darius was not there, but that will be the road he must follow—they then give him light and arm him with a naked Sword and Buckler they also present him with the Ornaments of the Knights of the East, he is then Conducted to the Great King Darius, brandishing and flourishing his sword as if fighting his way, he must also be accompanied by 4 princes; When he arrives before the Great King Darius he delivers the subject of his Embassy as follows, "I am come with my 4 Companions Knights Princes of Jerusalem with a deputation from the people of Jerusalem and as their Ambassadors to pray for justice against the Samaritans, who refuse to contribute to the rebuilding of Gods holy Temple, and to furnish the requisites for the sacrifices and other necessary matters." The Great King Darius then gives him a Letter, which having been received, he takes his leave of the Great King and Returns back by the same road he came, brandishing his sword as is fighting with his Enemies, when he arrives he is conducted to Prince Zerubabel and delivers him the Letter, who orders it to be read and is as follow. We Darius King of Kings, willing to

[189]

favour and protect our dear people of Jerusalem after the Example of our most Illustrious predecessor King Cyrus, having heard the Complaint against the samaritans. We will and do Ordain that they shall continue to pay the tribute which they owe for the support of the sacrifices of the Temple, otherwise we shall punish their further disobedience. Given in our Grand Court the 4th day of the 2^{d} month in the year 3534 and in the 3^{d} year of our Reign.

After which Zerubabel congratulates them on their success, and orders that the people be informed thereof and then gives the following Obligation.

The Obligation

I: A: B: Do promise and solemnly swear and declare on my sacred word of honor in the presence of Almighty God, and the most Excellent Princes of Jerusalem of the Grand Council here present never to reveal to the Knights of the East (or Knights of the sword) or any other person below this Degree the secrets which are now going to be communicated to me, under the penalty of being destroyed for ever, to be divested of all my Cloathing and my naked body exposed to every affliction, torture and hardship that can possibly be inflicted on me, my heart to be pierced with dagger untill all my blood is drawn forth,

[190]

I further promise and swear never to fight or Combat with one of the Brethren in this degree nor to dishonour him, but to do him all the Good in my power. So help me God. Amen.

After he has taken this Obligation he is conducted out of the Council, and goes from Jerusalem Accompanied by 4 of the Princes, in Imitation of Prince Zerubabel, whom he represents at the head of the Embassy; the road that he travelled in the Council represents the road which Zerubbabel travelled from Jerusalem to Babylon, the Combatting and fighting which he performed is figurative of that which Zerubbabel performed against the Samaratans in his Rout: his Travels being finished he is presented to Prince Zerubbabel to whom he gives an Account of his Journey and the subject of his Embassies.

1st He returns by the same road where he meets with the same Obstructions, which he combats and overcomes, in this he Imitates the celebrated Deputation which was sent from Jerusalem to the Great King Darius: being returned from his Journey he is again presented to Zerubbabel to whom he delivers the Letter he received from the Great King Darius, which indicates the return of the Embassy from Babylon to Jerusalem, Zerubbabel reads the Letter and gives Orders that the people be informed of the Success of the Embassy—he

[191]

departs the Council to return again with honor when he is shewn by particular friendship the magnificence with which the Embassy was received at Jerusalem, when the mysteries are made known to him, which represents the power given by the people of Jerusalem to their Ambassadors.

2dly As a Recompence for their glorious success; that being finished, the Signs, Tokens, the pass and sacred words are given to him, with the manner of Entering the Grand Council, at the time of his Knocking at the door for Admission.

PASS W^d^ The pass word is *Thebet*, which signifies the 20th day of the 10th month, on which day the Ambassadors made their entry into Jerusalem.

SIGN. The Sign is the right arms extended reciprocally the hands on each others left shoulder.

TOKEN. The Token is by takeing each others left hand little finger, placing the thumb on the middle joint thereof and striking 5 times with it thereon.

MARCH. The march is to take 5 steps on the Square.

SACR^d^ W^d^ The sacred word is the Innomenable name, which is also called *Adar*, signifying the 23^d^ of the 12th Month on which day thanks were given to the Almighty, for the reconstruction of the Temple.

AGE. The age of a prince of Jerusalem is 5 time 15.

[192]

THE HISTORY

The Samaritans having refused to pay the tribute for the sacrifices of the Temple, Zerubbabel sent 5 Ambassadors of Knights of the East to the Great King Darius whose residence was at Babylon to prefer his Complaints to him; The samaritans having notice thereof Assembled to oppose their passage, but those Knights being filled with zeal and Courage Valiantly fought and forced a passage to Babylon, where they made known the subject of their Embassy to the Great King Darius. The King to render them Justice, gave them a Letter in which he ordered the samaritans to submit themselves and pay a tribute to the Jews his Allies. On their return to Jerusalem they were received in Royal pomp and magnificence: The people met them without the City and accompanied them, singing songs of Joy and praise for their happy return. They proceeded to Zerubbabel to whom they delivered the Letter of the Great King Darius; Zerubbabel read it with a loud voice and gave Orders to inform the people of the Embassy, and that the Great King Darius had graciously granted their request and in Consequence of their fidelity and Courage they were appointed Governors and Princes of Jerusalem to render Justice to the people—they were Ornamented with habits of Gold stuff most rare and precious

[193]

they were decorated with a yellow Ribbon which hang from the right shoulder to the left hip, to which was suspended a medal of Gold upon which was engraved a ballance, to shew that they ought to conduct themselves with Justice and Equity: There was also a hand of Justice on the reverse side of the medal, as a mark of their Authority over the people as princes of Jerusalem which Dignity was offered to them as a recompence for their services rendered and the great Courage they manifested in protecting the workmen in the Construction of the Temple, and on their Embassy: They assembled in the two Chambers of the Temple to render Justice to the people. This my dear Brother is an Exact Abridgement of the Origin of the Princes of Jerusalem.

Duties and Priviledges of Princes of Jerusalem.

1st Princes of Jerusalem are Chiefs of Masonry they have a right to inspect all Lodges, and Councils, as far as the Knights of the East, they can revoke and annull all the work done in such, if found Repugnant to the Constitution and Laws of Masonry.

2d When a Prince visits a Lodge or Council of Masonry, he must be decorated with his proper cloathing and Orders to make himself known

[194]

he is a Prince of Jerusalem; Upon which the Sovereign or the Venerable Master must depute a Brother of that Degree (if there is such in the Lodge) to try and Examine him, this done he enters into the Council or Lodge to give an Account that the Visitor is such as has been announced. If it is in a Council the sovereign orders the door to be thrown open, he calls to order to form the Arch of Steel, he places him to his right hand, and does him all the honors due to him. If it is in a symbolick Lodge, the Visitor must be known as a Prince of Jerusalem to some brother in the Lodge of the same Degree otherwise he must pledge his word of honor that he is such. Then the Worshipfull deputes four of the most eminent Brothers of the Lodge, at the same time he ought not to deprive those of their places who are in Office; Those deputies accompany him to the door, which is then opened, and the Arch formed of Steel: They give him the most Eminent place, and if the Worshipfull is not a prince of Jerusalem, he must offer his place and mallet to the Visitor who is at Liberty to accept or refuse it; when he leaves the Lodge the same Ceremonies is performed as at the time of his Entry.

3dly If a Prince of Jerusalem presents himself to

[195]

a Lodge where there is no Brother of that degree and is without a Certificate as Prince of Jerusalem the Lodge must depute the most expert and enlightened Brother and the Worshipfull himself if found necessary, to Examine him as to his abilities in Masonry, After Examination he must give his word and honor, that he is a Prince of Jerusalem, After which he is to be received with the same Honor mentioned in the second Article.

4thly The Princes of Jerusalem have the Title in Council of the most valiant and Illustrious, To whom all Lodges of the inferior Degrees are obliged to give an Account of their work, they have a right to Examine the Constitutions, and no one can find any fault with such proceedings if they are five in number. They are Judges in the last resort of all Deliberations, held in Lodges, and when they have pronounced sentence, there is no appeal: They hold that power from their predecessors, which was given to them by the people of Jerusalem. They have a right of being covered in the Lodge and to address the Chair sitting, without asking permission for so doing.

5thly The Rights of the princes of Jerusalem are given to them, as a reward for their great services, which they rendered to the people of Jeru-

[196]

-salem and for their profound knowledge, and great services done to Masonry, their merit makes them equal to the great Zerubbabel of the Race of David.

6thly The Princes of Jerusalem must be upright, polite and strict observers of the Rules, In causing Justice to be done, and good order to be observed, particularly in Lodges.

7thly If a Prince of Jerusalem does not lead an Irreproachable life, and fails to be an honest man, he is to be punished by the Princes of Jerusalem, agreeable to a plurality of voices.

8thly If one Prince of Jerusalem should deride another he shall be deprived of assisting in Council for 3 successive Councils.

9thly If one Prince should give another a Challenge he shall ever be excluded the Council, his name erased, and advice thereof given to the Grand Council and to all Corresponding Councils and symbolick Lodges.

10thly If at an Election of Officers any prince of Jerusalem should demand a vote in his favor or in behalf of any other person he shall be excluded for ever.

11thly The Grand feast of the Princes of Jerusalem is on the 23d day of the 12th month which was the day that thanks was given to the Almighty for

[197]

the reconstruction of the Temple; On the same day the Officers of all the Councils of Princes of Jerusalem should be elected: On the 20th day of the 10th month a feast should also be celebrated in commemoration of the Triumphant entry of the Ambassadors who arrived that day at Jerusalem.

12thly A Council of Princes of Jerusalem must be composed at least of 5 Princes. The sovereign is Zerubbabel. The two Wardens are called the most Enlightened, the other Officers as in other Lodges. The Princes are called Illustrious, to announce at the Door of a Council of Princes of Jerusalem you must give 5 distinct knocks.

LECTURE OF THE PRINCE OF JERUSALEM OR PALESTINE.

Q: –1st Are you a Prince of Jerusalem?
A: – The Road to Babylon is known to me.
Q: –2d What was you before?
A: – A Knight of the East.
Q: –3d How came you to arrive to the dignity of Prince of Jerusalem?
A: – By the grand Zerubbabel and the Courage I have manifested in divers Combats.
Q: –4th How do the Princes of Jerusalem Travel?
A: – From Jerusalem to Babylon.
Q: –5th For what?

[198]

A: – On account of the Samaritans having refused to pay the Tribute for the sacrifices of the Temple, they were appointed to go on in an Embassy to Babylon to the Great King Darius to make known their Complaints.
Q: –6th How many Composed that Embassy?
A: – Five.
Q: –7th Who presided at that Embassy?
A: – The Grand Architect of the Universe and myself.
Q: –8th Did they meet with any Enemies on the road with whom they Combated?
A: – The samaritans against whom they were going to complain, armed themselves to oppose their passage, whom they encountered and vanquished.

Q: –9th What did they obtain of the great King Darius?

A: – A Letter in which he ordered those people to pat the tribute, on failure of which he should punish them.

Q: –10th How were they received in Jerusalem?

A: – With Royal and magnificent pomp, the people went out of the City to meet them and Accompanied them to the Temple with Canticles or Songs of Joy, thanking the Grand Architect of the Universe for their safety and success, and they were Elected Princes and Sovereign of Jerusalem.

Q: –11th Where did they assemble to administer Justice to the people?

[199]

A: – In two Chambers of the Temple.

Q: –12th How were they Cloathed?

A: – In Gold stuff; to decorate princes so respectable the choice was made of the Cloth that was most precious.

Q: –13th Was there nothing more remarkable or conspicuous in their Decoration?

A: – They had a yellow ribbon hanging from their right Shoulder to the left hip, at the end of which was pendant a Gold medal on which was Engraved a ballance, a two Edged sword, 5 stars with the Letters DZ, which signifies Darius and Zerubbabel.

Q: –14th Why all those Attributes?

A: – To remind them, that they ought at all times to Conduct themselves with Equity.

Q: –15th What does their habit represent?

A: – The Temple of Solomon rebuilt, 1 Square, 1 trowell, 1 ballance, 1 sword, 1 shield, 1 hand of Justice <and> 1 Equilateral.

Q: –16th What signifies those Attributes?

A: – The Temple of Solomon—the Courage that was displayed in the rebuilding of it. the square Compass and Trowel were the Tools which were made use of—The sword and the shield are the arms that the Princes Knights, made use of to

[200]

defend the workmen whilst they were constructing the Temple, the hand of Justice show the power of the Princes of Jerusalem.

Q: –17th Why is the habit vulgarly called an Apron?

A: – To remember that it was by its means they arrived to the high Degree of Princes of Jerusalem.

To Close the Grand Council.

Sov^{n} – Thrice Illustrious Brethren Valorous princes most Enlightened, what hour is it actually?

Genl – Most Illustrious most Valorous and most Equitable Sovereign, the sun has Traversed half his Career, and Justice has been done to the people.

Sov^{n} – Thrice Illustrious and most Enlightened princes, proclaim that I am going to Close this Grand Counsel by the Mysterious numbers.

Genl – Thrice Excellent and most valorous princes The Sovereign of the Sovereigns, Announces that the Grand Council is going to be closed.

A short silence then ensues, after which—They all arise, Then the Sovereign Strikes 5 with his sword on the Table and says, "This Council is closed," which is repeated by the Grand Wardens with the 5 Strokes Then all the brethren strike 5 and the Council is Closed.

Apron. The Apron is red, lined and bordered with yellow, on the flap a ballance equal held by the hand of Justice; In the Æra a Temple each side of the Temple a Cross and shield with the

[201]

letter *T* on one side or the other.

Ribbon. The Ribbon most be worn from the Right to the left, 4 Inches wide and yellow, bordered with red, to the end of which must be appended a gold Medal, on which must be 5 stars, one sword double Edged, in the middle of the Stars, on each side of the sword the Letters *DZ*.

Gloves. The Gloves are red.

[202]

The 17th Degree,

or Knights of the East and West.

The Origin of this Degree.

When the knights and princes offered themselves for the purpose of conquering the holy Land they took a Cross to distinguish them, and as a mark of being under the banners.

They also look an Oath to spend they last drop of their blood to Establish the True Religion. Peace being made they could not fulfill their vows, and therefore returned to their respective Countries, and resolved to do by their theory what they could not by practice, and resolved never to admit into their Ceremonies any but those who had given proofs of their friendship, Zeal and discretion, they Joined at Malta and formed a Connection relative to masonry, and took the name of Knights of the East and West, instead of that of Princes of Jerusalem, to teach all the world where that order Begun, and never changed in any wise their Customs and receptions.

In the year 1118, the first Knights to the number of 11, took their vows, between the hands of Garinous Patriarch and Prince of Jerusalem.

Form of the Council.

1st The Grand Council of Knights of the East must be red, spread with Stars of Gold.

[203]

2dly In the East of the Council must be a Canopy Elevated by seven steps, supported by 4 Lions or Eagles, and between them an Animal of the human kind with 6 wings.

3dly On one side of the Throne must be the Sun, and on the other must be the moon, to be done by a Transperency, under them a Rainbow, also at the East a Bason with perfumed water and a scull.

4thly On the North and South sides are 11 small Canopys elevated by three steps for the venerable Ancients, and opposite the Throne in the West are 2 Canopys elevated by five steps for the two Ancient Officers who act on the Council as Grand Wardens.

5thly A full Grand Council must be Composed of 24 Knights, the Venerable Master is called all Puissant. The Wardens and the 21 other Brethren are called Respectable Ancients. If there are more Brothers they are Stiled respectable Knights, and are placed north and South behind the small Canopys. The 1st Canopy at the right side of the Puissant is to be always vacant for the Candidate.

6thly All the Brethren are to be vested in white robes with a Circle of gold around their waists, each with a long white beard on, and a Golden Crown on their heads, the Knights in their Ordinary habits, carry a broad white Ribbon from their right shoulder to the left hip, with the Jewel

[204]

suspended thereto, and besides carry a Cross of the Order to a black Ribbon, hanging on their breast.

7thly The all Puissant has his right hand on a large book that lays on the Pedestal, to which book hangs 7 large Seals.

8thly A Draft of the Council is an Heptagon in a Circle, on one side in each Angle are the following Letters B. D. W. P. H. G. E. in the Center a man vested with a white robe, Centered with a Girdle of Gold, his right hand extended, and surrounded with 7 Stars, he has a long white beard, his head surrounded with a Glory, a two Edged sword across his mouth, 7 Candlesticks round him with these Letters H. D. P. I. P. R. C. over each Candlestick.

To Open the Council.

Q: – Venerable Brothers, Knights, Princes what is your Duty?
A: – To know if we are secure?
Q: – See and search if we are?
A: – We are so.
Q: – Respectable Brothers, This Grand Council of Knights of the East and West is opened, be attentive
A: – We shall always be attentive to every thing that the thrice Puissant shall propose.

Form of Reception.

The Candidate is Introduced by 7 knocks; 6

[205]

quick and 1 slow, when both the Wardens go and see who it is that knocks, and seeing the Candidate takes him by the hand and says, "Come my Dear Brother, I will show you surprizing things, he then leads him 7 times round, stops at each of the Angles, where he places his feet in a square, and so on to the last Angle, from which by 7 steps he advances to the Bason, holds his right hand to the all Puissant, who takes it between both of his, and gives him the following Obligation.

The Obligation.

I: A: B: do promise and swear to be faithfull in my Religion, and observe the Laws of the State as far as I can: I promise never to receive or Initiate, or Consent any to be received in this Degree, but Conformable to the Antient statutes and regulations, or by a power vested in me for that purpose, nor never will reveal the Mysteries of this Eminent Degree: All under the Penalties of my former Obligations, so God maintain me in Uprightness and Justice, Amen.

After this Obligation the Master of the Ceremonies takes the Candidate by the hand, raises him and brings him Between the Wardens, before the Draft. Then the Senior Warden says to

[206]

him, "Brother, Examine with Deliberation all the things which the All Puissant is going to Open to your view," After a little Silence the Senior Warden Continues and says, "is the mortal, here <that is> worthy to open the book and the seals.

All the Brethren cast their Eyes down and sighs. The Senior Warden hearing their sighs says to them, "Venerable and Respectable Brethren be not afflicted—here is a Victim (pointing to the Candidate) whose defeat will give you Content.

Q: – To the Candidate)—Do you know the reason why the Ancients have a long white beard?

A: – No, but I conceive you know it. I would wish to be informed?

A: – They are those who came here after passing great Affliction and having washed and dipt their robes in their own blood, (to the Candidate). Will you have such robes at such price?

A: – Yes. After which The wardens Conducts him to the bason, make both his arms bare, and puts a Ligature on each, and orders him to put them both in the water; The Wardens having each a Lancet retires back with a Spring, having a little red wine to drop from thence, then they give him a small stroke on the vien, and the supposed blood that comes forth is wiped on a Cloth

[207]

and each Warden show it to the Brethren and say, "he never was afraid to spill his blood, to see our surprizing things," Then the Ligatures are taken off, but his arms are left bare, When the Grand Orator makes him a Compliment on his Resolution.

1st Then the All Puissant opens the 1st Seal of the Great book, and takes out a Bow, and Quiver filled with arrows, and a Crown, gives them to one of the old men, and says, "depart and Continue the Conquest."

2ndly He opens the 2d Seal takes out a sword, and gives it to the next aged, and says, "go and destroy the peace among the prophane and wicked Brethren, that they never may have a residence in our Lodge."

3dly He opens the 3d seal and takes a ballance and gives it to the next aged, and says, "Endeavour that the wicked and prophane Brothers find Justice no where but in our Lodge.

4thly He opens the 4th Seal and takes out a deaths head, and gives it to the next aged, and says to him, "Go and Endeavour that the wicked might never find life amongst us.

5thly He opens the 5th seal and takes out a Cloth stained with blood, and gives it to the next aged and says,

[208]

"When is the time that we shall punish the Prophane and wicked Brothers who destroyed so many Brothers by their false Accusations.

6thly He opens the 6th seal and in that Instant the Sun becomes dark and looks black, and the moon stained with blood.

7thly He opens the 7th Seal and takes out Incense which he gives to a brother, and also takes out a Vase, with 7 Trumpets, and gives one to each of the 7 aged Brethren. After this the 4 old men in the 4 Corners shews their bladders full of wind Representing the 4 winds, (when the all Puissant says,) "never strike any prophane or wicked Brother untill I have discovered, the true and worthy Masons (Then the 4 winds puts up their bladders and one of the Trumpets sounds) when the 2 Wardens go and takes the Candidate covers his arms and takes from him his Aprons and Jewell—Then a second Trumpet sounds when the Junior Warden gives the Candidate a white robe, the Apron and Jewel of the Order. Then a third Trumpet sounds, when the Senior Warden gives him a long white beard, a fourth Trumpet sounds, Then the Junior Warden gives him a Crown of Gold, a fifth Trumpet sounds, the Senior Warden gives him a circle of Gold, Then a

[209]

sixth Trumpet sounds, when the Junior Warden gives him the sign, Token and word, Then the Seventh Trumpet sounds, on which all the 7 sound together, when the Senior Warden Conducts him to the vacant Canopy.

SIGN. One looks over their right shoulder, the other answers by looking over the left.

WORDS. The one says Adadon, the other answers Jabulon signifying Angel of Abyss.

TOKEN. You touch the left shoulder of a brother with your right hand, the person so touched, looks over his right shoulder, and so vica, versa.

JEWEL. The Jewel Iis [*sic*] an Heptagon of Silver or gold, in each angle on one side a Star of Gold and one of these Letters, B. D. S. H. P. F. G.* In the Center a Lamb on a book with 7 Seals, on the other side in each Angle these Letters B. D. W. P. H. G. F. and in the Center the two Edged sword, between an Equal Ballance, this Jewell is worn by the all Puissant, from the Center of his golden Circle, and by the other Knights, from their broad white ribbon, and all of them wear their Cross on the breast to a black Ribbon.

<APRON. A yellow silk bordered with red.>

PRIVILEDGES.

When a Knight of the East and West visits a symbolick Lodge of the 14th or other degrees, he cannot

[210]

dispence with wearing the Ribbon and Jewell he enters the Lodge with his hat on, a naked sword in his hand, a shield as a Prince of Jerusalem, and when he is going in, the Lodge door is to be thrown quite open, and he is Conducted by two Masters through the Arch, and if the Right Worshipful is not a Knight of the East and West, he offers the Prince Visitor the Hiram and Chair, who may accept or refuse it, he sits always on the right of the Master.

LECTURE.

Q: –1st Are you a Knight of the East and West?
A: – I am.
Q: –2^{d} What have you seen?
A: – Marvellous things.
Q: –3^{d} In what manner was you received?
A: – By water and the Effusion of blood.

* The retention of these letters is a French artifact. According to the *Baylot FM4 15 Ms.*, they represent "beauté, divinité, sagesse, honneur, puissance, force et glorie."

Q: –4th Explain that to me?

A: – A Mason is never afraid to spill his blood for Masonry.

Q: –5th What are the Ornaments of the Council?

A: – A Superb Throne, Sun, Moon, and Bason of Perfumed water.

Q: –6th What is the figure of the Draft?

A: – A Regular Heptagon placed on a Circle.

Q: –7th What is the representation of it?

[211]

A: – A man vested in <a> white Robe, girded with a gold Circle, round his right hand 7 Stars, his head surrounded with a Glory, a long white Beard, a two edged sword across his mouth, surrounded by 7 Candlesticks with these letters H. D. P. I. P. R. C.

Q: –8th What signifies the Circle?

A: – As the Circle is finished from one point, in the same manner ought a Lodge to be animated by its Union and Brotherly Love.

Q: –9th What signifies the Heptagon?

A: – Our mystick number inclosed in 7 Letters.

Q: –10 What are those Letters?

A: – B. D. W. P. H. G. and F. (that is) Beauty, Divinity, Wisdom, Puissance, Honor, Glory and Force.

Q: –11th Give me the Explanation of these words?

A: – Beauty, to adorn, Divinity, that is, Masonry is of Divine principles, Wisdom, a quality to Invent, Puissance, to Crush the prophane and wicked Brethren, and to reduce them in their Calumnies, Honor, is an Indispensible duty of a Mason, to teach him how to maintain in that respectable order, Glory, shews that a Good mason is Equal to the most High Prince, and Force, is necessary to Sustain us.

Q: –12th What signifies the 7 Stars?

[212]

A: – Seven Qualities by which Masons ought to be Conducted, namely Friendship, Union, submission, Discretion, Fidelity, Prudence and Temperance.

Q: –13th Why ought a Mason to be possessed of these Seven Qualities.

A: – Friendship is a sentiment that ought to reign among Brethren, Union, is the basis of Society submission, to receive a Direction from the Lodge without any murmuring, Discretion, to be upon your guard, so as never to be surprized—Fidelity, in observing strictly our Obligations, prudence, to rule our Actions, in such a manner that the prophane, may be always Jealous of our pleasures, without being able to blame our Conduct and temperance, and to shun all excess, against Body and Soul.

Q: –14 What signifies the 7 Candlesticks and their Letters?

A: – Seven faults, which Masons ought to shun, namely, Hatred, Discord, Pride, Indiscretions, Perfidy Rashness and Calumny.

Q: –15th What are the Reasons that Masons, ought to shun them?

A: – Because they are absolutely contrary to the Qualities which we are come to and acquired. A good mason never bears hatred against his Brother, even if he should be ill treated by him. Discord, is contrary to society and therefore we

[213]

must shun it. Pride must be banished, as it is contrary to humanity, Indiscretion is fatal to Masonry, Perfidy is horrible to an honest man. Rashness is treason to Masonry, and Calumny is a vice below a Mason, for he must endeavour to reeunite in himself a perfectness, and shun all other faults, that are a plague to human Nature.

Q: –16th What signifies the two Edged sword?

A: – It impresses the superiority of this over all other Degrees.

Q: –17th Are there any other higher Degrees than this?

A: – Yes, there are the respectable orders, of the Knights of the Sun, Knights of the white and black Eagle, and the sublime Degrees which are preceeding the last step of Masonry.

Q: –18th What signifies the book with the 7 Seals which none can open?

A: – A Lodge of Masons which the all Puissant has a right to open.

Q: –19th What is inclosed in the first seal?

A: – A bow and quiver with a Crown.

Q: –20 What in the second?

A: – A two Edged sword.

Q: –21st What in the third?

A: – A Ballance.

Q: –22d What in the fourth?

A: – A Deaths head.

Q: –23d What in the fifth?

[214]

A: – A Cloth with blood.
Q: –24th What in the Sixth?
A: – The power to darken the Sun, and tinge the moon with blood.
Q: –25th What in the Seventh Seal?
A: – 7 trumpets and perfumes.
Q: –26th Explain all these things to me?
A: – 1st the bow and quiver, with a Crown, signifies the Orders of the Lodge, which ought to be executed with such quickness and exactness, as the Bow sends forth the arrow; and receive those Orders with such submission as from a Crowned head: The sword signifies that a Lodge is always armed to punish. The ballance is a symbol of Justice; The Scull is the Image of a Brother who is excluded from a Lodge, this Idea must make all tremble, the more so, when they remember the penalties they have laid themselves under by their Obligations. The bloody Cloth, teaches us, that we are not to hesitate to spill the last drop of our blood for the good of Masonry: The power of Darkening the Sun and staining the moon with blood, is a representation of the power that a visiting brother of a Superior Degree has over the Lodge in interdicting the Officers, in case a Lodge does not work regular: Untill they repent of it by their amendment and submission. Lastly the 7 Trumpets and perfumes, signifies that Masonry is spread over the Earth on the wings offame [*sic*] and that she

[215]

will sustain it with every mark of honor. The perfumes Occasions a sweet Odour.
Q: –27th What age are you?
A: – Very Ancient.
Q: –28th What are you?
A: – A Patmean.
Q: –29th From whence came you?
A: – From Patmos.

To Close the Council

Q: – What is the Clock?
A: – There is no more Time.

Then the all Puissant strike 6 quick and 1 slow and says, "this Council is Closed," which is repeated by the Two Wardens, and the Council is Closed.

[216]

The 18th Degree,

or Knight of the white Eagle or Pelican, by the name of Perfect Mason or Knight of the Rose Croix.

This degree did not take its Original form of Scotch Masons, untill the last Temple, The Knights of Perfect Masons is in some Lodges of Masonry known under the name of Rose Cross, and is called the 4th degree in others by the name of the Knights of Saint Andrew the patron of Scotland, the 7th or last Degree, which many Lodges now understand, by the name of perfect Masons, and to follow after the Knights of the East and West. It is surprizing that a subject so pure and so perfect as masonry, should be susceptible of so many variations, particularly in the Title of this Degree, the reason whereof you will hereafter appear to you: Divers nations were too anxious to know the last Mysteries of the order, without attending to its Original Instructions. It is was reposed to some, whose Ignorance was so great, as not to be able to understand the first symbolic figures; upon that repose, the last knowledge of the order (foreign to the source) was fabricated by them to strangers some degrees a little like the matter, and who gave it after that, a new Title, which produces at this day the great differences in this matter, and some so far from the truth.

1st This degree is known by the name of Knight of the Eagle, a title that every body must know to be most Antient; Consequently it was Adopted by its

[217]

true name, which Origin is taken from Masonry Allegorick. The Eagle is the Image and representation of the supreme puissance, masons adopted like an Original Title has produced matter to this Degree.

2ndly It is called Knight of the Pelican, because the son of man is compared to the Pelican, who strikes his own Body with his bill and from thence brings out food to nourish its young: That Image is compared to the sacrifices of the Cross, which gives rise to this name, from the Justness of the Comparison.

3dly This Degree is called Knights of the Rose Cross because the Masons of Scotland in the primitive times had medals made, on which was a symbol relative to this degree, consisting of a Rose Cross, because the son of the Grand Architect of the Universe is compared to an Evangelick Rose, by his exemplary sweetness. Some of these medals have by accident passed into the hands of Lodges, the members whereof were Ignorant of their principles: they found that Emblem fine Enough to make a distinction, and therefore adopted the name of the Rose Cross to make their society conspicuous by an Elegant Emblem, which has continued for many ages without their knowing the Origin thereof.

4thly This Degree is also called and known by the name of *Harodim*, Masonry, because the first Lodge of it was kept on the summit of a mountain of that name situated between the West and the north of Scotland.

[218]

This Circumstance confounded the name of Rose Cross and they had nearly the same method of working, and in their Ceremonies they were much alike; there are some of them however that will not know one another by that name. Most part of the English Lodges do not know the Harodim and others not the Rose Cross; this last name is much increased in France and other parts. These two last kind of Masons are more reported in the Admi<minis>ration of their mysteries; they are well enough in their Initiations and agree in the Spirit of the subject but the large Viel is too thick for that Mystick subject they worked openly and shewed the superstition and prejudice of their morals, they knew nothing of the Ancient Allegory which the free Masons have always kept close in their hearts. The cause which produced this Disgrace to Masonry, is, that the Harodim and Rose Cross had made great progress in great Britain, and had multiplied with such Confusion, that the lowest masons were Initiated, which was the loss of the Dignity of the Order and overset the foundation. The religious Ceremony was destroyed by their prophane Conduct and Ignorance. Those masons who kept the Title of Knight of the Eagle, knew but little of the truth, but we can say to their praise, that they never have abused it, and have continued their masonry under the primitive Title: They teach nothing

[219]

but an amusing Allegorical moral; they always took care to guard against Fanaticks, that have given occasion to prophanation in those Lodges known by the name of Harodims and Rose Cross.

5thly This Degree is also called Knight of Saint Andrew which Origin came through Fanaticism: In Scotland in the earliest times, Masonry multiplied more than in any other place, they established many Lodges on the same plan, of virtue, Wisdom and Prudence, which presides in the said Orders. One of the Lodges had none of this, they had adopted the Custom Annually of holding their Grand meeting on Saint Andrews day, he being the patron of that Country, the people being Ignorant of the object of their Mystery, and only knowing that they were called Knights Masons and vulgarly so of Saint Andrew, and what contributed more to this name in the Eyes of the vulgar was, that their festivals and processions were held on Saint Andrews day, in a very pompous manner, the which made a strong impression on the people of the lower Class, who aspired with Ardor the remaining part of the year, to be Initiated, in order to share the pomp of the Celebrating day of their Patron. Afterwards this same lodge opened its doors easily to admit the people of the Lower sort, and only kept the name of Saint Andrew, because they were used

[220]

to their festivals and the said name, notwithstanding they learnt in their receptions that the title of this Degree was originally called the Knight of the Eagle, which was its true name. Afterwards having lost their Jewels, they could not get any Intelligence from any foreign or other Lodge who had not been exposed to the like Events, by Changes Ignorance and mistakes of the Antient form. Tranquility having been established, they took the model of the Cross of Saint Andrew, and formed a Jewel of it, on which that Saint was in full Length, though there was no relation between the Symbol of this Jewel and their work, yet it was sufficient for them that they had adopted the Cross. This was the principal reason, that those who wear the Cross of Saint Andrew, wear it as a Badge of Masonry; they are for the most part Ignorant why they wear it, and these Errors have been carried into Germany, where some travellers have constituted Lodges of this kind, such as that of Cologne, which was established a few years ago: Except that *they* govern themselves perfectly well; notwithstanding this it has a great many other improprieties in its Instructions, which is nothing else but that these changes have corrupted the Beauty of this Degree.

6thly In fine it is called the perfect Masons, because the Masons that we know in the Universe, and the

[221]

title of perfect Masons, makes of it the highest and most Eminent degree, and the last of their degrees which is the 7th there are some Lodges in England, who gave it to some Masons, who were not even Masters, a custom which is never practised, but strictly forbid in Lodges where perfect Masonry is practiced, and where you receive degree to degree, untill you come to the Degree of Perfection, as they do not give the knowledge of these sciences but by degrees, they conduct you from the 1st Temple to the 2d and to the 3d and in short to attain from one to the other even to the 7th which they give the name of perfect Master, which is the living Temple or the Allegory of the Redeemer. The 6 first degrees may be given to all sects who have a knowledge of the Ancient temple; but the 7th cannot be given but to those who submit to the new Law.

Disposition of this Lodge.

This Lodge must have two Apartments the 1st represents Mount Calvery, the 2d represents the Tomb of the Son of God, which shews Allegorically the death and resurrection of Jesus Christ. The first apartment must be in black and 33 lights on 3 branches of 11 each; which shows the age of Christ. In 3 Angles of the room must be three pillars Six feet high: on the Capitals of which must be wrote on the 1st in the North East

[222]

Faith, on the 2d in the East; *Hope*, and so on the 3d in the South East, *Charity*.

The Draft of the Lodge is an Oblong Square and figure, like Mount Calvary, with the tools of Masonry according to the description hereafter.

The Lodge is marked with Tribble lines, in which must be wrote between the Extremities, *Strength*, *Wisdom*, and *Beauty*, in the East, West, North and South with a dropping Curtain from a Canopy in the East: at the East and South angles are the Sun and moon, the heavens spread with Stars, and some <very> dark Clouds. In the East is an Eagle rising in the air, a symbol of the supreme puissance, 3 Squares in one, on each of the 3 Circles; Allegorically to represent mount Calvary, Opposite is a mount with a Cubic stone, as if it was sweating blood and water, to represent Christ in that state and on the Cubic stone a rose, a symbol of his sweetness with the letter, G, in the Center of the Rose, signifying Great Architect, or his expiring words.

In the Space between the Circles are Clouds to represent those on the Earth, at the time of that sacrifice. Below are the Antient tools of Masonry and the Columns broke in many pieces, the pavement also broke, to demonstrate that all the parts depending on the work of masons is destroyed when the architect is dead, and cannot be carried

[223]

on, and all the work divided, every thing ceased to be, by his death. A little higher is the viel or curtain of the Temple, that was torn in two parts at that time: on the outside of the Columns the 7 Knots of Union of perfect Masons. Before the Master must be a small Triangular Table, lighted with 3 lights: The Bible with the Evangelists, Compass, square and Triangle on it.

RIBBON All the Brethren must be dressed in black, with a long black ribbon from the Right Shoulder to the left hip,

APRON The Apron lined with black, those to be wore in what passes in the 1st apartment, where the Master and Wardens.

COLLAR Officers and Brethren must wear a black ribbon as a Collar,

JEWEL to the end of which is Ordinary Jewel, covered with black cloth the said Jewel is a crowned Compass, the points extended to a Circle of 60 degrees, a Cross within the Compass, and a pelican feeding its young, which are in a nest below, and on the other side of the said Jewel a white Eagle, with his wings extended as rising in the air; on both sides of the joint of the Compass a red rose.

In the second Apartment represents the Monument of the resurrection and ought to be hung with Tapestry full of Glory, without any human figures, and on 3 Candlesticks 33 lights inclosed in a large box, so cut with holes that the said

[224]

lights may look like stars. The draft of this apartment must be an Oblong square with quadruple lines, between which must be wrote Faith, Hope and Charity, also East, West, North and South round the border.

In the last part must be a Cross surrounded with the Glory, filled with Clouds and 7 Cherubims. In the Center of the Cross a Rose opened, and in its Center the Letter, G, below are 3 Squares on which are 3 Circles and on the opposite side a small mountain with 3 Triangles enclosed in each other; on the top of a Square Cubic Stone, which is allegorically the holy mount where Christ suffered: above the hill must be a blazing Star with 7 points, in the Center of which is the Letter G, which is the Allegorical representation of the Son of man risen in all his glory. In the South a Pelican feeding its young in their nest with his blood, and Image of his Eternal Goodness and tenderness. In the North an Eagle with his wings spread as rising in the air: The Image of the supreme puissance below is the Tomb. In the lower part of the said Square, in the middle line from the East to the West is the Thressel board, Cubic stone, hammer 2 feet rule and level, on the North side the rough stone and mallet setting tool and plumb, and in

[225]

the exterior of the East; a white dove and the 7 Knots of Union amongst masons.

Second part of the Disposition of the Lodge.

There must be a third apartment a little distance from the others, destined to be the Image of hell, in which must be represented the torments and horrors of that place: Seven Candlesticks with large flambeaus lighted; the Sockets of them must be Sculls and 2 Cross bones to each, the walls painted with human figures in flames as if damned, and painted so as to show, the most cruel tortures and Torments is experienced by the objects, in their distorted faces and Countenances, which they can possibly suffer in that place. In this Lodge the Master represents the personage of wisdom and reflection, and which gives him the title of most wise and perfect Master. The Wardens have the Title of thrice Excellent and perfect Wardens, and the rest of the Brethren as perfect Masters.

In the first point of reception, none shall take the name of Perfect, which Title is only given in the 2d Apartment, and for the second point of reception there is no other table, than a small one at the right hand of the Master, of a triangular figure with the 3 lights, Evangelists

[226]

and other articles upon it as mentioned before.

In the 2d apartment all the Brethren shall wear their Jewel to a black ribbon.

To Prepare the Candidate

The Candidate must be dressed in black, and red ornaments of ribbon and apron, with a sword and Sash: The Master of Ceremonies goes to him in Order to prepare him, and says, "All the Masons Temples are demolished, the tools and Columns broke and the Masters word is lost; since your last reception in spite of all the precautions we have taken and our endeavours not to be surprized, we are deprived of knowing ourselves and the order in general is in the greatest consternation." After the Master of Ceremonies has thus spoke to him; he leaves him in that room in darkness, and comes to the Lodge to be present at the opening of the perfection Lodge.

To Open.

All the Brethren being placed in Order the Master by the name of the most wise, shall open the Lodge thus.

Q: – Thrice Excellent Wardens what is the duty of a Mason?
A: – To see if we are well Tyled.

Q: – Do your duty then?
A: – We are secure.

[227]

Q: – What is the Clock?
A: – The hour of Perfect Masons.
Q: – What is that hour?
A: – That Instant when the viel of the Temple was rent in Twain, darkness and Consternation is spread on the Earth, the light departs from us the tools are broken, the blazing Star is obscured the Cubic stone sweats blood and water and the Masters word is lost.

Then the Master proceeds—"My dear brethren As Masonry proves to be in just tribulation let us employ all our time by a new labour to recover the word; this Lodge of Knight of the Eagle and Perfect Master is opened." The Wardens reply, Huzza 3 times—after which there is a silence for some time.

Form of Reception.

When the Candidate is ready to be introduced the Master of Ceremonies conducts him to the Lodge door and knocks thereon 7 times: the Junior Warden answers the same on the mallet of the Senior, and he the same number on the mallet of the Junior Warden, on which the Junior Warden in duty goes to the door to see who knocks there; then says to the Senior Warden, "there is one at the door who knocks like a Knight of the East and West: The Senior Warden reports the same to the Master, who orders him to his duty

[228]

he then sends the Junior Warden to see who it is that knocks: The Master of the Ceremonies informs him, that there is a wandering brother Mason among the woods and mountains since the destruction of the Temple, who has lost his reward and comes here with a desire to recover it by your consent—On which the Junior Warden shuts the door and repeats it to the Senior Warden who does the same to the Master, who then says "Brethren do you consent that the wandering brother shall be introduced into this Lodge to satisfy his desire," on which all the brethren manifest their approbation by raising their right hands, and then they all seat themselves as if in a great consternation, their right hands on their hearts, and their heads leaning on the left, the palm covering their Eyes, and the Elbow on their knee. The Master has his left hand on his forehead, his Elbow on the Table and his right hand on his heart; When the Lodge is in this situation the

Candidate is introduced between the Wardens: Then the Senior Warden says to the Master, "here is the Knight Mason who desires the Masters word. On which the Master addresses the Candidate thus.

Q: – What is the name of the 3 pillars?
A: – Faith, Hope, and Charity.
Q: – How are we to find these pillars?

[229]

A: – By travelling and searching in the most profound darkness.
Q: – And what time will that take?
A: – Three days.

Then the Master says, "let us travel my dear Brethren, from the East and North, from the North to the West, from thence to the South, and then not to loose the point in view of the good end that leads us. All the brethren follow the Master as described above, thirty three times, but may be reduced to 7 times, after which the Master goes from that apartment to the next, where they all take their red Jewells and Ornaments and from thence they proceed to the third or hell apartment, having left the Candidate with the Master of Ceremonies in the second apartment, who is conducted to the door of the third, on which he knocks 7 times A brother waiting at the door, gives him the pass word *Emanuel*,—which the Master of Ceremonies orders the Candidate to pronounce when his is going in. The Tyler demands the pass, on which the Candidate says, "that he is one of the Brothers who search for the secret of the new Law, and the 3 pillars of Masonry. The Tyler knows by that Answer that he is the Candidate, and directly seizes him and takes

[230]

from him his black ribbon and apron, and says, "the marks you are now decorated with are not the marks of humility, and for recovering what you are looking for, you must yet undergo more rigorous proofs than before.

He then covers him with a black Cloth besprinkled with ashes, in such a manner that he cannot see any thing through it, then says follow me and I will conduct you into the most Dark place where the most mysterious word shall arise Triumphant in Glory, with the great advantages of Masonry: but you must confide in me." After this he Conducts the Candidate into a room to mount and descend as often as possible and then conducts him to the third Apartment or hell, and lifts up the Cloth, that he may see and perceive all the horrid objects for about a minute or two. Then he conducts him 3 times round the room and says, "This is in memory of the Mystic voyage of our Saviour when he was in darkness for 3 days," he then returns to the door, drops the viel and says, "All the horrors you have already perceived is nothing in comparison to those you will suffer if you have not all the requisite firmness": Then the Tyler conducts him back to the second Apartment, at the door of which he knocks 7 and tells him, "Remember to answer

[231]

all the questions that shall be made to you, and that you come from Judea; That you have passed by Nazareth, and if they ask you my name, tell them it is Raphael, and that you are from the Tribe of Judah; without which you cannot guard yourself from the most unhappy things, that will befall you." The Junior Warden waits sometime after the knocks, before he goes to the door, in order to give the Tyler time to instruct the Candidate. He then opens the door and asks the following Questions.

Q: – Who comes there?
A: – A Knight of the East and West, who having travelled a space of the most profound darkness; offers himself to you, and the fruits of his labour to assist in the work.

The Junior Warden reports the same in form; on which the Master orders the Candidate to be Introduced: The Senior Warden then addresses the Chair, and says, "This is the Knight of the East and West, who by his help, hopes to recover the word that was lost, and becomes by that a perfect Mason." On which the Master asks the Candidate the following Questions.

Q: – Where do you come from?
A: – From Judea.
Q: – Which Town did you pass by?
A: – By Nazareth.
Q: – What was the name of your Conductor?

[232]

A: – Raphael.
Q: – What Tribe do you belong to?
A: – To the Tribe of Judah.
Q: – Give me the Initials of the 4 above words?
A: – I. N. R. I.
Q: – Put these Letters together?
A: – Inri.

Then the Master says, "Brethren the word is found, give this our Brother the light," Then the Wardens take off the viel or black Cloth. When all the brethren Clap with their hands 3 times all together and say Huzza! Huzza! Huzza! Then the Master tells him, "come to me, that I may communicate to you the last mysteries of the Order." The Senior Warden then Conducts him to the Master, who gives him the Sign, Token and Word, and says to him, "I wish you Joy my Brother on the recovery of our Mysterious Word, which gives you the Title of perfect Mason.

1st Sign. Is to raise your Eyes to heaven; Clinch the fingers of both hands, the palms of your hands opposite your forehead, then let them fall down to your waist: this is the Sign of Admiration.

2d Sign. Is in answer to the 1st and is to lift up your right hand, put up the 1st finger and clinch the others, which signifies that there is but one God, the source of purity and Truth.

Token. The Token is to Cross your hands, and clasp them reciprocally on each others breast—this token

[233]

is called the Good Shepherd.

Pass Wd. The pass word is Emanuel.

Word. The Word is Inri.

The Discourse.

The Masons from the Reedification of the Temple having neglected their work and abandoned to the Viscissitudes of the times the precious Edifice, which they had reared with so much pains: The work of the wise workmen corrupted, the Strength of the Materials and the beauty of the Architecture gave place to disorder and vice. The great Architect of the Universe determined to manifest his glory, and abandoned the Temple, to elevate by his divine, Supreme Geometry a Spiritual Temple whose Existance would not be attached by human greatness, and which might exist to Eternity by that Puissant resolution. That men have seen the miraculous Phenomena; the prodigy of Prodigies, the Cubic Stone pierced, sweating blood and water, and suffered all the Anguish of the soul: This was when the corner stone of the Edifice was broke by the workmen of the foundation of the Temple, for where the Rubbish of the Temple at that time was thrown, the masonic rose was sacrificed on a Cross, planted on the top of a mountain, from the surface to be elevated to the Celestial Globe by 3 squares, 3 triangles and 3 Circles, cut in points of Diamond

[234]

Human Masonry was in an Instant destroyed, the viel was rent, and Earth was covered with darkness, the light was withdrawn, the tools of Masonry was broke, the flaming star vanished and the word was lost. You may easily Judge what sufferings the Good Masons underwent in that moment: what consternation and affliction can be more expressed, they were obliged to travel in the most profound darkness for 3 days, uncertain, whether they were to live longer, or if any new accident should happen to them; they were so far reduced in perplexity of heart, that they feared the end of time was come. The will of him that Conducts all events and things, after finishing the time of their surprize caused the light to shine again at the end of 3 days, and this was not done without some new and surprizing thing or phenomena, the tools of masonry which were broke before, retook their ordinary forms, the blazing Star returned in a more brilliant manner, and the word was recovered: this was the scourge of the Masons for their negligence and Obscurity which their neglect had plunged them into. Some of them after travelling the space of 33 years, searching for the word, learnt to some others the method to find it was to know the 3 pillars of Hope, faith and Charity and to embrace

[235]

the new Law, in order to hope to enter into the Mystic work of the Order and that, that was not by any new principles that masonry appeared to the Eyes of man, but on some theorick rules, that conducts them Allegorically to the practice of their actions—since which time the masons do not build any material Edifice, but the spiritual are their work, they enforce their works by temperance, prudence, Justice and fortitude and never are affraid of the Viscisitudes of the times. I wish my dear Brother these pillars may never fall and that the great Architect of the Universe may be your help.

To Close

The Junior Warden knocks 7. The Senior Warden knocks 7.

Jun[r] W[n] Whats the Clock?

Sen[r] W[n] The hour of perfection.

Jun[r] W[n] What was that hour?

Sen[r] W[n] The moment the word was recovered the Cubic stone was changed to a mystick rose the blazing star returned with more splendor, our tools have taken their former shape, the light is come to us with the greatest brilliancy, darkness is vanished, and the new Law shall reign universally among us.

Junior Warden, "let us follow the Law

[236]

which was grounded by the most miraculous Events," this being repeated they all Cry <Huzza!> Huzza! Huzzah!—and the Lodge is Closed.

[236]

or Sublime Scotch masonry, called by the name of Grand Pontiff

The hangings of this lodge must be blue spread with golden Stars. The Master in this Lodge goes by the Title of Thrice Puissant Grand Pontiff, he is vested in a white Sattin robe, and sits under a blue Canopy on a throne; behind which in a Nich is a transparent light sufficient to light the whole Lodge, he holds a scepter in his hand: There <is> only one Warden who sits right opposite the Thrice Puissant in the west and holds a staff of gold in his hand: All the

[237]

rest of the brethren are vested in white robes and have the Title of faith full and true brothers. All must have a blue sattin fillet round their foreheads with 12 Golden Stars embroidered thereon. The thressel board or draft of the Lodge represents a Square City or the Celestial Jerusalem on Clouds descending from heaven to crush the remains of the present Jerusalem, and a 3 headed Serpent or Hydra in chains, representing the badness of the Infidels, Jews and vagrants yet remaining there. This Celestial Jerusalem has 12 gates, 3 on each side and in the Center of the said City you see a tree that bears 12 different kinds of fruits: the present Jerusalem underneath seems to be turned upside down and the chained 3 headed Serpent seems as of the Celestial Jerusalem crushes him. On one side of the Draft you see a high mountain.

To Open.

The thrice Puissant strikes 12 at equal distances and then asks the following Questions Viz^{t}.

Q: – Brother whats the Clock?
A: – The hour foretold.
Q: – Brethren the whole is Alpha and Omega, Emanuel. Let us work.

Then the Warden strikes 12 as above and says "Faithfull Brethren the Lodge of Grand Pontiff is open.

FORM OF RECEPTION.

The Candidate must be decorated with the badge of

[238]

Knights of the East and West, a blue sattin fillet with 12 Gold stars thereon, tied round his forehead before he enters, he is then immediately introduced into the Lodge, where the Warden places him on the top of the mountain and asks him, "Brother, do you detest and hate the perfiduous? Do you promise to break all Communication, Correspondence and friendship with them? The Candidate answers I promise and swear. Then the Warden leaves the Candidate on the mountain, and goes down backwards towards the Celestial City, and with a surveyors chain measures the 4 sides of the said City, he then goes to the Candidate and again and tells him, "Brother that City (pointing to it) measures 12,000 Stadia each side. Then he takes the Candidate by the left hand, and both come down backwards, he then conducts him before the Draft facing the Thrice Puissant at the right hand of the Warden, after a minutes silence he directs him to make 3 Square Steps to the Chained Serpent, and 1 step on each of the 3 heads, he then directs him to advance to the Celestial City, advancing with his left foot only bringing his right foot to the heel of the left every step, and then kneel 3 times with his right knee holding at the same time his right hand horisontally towards the thrice Puissant. N:B: this is

[239]

in Lieu of the Obligation. Then the thrice Puissant directs him to walk 3 steps backward which brings him again at the bottom of the Draft where the Warden gives him the Sign, Token and word—Vizt.

SIGN. The Sign is to hold your right hand horisontal the fingers extended, and then drop 3 fingers perpendicularly down.

TOKEN. The Token is to put reciprocally the palms of the right hand on the forehead of each other.

WORDS. The Words are 4—one says *Hallelujah*; the other answers, Let us praise the Lord. The first says Emanuel, the other answers God grant.

RIBBON. The Ribbon is a broad red one, strewed with 12 gold stars, to which hangs the Jewel.

JEWEL. The Jewel is a square of gold, on one side the word *Alpha*, and on the other side Omega. The Ribbon must be wore from the right shoulder to the left hip

The Doctrine.

Q: – 1st What are you?
A: – I am a sublime Grand Pontiff.
Q: – 2d Where have you received this Degree?
A: – In a place that required no other Light but that of the Sun and Moon.
Q: – 3. Explain this to me?
A: – As the Lodge of grand Pontiff never wants any

[240]

artificial light, so the faithfull and true Brothers the Sublime Grand Pontiffs do not want riches or titles to be admitted into this Sublime Degree as they prove themselves in their attachment to Masonry and faithfullness in their several Obligations, their virtue and true friendship for their brethren in General.

Q: – 4. What does the Draft of this Lodge represent?
A: – A Square City of 4 equal sides with 3 gates on each side; in the middle of which is a Tree that bears 12 different fruits; the said City is suspended as on clouds, and seem to crush a 3 headed serpent.
Q: – 5. Explain this to me?
A: – The Square City represents Antient Masonry under the Title of Grand Pontiff, which comes down from heaven to replace the Antient Temple destroyed, where the Grand Pontiff comes to make it appear, as it is represented by the ruins and 3 headed chained serpent underneath.
Q: – 6. How comes Masonry fallen to ruins, as we <are> tied and attached indispensibly by our Obligations which cannot be Equivocal?
A: – It was so decreed in all times, which we learn by Saint John, who we know was the first Mason that held a perfection Lodge.
Q: – 7. Where does Saint John say this?
A: – In his revelations where he talks of Babylon and Celestial Jerusalem.

[241]

Q: – 8. What signifies the Tree with the 12 different fruits which stand in the Center of the said Square City?
A: – The Tree of life is placed there to make us understand where the sweets of life are to be found and the 12 fruits signify that we meet in every month to instruct ourselves mutually and to sustain one another against

our Enemies.

Q: – 9. What signifies the sattin fillet which the Candidate is blinded with, and the 12 golden Stars?

A: – It procures those who wear it, the Entrance of our Lodge, as it procured the entrance into the Celestial Jerusalem to those who wore it, thus Saint John explained himself.

Q: – 10. What signifies the 12 Golden Stars on the fillet of the Candidate and those of the Brethren?

A: – They represent the 12 Angels who watch the 12 Gates of the Celestial Jerusalem.

Q: – 11. What signify the blue hangings and gold stars thereon?

A: – The blue is the symbol of Lenity, fidelity and sweetness, which ought to be the share of all faithful and true brothers: and the Stars represent those masons who have given proofs of their attachment to the statues and rules of the order, which in the end will make them deserving of entering the Celestial Jerusalem.

Q: – 12. What age are you?

[242]

A: – I reckon no more.

Q: – 13. What remains for you to acquire?

A: – The sublime truth of the Princes Adepts and the Royal Secret.

Q: – 14. What is your name?

A: – Faithfull and true brother.

To Close

Q: – What is the Clock?

A: – Thrice Puissant the hour accomplished.

Then the thrice Puissant says *Alpha* and Omega, let us rejoyce my brothers.— he then strikes 12, which is repeated by the wardens and the Lodge of Grand Pontiff is Closed.

[243]

The 20th Degree,

Venerable Grand Master of all Symbolick Lodges, Sovereign Princes of Masonry or Master Advitam.

THIS LODGE MUST BE DECORATED with blue and yellow: The Grand Master sits on a throne Elevated by nine steps under a Canopy: before him an Altar, on which is a Sword, Bible, Compass, Square, Mallet, &c.—the same as in a Symbolick Lodge, between the altar and the South is a Candlestick with 9 branches, which is always lighted in this Lodge, there are 2 wardens in the west. The Grand Master represents Cyrus Artaxerxes &c with all his Royal Ornaments and a large Blue and Yellow ribbon across each other.

To Open

The Grand Master says, "I desire to open the Lodge, he then goes down on the lowest step of the throne, when he is assured that the Lodge is well Tyled, he knocks 1 and then two separate with his mallet, each Warden repeats the same which makes 9—The Grand Master then asks the following Questions.

Q: – Where is the Grand Master?
A: – In the East.
Q: – Why in the East?
A: – Because the Sun rises in the East.

The Grand Master then says, "As it rises in the East, I open this Lodge," which is repeated

[244]

by the Wardens, and all the Brethren Clap 1 and then 2.

The Order of Reception

The Candidate represents *Zerubabel* who comes by himself, without being introduced, decorated with his Jewels and Badges of his highest degrees. The Wardens takes him by the hand and place him in a blue Elbow Chair opposite the Master, who asks him all the Questions from an Entered Apprentice to the Grand Pontiff and after he has satisfied the Grand Master and is found worthy to hold a Scepter, they make him travel 9 times the Lodge, beginning in the South and then by 9 Square steps he advances to the throne walking over swords laid across. There must be a pot with coal fire close to the Throne, so that the Candidate may feel the heat of the fire whilst he is taking the Obligation which he takes by putting his right hand on the Bible, covered by the Grand Masters right hand and then repeats the

Obligation.

I: A:B: Promise and swear evermore, that by my former Obligations, and on the greatest penalties, to protect Masonry and Masons with all my might, and not to acknowledge anyone for a true Mason who is not made in a lawfull Lodge. I promise that I shall strictly observe and adhere to all the Statutes and regulations.

[245]

I further Promise never to disclose this Degree but by a full power in writing, from the Grand Inspector or his Deputy: and then to no one but such as has been a Master of a Regular Lodge Under the penalty of being dishonored and despised by the Order in General. he then kisses the Bible.

Exercise of the Signs.

1st The 1st Sign, is to make 4 times a square with your right hand and Arm, the fingers clinched and the thumb up, Clapping your hand twice on your heart, then put your left hand on your left hip the thumb and fingers making also a square as well as the Arm, at the same time putting your two heels together forming another Square.

2d The 2d Sign Is that of Aaron the High Priest which he made when the Tabernacle was finished, which is kneeling down with both Elbows on the ground, the head reclining on the left side downwards.

3d The 3d Sign is that of Solomon when the Temple was finished, which are 5 squares, dropping both your hands on your breast, both the thumbs upwards which are 4, then putting your heels together makes a 5th Square.

Token. The Token is to take each others Elbow with the right hand, square it 4 times reciprocally, then

[246]

slip the hand down and give the Masters Gripe.

WORD. The word is *Jechson*, which signifies I am what I am, this is also the name of the man who found out the Cavern where the Lion used to keep, who kept in his tusks the key of the Ark of Alliance which was lost, as is mentioned in the Degree of the Royal Arch.

1st PASS WORD The answer to this word is *Nicklots*, a pass word.

2d PASS WORD Is *Jubilum*, which is the name of him, who found the Lion in the Said cavern, the Lion had a Gold Collar on which was engraved the word *Jechson*, the rest is an Enigma to you, and is only known to the Sublime Princes of the Royal secret, a Degree you cannot receive unless you crush the serpent of Ignorance.

3d PASS WORD Is *Zanabazare*, and is the name of him who laid the foundation of the 1st Temple, which was afterwards rebuilt by the Princes of Jerusalem.

JEWEL. The Jewel is a Triangle on which is engraved the word *secret*, appended to a large ribbon of yellow and blue.

INSTRUCTIONS BY WAY OF LECTURE.

Q: – 1st Are you a Grand Master of all Lodges?
A: – They know me all at Jerusalem to be such.
Q: – 2d How shall I know that you are a Grand Master of all Lodges?
A: – Seeing my zeal in rebuilding the Temple.
Q: – 3d In what manner have you travelled?

[247]

A: – From the South to the East.
Q: – 4. How many Voyages?
A: – Nine.
Q: – 5. Why so many?
A: – In memory of the 9 Grand Masters that travelled to Jerusalem.
Q: – 6th Can you give me their names?
A: – Their names were *Zerubabel* [BLANK SPACE], *Josue*, *Eliab*, *Joyada*, *Nehemias*, and *Malachias*.*
Q: – 7th What are the pass words?
A: – *Nichlots*, *Jubilum*, and *Zanabazare*.
Q: – 8. What struck you most, when you entered the Lodge of Grand Master?

*Other manuscripts demonstrate a variety in the names. For example, a manuscript which belonged to Colonel John Mitchell, first Sovereign Grand Commander of the Supreme Council, 33°, includes *Esdras*, *Zerubabel*, *Phalehi*, *Josue*, *Eliab*, *Joyada Nehemias* & *Malachias*, while the *Francken* Mss. (1771, 1783) have *Esdras*, *Zerubbabel*, *Phalehé*, *Josue*, *Eliab*, *Joyada*, *Homen*, *Nehemias* & *Malachias*.

A: – The Candlestick with 9 branches.
Q – 9. Why do they always burn in this Lodge?
A: – To remind us, that there can be no less than 9 Masters to form a Grand Masters Lodge.
Q: – 10. What is the reason you desired to be admitted in this Lodge of Grand Master?
A: – To receive the Two lights I was not acquainted with.
Q: – 11. Have you received these Two lights and how?
A: – I received first the small Light.
Q: – 12. Explain this to me?
A: – That is to say, that I am received by steel and fire.
Q: – 13. What signifies the Steel?
A: – In remembrance of the steel by which Hiram Abiff lost his life, and I hand sworn to make

[248]

use of it, whenever I can revenge, the said murder, on Traitors to Masonry.
Q: – 14. Why the fire?
A: – In remembrance that our forefathers have been punished by fire.
Q: – 15. By whom was you received?
A: – By Cyrus.
Q: – 16. Why by Cyrus?
A: – Because it was he who ordered Zerubabel to rebuild the Temple.
Q: – 17. What did you promise and swear when you received this Degree?
A: – I promised and swore, that I will see the Laws Statutes and Regulations well observed in my Lodge.
Q: – 18. What is your name now?
A: – Cyrus.
Q: – 19. What was your name before you received this Degree?
A: – Zerubabel.
Q: – 20. What means the word Jechson?
A: – I am what I am, which is the name of him that found the Cavern, where the Lion used to keep.
Q: – 21. Why is the Lodge decorated with yellow and blue?
A: – In memory of the Eternal appearing in clouds of Gold and azure on mount Sinai, to dictate the laws to Moses (and established him Moses) the greatest Sacrificer of the people.
Q: – 22[d] Where do you find the history of our Mystery?

A: – It is found in the Archives of Kelwillin[†] in the

[249]

north of Scotland.

Q: – 23. How comes it that you travel from the South to the East?

A: – To prove the power of the Great Architect of the Universe, that he extends himself from one end of the world to the other without bounds.

Q: – 24. Why do you wash your hands in the 14th Degree?

A: – To prove our Innocence.

Q: – 25. How comes the history of Hiram Abiff so much revered?

A: – As we know, that he chose rather to sacrifice his life than to give up the secrets of Masonry.

Q: – 26. How comes the triangle with the word secret on it, to be the most precious Jewel in masonry and with which you are now decorated?

A: – Because its justness, Equality and proportion represents our redemption.

Q: – 27. What was the mark of the place where Hiram Abiff was found underground?

A: – The mark left there was a Sprig of granate.

Q: – 28. Why then do the Master Masons in the Symbolick Lodges call it a Sprig of Cassia?

A: – The sublime Grand Elected, descendants from the Ancient patriarchs, did not think proper to give the real name, or truth of Masonry, therefore agreed among themselves to say it was a Sprig of cassia, because that plant stunk very much

[250]

Q: – 29. What are the reasons of the different knockings at the door to get admittance?

A: – To know and be assured, that they have passed the different Degrees, which numbers we must understand.

Q: – 30. How comes it that we keep our Mysteries with so much Circumspection secret?

A: – For fear that some Traitors of the Stamp with those 3 fellow Crafts that murdered Hiram Abiff might be found amongst us.

Q: – 31st What is the reason that the Grand Master of all Lodges are received with so much honor in the Symbolick Lodges?

A: – Those homages are due to their virtues and Qualities as Princes Ma-

† **Kelwillin**. This is the mythical mount Kilwinning.

sons: the firmness which they have shewn on so many Occasions, in spilling their blood for the Support of Masonry and the fraternity.

Q: – 32. How comes it that we applaud with our hands?

A: – By that we express our happiness whenever we do a good thing and render Justice.

Q: – 33. What subject of meditation offers itself us, or what can we say of the Conduct of Solomon?

A: – That a wise man can err, and when he is sensible of his fault, corrects himself in acknowledging that fault and thereby claims the Indulgence of his brethren.

Q: – 34. Why do the blue Lodge Lodges take the name and Title of Saint John of Jerusalem?

[251]

A: – Because in the times of the Crusades the perfect masons, Knights and Princes communicated their Mysteries to the Knights of that Order and then, it was resolved that they should celebrate their festivals annually on that Saints day being all under the same Law.

Q: – 35. Who was the first Architect that conducted the works of Solomons Temple?

A: – Hiram Abiff, Signifying the inspired Hiram.

Q: – 36. Who laid the first stone?

A: – Solomon himself cut that stone and laid it, which stone afterwards supported the Tabernacle.

Q: – 37. Was any thing inclosed in that Stone?

A: – Yes, some Characters which was like the name of the Grand Architect of the Universe, as it was known by Solomon at that time.

Q: – 38. What Stone was it?

A: – An Agate stone of one foot square.

Q: – 39. What was the form of it?

A: – A Cube.

Q: – 40. At what hour or time of day was it when that stone was laid?

A: – Before Sunrise.

Q: – 41. What was the reason thereof?

A: – To shew, that we must be early, and begin our work with Vigilance and Assiduity.

[252]

Q: – 42. What Cement did he make use of?

A: – A Cement composed of the purest and finest flour, milk, Oil, and wine.

Q: – 43. Is there any meaning in the Composition of this Cement?

A: – Yes, For when the Grand Architect of the Universe was willing to create the world, he employed his sweetness, his Bounty, his wisdom and his might.

Q: – 44. What is the reason that the Number 81 is held in such esteem, among Princes of Masons?

A: – Because that number explains the tripple alliance which the Eternal operates, by the tripple triangle which was seen at the time Solomon Consecrated the temple to God: and also that Hiram Abiff was full 81 years of age when he died.

Q: – 45. What was perceived more at the Consecration?

A: – A perfume which did not only surround the Temple but all Jerusalem.

Q: – 46. Who destroyed the Temple?

A: – *Nebuchadnezer.*

Q: – 47. How many years after it was built?

A: – 470 years 6 months and 10 days after the foundation was laid.

Q: – 48. Who built the Second Temple?

A: – Zerubabel by the Grant and help of Cyrus <King> of Persia, set about building, and finished it in the

[253]

Reign of Darius. When he was known to be a Prince of Jerusalem, Cyrus not alone gave Zerubabel and the Captive Masons their liberty, but ordered that all the treasure of the old Temple should be restored them in order to embellish the second Temple which he had given orders to Zerubabel to build.

Q: – 49. What signifies the Jewel of the Knight Grand Master of all Lodges being in a Triangle?

A: – He wears it in Remembrance of the presents given by Monarchs, and the protectors of the order in recompence for our zeal, fervor and Constancy.

Q: – 50. Which way have you travelled or posted to become a right Worshipful Grand Master of all Lodges and Grand Patriarch?

A: – By the 4 Elements.

Q: – 51. Why by the 4 Elements?

A: – To put me in mind of the Troubles of the world, to cleanse and purify myself of all my impurity and render myself worthy of perfect virtue.

Q: – 52. Where was the Lodge of Grand Master first held?

A: – To the East of the Temple in the Sacred Vault.

Q: – 53. Where is that Lodge held at present?

A: – All over the world, conformable to the Order of Solomon, when he told us to Travel and to spread over the Universe, and to teach Masonry to those who should be worthy of it, and Especially to those who received us kindly, and were virtuous men.

[254]

Q: – 54. What did Solomon give you on your departure to remember him?
A: – He recompensed the merits of all the workmen and shewed to the Chief Masters the Cubic Agate stone on which was engraved on a Gold plate the name of God.
Q: – 55. How was that Agate stone supported?
A: – It was placed on a pedestal of a triangular form, surrounded by 3 brass pillars, which pillars were again surrounded by a Circle of brass.
Q: – 56. What signifies these 3 pillars?
A: – Wisdom, Strength, Beauty.
Q: – 57. What was in the middle of that Circle?
A: – The point of exactness, which teaches the point of perfection.
Q: – 58. What did Solomon give you more?
A: – The great Sign of Admiration and Consternation by which I am known to my brothers, he also put a ring on my finger in remembrance of my Alliance with virtue, and loaded us with kindness.
Q: – 59. Why have you a Sun on the Jewel of perfection?
A: – To shew that we have the full light and know Masonry in its full perfection.
Q: – 60. Who destroyed the second Temple, which was finished by the Princes of Jerusalem?
A: – Pompey began its destruction and King Herod the great finished it.
Q: – 61. Who rebuilt it again?

[255]

A: – King Herod, repenting the action he had so unjustly done, ordered to recall, all the Masons that were fled and spread into different Countries back again to Jerusalem for the reconstruction of the said Temple.
Q: – 62. And who destroyed this 3d Temple?
A: – *Titus*, the Son of the Emperor Vespasian, the Masons who saw with sorrow the Temple again destroyed; departed for Rome, where they became Catholicks, and took a resolution never to assist in raising another Temple.
Q: – 63. What became afterwards of these Masons?
A: – After residing a long time at Rome, most of them died there and the remaining Masons divided themselves, and went into several parts of Eu-

rope, but the greatest part of them went into Scotland, where they built a Town called Kilwellin, and where at this time is a Lodge of that name.

Q: – 64. What happened afterwards to these Masons?

A: – 27000 of these Masons in Scotland, resolved to assist the Christian Princes and Knights that were at that time at Jerusalem, in a Crusade, in order to take the holy City and Land from the Barbarians, who was then in possession of it, and they obtained leave from the Scotch Monarch.

[256]

Q: – 65. What happened the most remarkable to them?

A: – Their bravery gained them the Esteem and respect of the Knights of Saint John of Jerusalem, and the General of that Order and all the great Officers took the resolution of obtaining the Secret of their Masonry, which when they had received, they also admitted those Scotch Masons into their Order, by the name of Rose Cross or Pelican.

Q: – 66. What became afterwards of those Masons?

A: – After the Crusades was over, every one retired to their respective Country, at which time Masonry was spread over all Europe, and was for a long time in full vigour in France and England, but after the destruction of the Temple they neglected the Craft for many years, nay ages in France England &c. but the Scotch only, to their praise, be it said, kept up the practice of it.

Q: – 67. How came it again in vogue in France?

A: – A Scotch Nobleman who went to France, became for a long time a resident at Bourdeaux, where he established a Lodge of Perfection, from the members of the said Lodge in 1744, being assisted by a French Gentleman who delighted much in all the Degrees of Masonry, and this Lodge is still kept up in the most splendid manner in the new structure there.

Q: – 68. What means the fire in our Lodge?

A: – My submission, the purification of my Morals and my equality among my Brethren.

[257]

Q: – 69. What signifies the Signs of the Air?

A: – The purity of virtue and truth of this Degree.

Q: – 70. What does the sign of the Sun mean?

A: – It signifies that some of us are more enlightened than others in the Myster ies of Masonry, and for that reason we are often called Knights of the Sun.

Q: – 71. How many Signs have you in the Degree of Grand Pontiff, Worshipful Grand Master of all Lodges?

A: – We have 12 Signs.

Q: – 72. Explain these to me?

A: – The 1st sign is that of the Earth or Apprentice, the 2[d] is that of water or fellow Craft, the 3[d] is that or Terror or the Masters, the 4th is that of Fire, the 5th is that of Air, the 6th is that of the point in view, the 7th is that of the Sun, the 8th is that of Astonishment, the 9th is that of horror, the 10th is that of stench or a strong smell, the 11th is that of Admiration, and the 12th is that of Consternation.

Q: – From whence came you?

A: – From the sacred vault of Jerusalem.

Q: – What are you come to do here?

A: – I am come to visit and see your works, and show you mine, to work together and rectify our Morals and if possible to sanctify the prophane, but only by the permission of a Prince Adept or Sublime Prince of the Royal Secret (if one present)

[258]

Q: – What have you brought?

A: – Glory, Grandeur and Beauty.

Q: – Why do you give the name or Title of Saint John to our Lodge?

A: – Formerly all the Lodges were under the name of Solomons Lodges, as he was the founder of Masonry; but since the war of the Crusades, we have agreed with the Knights Templars, Hospitalers, or Saint John to dedicate them to Saint John as he was the Support of the Christians and new law.

Q: – What do you ask here?

A: – Your good will and pleasure; as you may find me worthy, Obedient and Virtuous.

To Close

The Grand Master says, "My brothers enter into the Cave of *Siloe*, work with the Great Rafodam measure your steps to the Sun, and then the great black Eagle will cover you with his wings to the End of what you desire by the help of the most sublime Prince Grand Commander."

He then strikes 1 and then 2, and makes the Sign of 4 Squares, which is repeated by the Warden and the Lodge is Closed.

[259]

21st Degree,

Prusian Knight or Noachite, in 2 Degrees, otherwise called the Masonic Key

You must absolutely have been Initiated into the Degree of Knight of the white Eagle, to be admitted into this Degree, though it is looked upon as the Knights Servants of the K:H, or Knights of the white and black Eagle, as it is now called for known reasons: formerly it was sufficient to be a Master Mason to be Initiated into this Degree, which cannot be at present done for the reasons which will be given in due time.

The Origin of this Degree.

The most Antient order of Noachite known this day by the name of Prusian Knights Servants of the Princes of the white and black Eagle is translated from the German, by Brother *Berage*, Knight of Eloquence, or Grand Orator of the Chapter & by Brother *Gelois*, Grand Inspector and Knight, Lieutenant Commander, General of the Prusian Council or Noachite in France in the year 4664. The Grand Master General of the order who is stiled Knight, Prince, Grand Commander, is the most Illustrious *Frederick* of Brunswick King of Prussia, whose Ancestors have for these 300 years, been the protectors of the said Order and is Celebrated by the Prusian Knights, in memory of the building of the Tower of Babel, and

[260]

the confusion which happened there. Formerly this Degree was known by the name of Noachite which is descendants of Noah. The Pagans knew this Order under the name of Titans who attempted to scale the heavens and dethrone Jupiter; but the present Knights acknowledged no other God but the great Architect of the Universe, and our happiness consists in adoring him. We celebrate every year in the month of March during the full moon the Confusion of the Languages and the destruction of the Tower of *Babel* which destruction is one of the greatest wonders of the Creator; and is the Epocha of that day of Gods wonder and revenge, that we celebrate and meet for that purpose on the aforesaid night in March. Every other month during the full moon Candidates may be received, but no other light than the moon and Stars are allowed at a reception and the holding a Chapter.

Grand Officers of the Chapter

1st The Master of the Chapter is called Lieutenant Commander, and is decorated with a large black ribbon in a triangular form round his neck, with an Equilateral Triangle hanging on the breast.*

2d The Senior Knight of the Chapter, officiates as Senior Warden, and is a Grand Inspector, wears the same Jewel to a narrow black ribbon, to the 3d button hole of his Coat.

3d Another Knight acts as Junior Warden and is

[261]

called Introductor and wears the same Jewel.

4th Another Knight of the Chapter is called Knight of Eloquence or Grand Orator, wears the same Jewel to the 3d button hole of his waistcoat.

5th Another Knight is called Chancellor or Grand secretary, wears the same Jewel, in the same manner as the Grand Orator.

6th Another Knight is called Knight Treasurer, and wears the same Jewel, in the same manner as the Grand Orator and Grand Secretary.

7th Another Knight of the Chapter is called Knight Captain of the Guards, and wears the same Jewel in the same manner as the 3 last mentioned Officers.

All the Knights besides the 7 Officers wear the same Jewels to the 3d button hole of their waistcoat, with their hats off, but the 7 Grand Officers wear their hats in a Grand Chapter. In case of a scarcity of Officers, 3 of the above named can hold a Chapter, Vizt. The Knight Lieutenant Commander and the 2 Senior Officers, who officiate as Wardens.

Draft The Draft of the Chapter is, only the firmament with the full moon and Stars, on which the Eyes must be always fixed.

---

* Earlier French rituals depict the jewel with the letters S, C, J and P, meaning *Sem*, *Cham*, *Japhet*, and *Phaleg* (*Shem*, *Ham*, *Japhet*, and *Peleg*, in English Bibles).

The place where a Chapter is to be held should be so situated, that the full moon and Stars may enlighten it, either through the top or windows, as it is especially forbid, that the Sun or any artificial light should enlighten our Chapter.

[262]

To Open the Grand Chapter

The Lieutenant Knight Commander opens the Chapter in the East with 3 distinct knocks, very slow, and at an equal distance. The Senior Knight in the west answers by striking one blow with a mallet on the pummel of his Sword, on which the Lieutenant Commander says, "To Order," on which all the Knights rise, put up both their hands to heaven, the fingers extended, and look towards the East where the Moon rises, and while in this position or attitude, the Lieutenant Commander asks the following Questions.

Q: – Brother Senior Knight who are you?
A: – If you are Curious to know, let me first know who you are.
Q: – Do you know the Sons of Noah?
A: – I know three of them.
Q: – Who are they?
A: – I will tell you in the manner of our Spelling.
Q: – Then let us hear?
A: – You begin and I will answer.
Q^{r}:– *S.*—Answer, C.—Question^{r} *J*: well what signifies these three Letters?
A: – They are Initials of 3 names.
Q^{r}:– *Shem*, *Cham*, and *Japheth*, now give me the Sign?
A: – Here it is. (he makes the sign)
Q: – Give me the pass word?
A: – Phalag. (pronounced very slow.)

[263]

Then the Lieutenant Commander says, the Chapter is open,—then all take their seats.

The rest of the Lecture.

Q: – 1st What name is that?
A: – It is the name of the Architect who formed the plan, and conducted the building of the Tower of Babel.
Q: – 2^{d} Who taught you his name?
A: – The Lieutenant Commander of the Prusian Knights.

Q: – 3d In what place did he give you that name?
A: – In a place where the moon alone gave light.
Q: – 4th Could they get no other Light?
A: – No.
Q: – 5 Was the building of that Tower praise worthy?
A: – No. Because the perfecting of it was Impossible.
Q: – 6 Why was it impossible?
A: – Because presumption, Vanity and Arrogance was the foundation of it.
Q: – 7 Is it in Imitation of the sons of Noah that you keep this in memory?
A: – No, on the Contrary; but only for the reason to have their faults always before my Eyes.
Q: – 8 Where lies, or is deposited the body of *Phaleg*?
A: – In a Tomb made of Grey stone.
Q: – 9 Has he been rejected or disowned for his Sins?
A: – No, because by Characters which were engraved on an Agate Stone (which was found among the

[264]

dust of his Body in a durable Coffin of grey stone in the said Tomb,) we learn that God had forgiven him, as he had repented of his Sins and was become humble.
Q: – 10. In what manner was you Initiated a Prusian Knight?
A: – By 3 genuflections, and by 3 times kissing the pummel of the Lieutenant Commanders sword.
Q: – 11. Why did you make 3 genuflections?
A: – To put me in mind of practicing humility.
Q: –12. Why do the Knights wear a Triangle?
A: – In memory of the Triangle before which Phaleg the penitent did pray.
Q: – 13. Why is the arrow in the Triangle reversed?
A: – That is in memory of what happened at the Tower of Babel.
Q: – 14. Why a black ribbon?
A: – The black shows grief, sorrow, and repentance of the workmen of the said Tower.
Q: – 15. Did they work by day and by night?
A: – Yes, in the day by favor of the Sun and in the night by the light of the moon.
Q: – 16. Where is the Grand Lieutenant Commander placed?
A: – Always opposite the moon.
Q: – 17. And where are the Grand Officers placed?
A: – Opposite the Lieutenant Commander.

Q: – 18. Where are the other Knights placed?
A: – Any where to the right and left, but their Eyes

[265]

must be always fixed on the Lieutenant Comman[r].
Q: – 19. What is the reason thereof?
A: – Because a Prusian Knight has renounced all pride and Ostentation, to substitute humility and therefore requires no rank in a Chapter.
Q: – 20. Have you any more particular signs?
A: – Yes, and I will answer them if properly questioned.
Q: – 21. Where is your father?
A: – (The answer or sign) is to look up to heaven.
Q: – 22. Where is your mother?
A: – (The answer or sign) is to look mournfully on the Ground.

Form of the Reception.

The Candidate is introduced bareheaded, in his Ordinary Clothes, without a sword; decorated with a plain white Apron. The Junior Warden called Introductor is always the protector of the Candidate, who goes to the Anti Chamber and conducts him to the door of the Chapter, on which he knocks 3 times. When the Senior Warden says, "who knocks there," the Captain of the Guards goes to the Junior Warden; returns, and informs the Senior Warden, that the Junior Warden requests to enter the Chapter. He is then admitted on pronouncing the password Phaleg, and informs the Lieutenant Commander that he has left at the door a Candidate decorated with the Attributes of a Master Mason of Hiram, who

[266]

begs the Lieutenant Commander to receive him a Prusian Knight. The Lieutenant Commander then orders, that he be introduced on pronouncing the word password Tubal Cain. The Lieutenant Commander then asks the following Questions.

Q: – Brother Junior Warden do you answer for the Master Mason you present me?
A: – I answer for him, as myself.
Q: – If so let him advance to the foot of my throne.

On which the Candidate Advances and gives the Sign, Token and Word of a Master Mason. Then the Lieutenant Commander says, "Brothers Knights, here present: A perfect Mason of Hiram is desirous of becoming a Prusian Knight, do you consent that he shall be received." All the Brethren draw their swords and point them towards the Candidate without speaking (which signifies their consent.) Then the Lieutenant Commander says to the Candidate, "In the name of all the Prusian Knights here present, I consent to your request, *provided*, you will renounce all pride and Ostentation during your future life? Answer me? What do you say?

A: – The Candidate Answers and says, "I consent and promise that I will from this moment, divest myself in my future of pride and Ostentation.

The Lieutenant Commander says, "If it is so, and you are sincere, come and make a beginning in

[267]

and Act of humility. He is then conducted by the Junior Warden and Captain of the Guards to the footstool of the throne, where he makes 3 genuflections with his left knee, and at the third he continues on his knee, The Lieutenant Commander comes to him, presents the pummel of his sword to him, which the Candidate kisses 3 times. Then the Knight of Eloquence or Grand Orator harangues him, and puts him in mind of the proud and Ostentatious attempt of the sons of *Noah*, And likewise of the repentance and humility of Phaleg, the great Architect of the Tower of Babel &c.—after this Discourse all the brethren Knights, sheathe their swords, and observe a profound silence for a little while: they then make the Sign of a Master Mason of Hiram altogether. Then the Lieutenant Commander administers the following Obligation.

The Obligation

Q: – 1st Do you promise me never to reveal the Mysteries of our Order to any of Adams Children, unless you are convinced that he is a Prusian Knight?

A: – I swear and Consent.

Q: – 2d Do you promise me on the peril of your life that you will never suffer a Son of Adam to wear the Jewel of the order, unless you are possitively assured that he is a Prusian Knight

A: – I swear and Consent.

[268]

On which he is relieved, and the Lieutenant Commander orders the Senior Warden to give the Sign, Token and Words to the Candidate

Sign. The Sign is to put both up your hands, the fingers extended upwards, the

thumbs opposite your Ears, and makeing 3 Genuflexions.
PASS W[d] The pass word is *Phaleg*, 3 times repeated very slow
MYSTERIOUS WORDS} The Mysterious Words, are Shem, Cham, and Japheth, at the same time you give the Token
TOKEN by taking the two fore fingers of a brothers hand Between your thumb and fore fingers press them with your thumb and say,
WORDS "Shem," the other answers by pressing in the same manner and says, "Cham," the first presses again and says, "Japhet."

There is another Sign, Token and Word, to enter into a Chapter, which is called the Sign, Token and word of Entrance, Viz[t]

2[d] SIGN he that wishes to enter the Chapter shows 3 fingers, the other answers him with the same sign, then he that made the sign first,
2[d] TOKEN takes the 3 fingers of the other Brother in his hand and says, "*Frederick*, the 3[d]."
WORDS The other answers by saying "*Noah*," three times. This last Sign and Token and Words, signifies that Frederick King of Prussia the 3[d] of that name, is the Chief of this Degree, and that to him we are beholden for the precious Treasure and sublime knowledge which is deposited with him in succession from his Ancestors. Then follows, the Historical discourse

[269]

by Brother Eloquence.

THE HISTORY.

The descendants of Noah (notwithstanding the Covenant with God, which was made buy the sign of the Rainbow, that he never would destroy the Sons of Men again by a General Deluge) resolved to build a Tower so high, that they thereby could defy the divine vengeance of the Almighty God: They chose for that purpose a plain called *Sinari*, in Asia. Ten years after the foundation of the said Tower was laid, the Almighty looked down on earth and seeing the Pride and Audacious attempt of his people: Descended in order to confound their project, he therefore caused a Confusion of Languages among the workmen, which is the reason that the said Tower was Called Babel, which signifies Confusion. Sometime afterwards *Nimrod*; (who was the first that established distinction among men, and who vindicated the right of Adoration due to the Divinity;) founded a City which for the above reason he gave the name of Babylon, in other words a Circle of Confusion. It was in the time of the full moon that God, worked this wonder, which is the reason that the Prusian Knights or Noachites hold their festivals every year in the month of March during the full Moon

[270]

As the workmen could no longer understand one another they divided themselves and departed.

Phaleg who gave the plan of the said building and who was also the Chief Conductor thereof, finding that he was guilty, and had greatly sinned against God, in that which he had done, condemned himself to a very severe penance, and retired from the sinful spot, and went into the North, now called Germany, where he arrived after undergoing a great deal of trouble and fatigue in crossing large deserts on which he found nothing else for sustenance, but the roots of the Earth and wild fruits. He fixed himself in that part which is now called Prusia and with great labor he constructed several huts, where he sheltered himself from the weather, and in process of time he built himself a little Temple of a Triangular form where he used to shut himself up very often to implore the forgiveness of God, for the Sins he had Committed. In the year 1553 in diging for Salt mines (which are frequently found in Prusia) they found ruins of a triangular Edifice, 15 Cubits deep; in the Center of which stood a Column of white marble, on the base of which was engraved in *Syriac* Characters the whole history of the penitent *Phaleg*. By the side of the said Column they found a Coffin, or Tomb of Grey stone, in which they perceived some dust

[271]

and a black agate stone on which was cut in Syriac Characters, "Here lies the Ashes of the great Architect of the Tower of Babel; the Almighty pitied him, because he became humble and penitent."

They continued to dig, and found a quantity of other Agate stones and some of white marble, which had on them also, divers curious, as well as interesting descriptions, part of which are already translated in the German tongue and some others which are not as yet decyphered or translated. All the descriptions cut or engraved on these Agate and other stones, are very interesting mysteries; which we cannot communicate but to those who have from time to time given the greatest proofs of their discretion; and who have been Initiated into the highest and most sublime knowledge of our Mysteries: because we are not to doubt of their Sagacity and prudence when they are come to that perfect point, and all Confidence ought and may be reposed in them.

All these curious pieces of Agate, Marble, the Coffin and Column, are deposited in the Archives of the King of Prusia, being a secret place. N:B: The Epitaph does not say that *Phaleg* was the Architect of the Tower of *Babel*, but the inscription on the base of the Column, instructs us that *Phaleg* was the Son of *Shem*; the Eldest Son of Noah. These my Brother you have

[272]

part of the secret of our Order, which is not known by any one of the Sons of Adam (that is) the prophane. I have entrusted you with this with pleasure: If you are so rash as to become indiscreet, pursue the example of the great *Phaleg*, and practice humility and those Lessons which the Knights philosophers have taught, that is to say, the Knights Adepts of the Sun. The Noachites are called this day Prusian Knights, and are descendants of *Phaleg*, Architect of the Tower of Babel, therefore the Origin of this Order is long before the Æra of Hirams, or Solomons Masonry because every body knows that the Tower of Babel was built many Centuries before the Temple of Solomon, and in former Ages it was not required that a Candidate should be a Master Mason of Hiram, but in the times of the Crusades the Knights of the different orders of Europe were Initiated into this Degree by the Christian Princes to conquer the holy Land, which was invaded by the Infidels. The Masons descendants of Hiram by the affection they had for the Noachites, as they were much venerated and Esteemed, therefore desired to be Initiated into their order and were admitted Prusian Knights according to the Mystery of Masonry, and from that time they resolved not to admit a Candidate unless he is at least a perfect Mason according to the statutes and regulations

[273]

of the order deposited also in the Archives of the King of Prusia. It is especially forbid by the statutes of our order, to make use of any tables eating or drinking or any Artificial Light in this Chapter: but the Lieutenant Commander the only expositor of the Instructions and doctrine of this Degree, has the power for the instruction of the Candidate, to open a table or fellow Crafts Lodge (after the Chapter is Closed) on which table there must be nothing served up of any kind of Animal food, but only Roots, fruits and Vegetables, in memory of the Penitent *Phaleg*, who lived on Vegetables during his penitence.

The Second Part of the Degree of Prusian Knight called the perfect Prusian Knight

To Open.

Q: – Where is thy Father?
A: – (The answer is) by looking up to heaven.

Q: – Where is thy Mother?
A: – (The answer is) by looking down on the Earth.

Then the Lieutenant Grand Commander says "this Chapter of perfect Prusian Knight is open

Further Interesting Explanations.

In the Grey stone Coffin of *Phaleg,* among his dust was found, beside the black Agate stone

[274]

(as mentioned in the first part of this Degree) several others Viz[t].

1st One Agate stone of a triangular form, on which was cut or engraved in Hyroglyphic Characters, which were not, before the reign of this present King of Prusian Explained, but contain, and we thereby learn that 9000 years before the Æra of Adam this world Existed.

2[d] On another Stone in the same Characters and Hyroglyphicks was engraved, that our forefathers had built many Edifices underground, for fear they should be prophaned by Infidels and others, of which that of *Enoch,* was one and perhaps the first.

3[d] There was also found 6 Stones of white marble on which were also hyroglyphical Characters but these will not be explained untill the true Elected are all united under the banner of one sovereign and one Law, which Law is that which is practised by the Knights Adepts and which will bring us to the knowledge of it: but we must absolutely crush entirely the Serpent of Ignorance and prejudice in matters of Religion in hope and full Expectation of the Eternal Beatitude. This Lodge must be Closed in the same manner as opened.

[275]

Knights of the Royal Ax, or Hache, sometimes called Grand patriarch, by the name of Princes of Lebanus

This meeting is called a College.

To Open a Colledge.

The chief prince says, "to order brethren," which is repeated by the Senior and Junior Grand Officers; after some silence is observed, the Chief Prince holds up his hands, the fingers and thumbs extended as wide as possible and says, "The trees of Lebanon are grown up and fit to be cut," on which all the brethren hold up their hands in the same manner, then let them fall on their thighs, in allusion that they were felled and cut down; in order to be used for holy purposes, Viz^t^.

1st They were used for building Noahs Ark.

2^d^ They had been used for the Construction of the Ark of Alliance.

3^d^ For the use of Solomons Temple.

The Chief Princes then say.

1st Noah	the answer to these	Japhet
2 Bezaleel	words are made	Eliab
3 Sidonians	by the Senr Officer	Lebanus

There is no Token in this Degree.

Origin of this Degree

This Degree was established on the 3 above

[276]

mentioned Occasions of cutting Cedars for holy enterprizes. The explanation of the Letters on the Ax or jewel will teach you.

L. on one side of the blade means.................................Lebanon
S. on the top of the handle.......................................Solomon
A. on the same side means..Abda
AD on...............................d° ....Adoniram
C. on...............................d° ....Cyrus.
D. on...............................d° ....Darius.
X. on...............................d° ....Xerxes.
Z. on...............................d° .... Zerubabel.
A. on...............................d° .... Annanias.

On the other side of the Ax are the following Initials

S. on the blade, means ....Sidonians
N. at the top of the handle..Noah.
S. at the same side means. ....Shem.
C. on...............................d° .... Cham.
J. on ....d° .... Japhet.
M. on...............................d° .... Moses.
B. on...............................d° ....Bezaleel.
E. on...............................d° .... Eliab.

The said Ax or Jewel must be crowned, and should be of gold, it must hang on the breast to a ribbon of the Colour of the Rainbow, it may be also worn from the right shoulder to the left hi The Sidonians were always very zealous for the promoting holy enterprizes; for before the deluge

[277]

they employed themselves in cutting the Cedars of mount Lebanus, for the Construction of Noahs Ark, under the Conduct of Japheth: the descendants of them likewise did cut the Cedars, (that were grown up again,) for the Construction of the Ark of the Covenant; and their posterity also cut in the same forest again, under the Conduct of the Princes of Harodim for the Construction of the first Temple of God, by the orders of King Solomon. The same nation assisted in bringing the Timber down from the said mountain to the sea side, to be transported from thence to Joppa. Those zealous peoples descendants have since been employed to fell the Timbers of the said mountain for the Construction of the Second Temple, by the orders of Cyrus, Darius and Xerxes, under the conduct of Zerubabel. This celebrated nation formed on the said mountain Colleges or meetings, and always on their works adored the Great Architect of the Universe; they had the same signs, and their different words were taken from the different

Inspectors and Conductors: as Noah and his 3 Sons, Noah being the first Chief, and his Sons the Conductors. We owe to these Conductors and Antient Patriarchs, that we are come to the knowledge of these Events, in succession of time since the Deluge. In the earliest days and times Colled<ges>

[278]

were established on the said Mountain for the Construction of the Ark of the Covenant; and in an Epocha afterwards, the same rule was observed, and Colledges were held for the Construction of Solomons Temple. That wise King ordered that a small Palace should be built on Mount Lebanus, which when finished he used to go to, to see what progress the workmen made in hewing and squareing the Cedars.

Thus, by their Example we preserve with the greatest respect, the names of those Venerable Patriarchs and also the memory of the Sidonians.

The Initials of the Jewel form an Abridgement of this interesting history, as well as the figure of the Draft. This Colledge is Closed in the same manner as it was Opened.

[279]

The Key of Masonry Philosophical Lodge, Knights Adepts of the Eagle or Sun

This council must be illuminated by a single Light, and is enlightened by 1 Divine light because there is 1 single light that shines among men, who have the happiness of leaving the darkness of Ignorance, and of Vulgar prejudice to follow the only light that leads to the Celestial truth.

The light that shines in our Lodge is composed of a glass Globe, filled with water, and a light placed behind it, which renders the light more clear through the glass by reflection. The globe and the light is placed in the south.

Decoration of Officers

The Grand Master or thrice Puissant is called father Adam, and is placed in the East, vested in a robe of pale yellow, like the morning, he had his hat on, in his right hand a Scepter, on the top of which is a Globe, gilt, the handle or extremity <of> the said Scepter is also gilt. The reason that Father Adam carries the Globe above the scepter in this Council is, because he was constituted Sovereign Master of the world, and created Sovereign father of all mankind. He carries a sun suspended by a gold chain round his neck and on the reversion of this gold Jewel is a Globe. In this Degree no other Jewel is worn, and no

[280]

Apron. There is only 1 Warden who sits opposite father Adam in the West and is called brother Truth he is decorated with the same Jewel and order as Father Adam, and wears besides a large white water Ribbon as a Collar, with an Eye of Gold embroidered thereon, above the gold Chain and Jewel of the Sun. The number of the other Officers are 7 and are called by the names of the Cherubims as follows. Zaphriel, Zabriel, Camael, Uriel, Michael, Zaphiel, and Gabriel; These ought to be decorated in the same manner as the Thrice Puissant father Adam. If there are more than that number of Knights of the Sun, they go by the name of Sylphs, and are the preparers of the Council and Assistants in all the Ceremonies or Operations of the Lodge: these wear the <same> Jewel, but to a ribbon of a fiery Colour hung to the third button hole of their Coats.

To Open the Grand Council

Father Adam says, "Brother Truth what time is it on Earth?"

A: – Mighty Father, it is midnight among the prophane or Cowans, but the sun is in its Meridian in this Lodge.

Then Father Adam proceeds and says, My dear Children profit by the favour of this Austere luminary at present showing its light to us, which will conduct us in the path of Virtue and to follow that

[281]

Law which is eternally to be engraved on our hearts and which is the only Law that can conduct us, and by which we cannot fail to come to the knowledge of pure truth. Then father Adam makes the sign—and puts his right hand on his left breast, on which all the brethren put up their fore finger of their right hands above the height of their heads, the other fingers clinched, showing thereby that there is but one God, who is the beginning of all truth. Then father Adam says, "this Lodge is open." Whenever the Thrice Puissant father Adam says, "to order my Children," they put their hands on their breasts and he puts up his forefinger, and so vica versa.

Form of a Reception.

After the Lodge or Council is opened the Candidate is introduced in an antichamber, where there are a number of Sylphs each with a pair of bellows, blowing the fire under a large pot, which the Candidate sees but they take no notice of. After that he is left in this situation for about 2 or 3 minutes, the most Antient of the Sylphs goes to the Candidate and covers his face with a black Crape (he must be without a sword) and tells him that he must find the door of the sanctuary and when he has found it, he must knock 6 times on it with his open hand; after he had knocked

[282]

thus. Brother Truth goes to the door and opens it a little, and asks the Candidate the following Questions, which he answers by the help of the Sylphs.

Q: – What do you desire?
A: – I desire to go out of darkness, to see the true light and to know the holy Truth in all its purity.
Q: – What do you desire more?
A: – To divest myself of Original Sin, and destroy the Juvenile prejudices of error, which all men are liable to, namely the desires of all worldly attachment and pride. On which Brother truth comes to Father Adam and relates what the Candidate has told him, when Father Adam gives orders to Introduce the Candidate to true happiness. Brother Truth then opens the door, takes the Candidate by the hand, and conducts him to the middle of the Lodge or sanctuary (which is also covered with a black Cloth,) when father Adam addresses him thus, "My Son! Seeing that by your labour in the Royal art, you are now come to the desire of knowing the pure and holy truth, we shall lay it open to you without any disguise or covering, but before we do this, consult your heart and see in this moment, if you feel yourself disposed to obey her (namely Truth) in all things that she commands: If you are disposed as I have desired, I am sure she is already in your heart, and you must feel an emotion

[283]

that was unknown to you before, this being so, you must hope that she will not be long to manifest herself to you. But have a Care not to defile this sanctuary by a spirit of Curiosity, and to take care not to increase the number of the vulgar and prophane that have for a long while ill treated her untill she (Truth) was obliged to depart the earth and now can hardly trace any of her footsteps: But she always appears in her greatest glory without disguise to the true, good and honest free Masons, that is to say to the zealous extirpators of superstition and Lies. I hope my dear brother you will be one of her Intimate favourites; the proofs that you have exercised assures me of every thing I have to expect of your zeal, for as nothing now can be more a secret between us, I shall order Brother Truth that he will instruct you in what you are to do, to come to the Center of true happiness." After this discourse of Father Adams the Candidate is unveiled, and then is shown the form of the Lodge or Council, without explaining any part thereof. Then Brother Truth proceeds, "My dear Brother, By <my> mouth holy Truth speaks to you; but before she manifests herself to you she requires from you proofs by which she is satisfied: In your entrance into the Masonic Order, she has appeared to you in many things, which you could not have apprehended or

[284]

comprehended without her Assistance, but now you have the happiness of arriving to this brilliant day, nothing that you have heretofore seen can be secret to you: Learn then the moral use that is made of the 3 first parts of the furniture which you saw, when you was received an Entered Apprentice Viz[t]: The Bible, Compass and Square.

THE BIBLE. By the Bible you are to understand that it is the only Law you ought to follow, it is that which Adam received at his Creation and which the Almighty engraved on his heart: This Law is called natural Law, and shews that there is not any other but one God, and that we ought to adore him without any Subdivision or Interruption.

COMPASS. The Compass gives you the faculty of Judgeing for yourself, that whatever God has created is well and the Sovereign Author of every thing existing in himself is neither good nor evil, because we understand by this expression, an action done which is not excellent in itself but is relative and submits to the human Understanding or Judgement to know the price or value of the same, and that God with whom every thing is possible, communicates nothing of his will but such as his great goodness pleases and every thing in the Universe is governed as he has decreed it; with our just being able to compare it to the Attributes of the Divinity. I equally say, that in himself there

[285]

is no evil, because he has made every thing with Exactness, and that every thing exists according to his will, consequently as it ought to be. The distance of good and evil with the Divinity cannot be more justly and clearly compared, than by a Circle formed with a Compass, for the points when reunited form an entire Circumference and represents the Immensity of God, who is the beginning of all things, for as the point forms a circumference by its union, so the points when seperated is the beginning of all Solids, existing or possible, and when any point in particular equally approaches or seperates from its point, it is then only a faint resemblance of the distance between good and evil which we compare to the points of a Compass forming a Circle, which Circle when completed is representative of God.

SQUARE. By the square we discover that God has made every thing equal, in the same manner as you are not able to dig a body in a Quarry compleat or perfect; thus the will of the Eternal in creating the world by a liberal act of his own will, foresaw every matter that could possibly happen in consequence thereof, that is to say, that every thing therein contained at the time of the Creation was Good. You have also seen a Level a plumb and a rough stone.

LEVEL. By the Level you are to learn to be right and

[286]

sincere, and not suffer yourself to be drawn away by the multitude of blind and Ignorant people, to be always firm and Steady to sustain the right of the natural law and the pure and real knowledge of that truth which it teacheth.

PERPENDICULAR AND ROUGH STONE} By the Perpendicular and rough Stone, you ought to understand, the prejudiced man, polished by reason, and that Censure is put away by the Excellence of our Master.

THRESSEL BOARD} You have seen the thressel board, to draw plans on, this represents the man whose whole occupation is the art of thinking, and who employs his reason to that which is just and reasonable.

CUBIC STONE} You have seen the Cubic stone, the moral of which and the sense you ought to draw from it is, to rule your actions, that they might be equally brought to the sovereign Good.

PILLARS.} The 2 pillars teach you that all masons ought to attach themselves firmly, to become an ornament of the order as well as the support thereof, as the pillars of Hercules formerly determined the end of the Antient world.

BLAZING STAR.} You have seen the blazing Star, the moral sense of which is, a true Mason perfecting himself in the way of Truth, that he may become like a blazing star, which shineth equally through the thickest darkness: that is to say, it is useful to

[287]

those that it shineth upon, and who are ready and desirous of profiting by its light.

These first Instructions have Conducted you to the knowledge of the slaughter of Hiram Abiff and the enquiries that were made to find him out. You have been informed of the Signs, Words and Tokens, which were substituted in the room of those we feared, to have been surprized, but of which you have since learnt, that the treacherous villians had not been able to receive any knowledge of; and this ought to be an Example an salutary advice to you to be always on your guard and well pesuaded that it is difficult to escape the snares that Ignorance joined to conceited opinions lay every day against us, in order to overcome is: And the most virtuous men are liable to fall, because their Candor renders them unsuspecting; but in this case you ought to be as firm as was our respectable father Hiram Abiff who chose rather to be masacred than to give up what he had obtained. This will teach you, that as soon as truth shall be fixed in your heart, you ought no more to consider the resolution you should take; You must live and die to sustain the light by which we acquire the sovereign good, never to expose ourselves to the conversation of Cowans, to be circumspect with those who are most Intimate

[288]

in our Mysteries and not to deliver ourselves up to any, except those whose characters and behaviour have proved to be brothers, that are worthy to come and appear in the sacred sanctuary where holy truth delivers her Oracles. You have past the secret and Perfect Master the fourth and fifth Degrees of Masonry: You have been decorated with an Ivory kee, a symbol of your discretion: You have received the first pronounciation of the Ineffable name of the great Architect of the Universe, and have been placed at the first Balustrade of the sanctuary: You have had the rank among the Levites after you knew the word *Zizon*, which signifies a Balustrade of the Levites, where all those are paced as well as yourself to expect the knowledge of the most sublime mysteries.

COFFIN GRAVE AND ROPE} In the Degree of Perfect Master, they have shewn you a Grave a Coffin and a white Rope, to raise and deposit the body in a sepulcher made in the form of a Pyramid, on the top of which was a triangle, within which was the sacred name of the Eternal, and on the pavement were the 2 Columns of Jachin, and Boaz, laid across.

IVORY KEY} By the Ivory key in the 4th Degree, you are to understand, that you cannot open your heart with safety but at the proper times.

CORPS AND GRAVE} By the Corps and Grave is represented the state of man before he had known the happiness of

[289]

our Order.

ROPE. The Rope to which the Coffin is tied, in order to raise it, is the symbol of raiseing and Unity, as you have been raised from the Grave of Ignorance to the Celestial place where Truth resides.

PYRAMID. The Pyramid represents the true Mason that raises himself by Degrees untill he reaches heaven, to adore the sacred and unalterable name of the Eternal supreme.

INTIMe SECRETY} This new Degree leads you near Solomon and honor, and after you redoubled your zeal, you did gain new honors and favors, haveing nearly lost your life by your Curiosity, which attachment in masonry, gave you the good Qualities of your heart, and which found you grace, and led you to the Degree of Intendant of the Buildings, and where you saw a blazing Star, a large Candlestick with 7 branches, with altars, Vases of purification and a Great Brazen Sea. By the Expression of purification, you are to understand, that you are to be cleansed of Impiety and prejudice, before you can acquire more of the sublime knowledge, in passing the other Degrees, to be able to support the brilliant light of reason, enlightened by Truth, of which the blazing star is the figure. By the candlesticks with 7 branches you are to remember

the Mysterious number of the 7 Masters who were named to succeed one; and from that time;

[290]

it was resolved that 7 Knights of Masonry united together were able to Initiate into Masonry, and show them the 7 Gifts of the Eternal which we shall give you the perfect knowledge of, when you have purified in the Brazen Sea. You have past from the Secret to perfect Master and from that to Intimate Secretary, Prevost and Judge and Intendant of the Buildings. In those Degrees they have shewn you an Ebony box suspended, a key, a ballance and an Inflamed Urn.

Ebony box.} The Ebony box shews you with what a scrupulous attention you are to keep the secrets that has been confided in you, which you are to reserve in the Closest of your heart, of which the Box is an Emblem and when you reflect on the black colour of the said box, it shows you to cover your secrets with a thick viel, in such a manner that the prophane Cowans, cannot possibly have any <knowledge> thereof.

Key. The key demonstrates that you have already obtained a key to our knowledge, and part of our Mysteries, and if you behave with Equity, fervor and Zeal to your brothers, you will arrive shortly to the knowledge and meaning of our Society, and this Indicates also, the reason of the ballance.

Inflam^{d} Urn} By the Inflamed Urn, you are to understand, that as soon as you come to the knowledge of the Royal and sublime art, you must by your behaviour leave behind you in the minds of your

[291]

brethren, (and even the vulgar;) a high Idea of your virtue, equal to the perfume of the burning Urn. In the Degree of Intimate secretary you have seen and heard Two Kings who were entering into their new Alliance and reciprocal promise, and of the perfection of their Grand enterprize,—they spoke with regret of the loss of Hiram Abiff our Excellent Master; you saw Guards and a man overseen, and very near being put to death for his Curiosity in peeping,—you also heard a project of a place called the vault to deposit the precious Treasure of Masonry when the time should be fulfilled, and afterwards you became a brother. The Conversation of the two Kings is the figure, request and report that our bye laws must have with the natural Law, which forms a perfect agreement with the Covenants and promises to those who shall have the happiness to be contracted to you in the same manner and perfect Alliance as they will afterwards come to the Center of the true knowledge. The Tears and regret of the two Kings, are the Emblem of the regret you ought to have, when you perceive a brother depart from the road of Virtue. The man you saw peeping and who was discovered and seized, and conducted to death, is an Emblem of those who come to be Initiated into our sacred Mysteries through a

[292]

motive of Curiousity, and if so indiscreet as to divulge their Obligations; we are bound to cause their death, and take vengeance on the Treason by the destruction of the Traitor. Let us pray the Eternal to preserve our Order from such an Evil: you have seen an Example thereof in the 9th Degree, to which you came by your zeal, fervor and Constancy. In that Degree you have remarked that from all the favorites that were at that time in the Apartment of Solomon, only 9 were Elected to revenge the death of Hiram Abiff: this makes good that a great many, often are called, but few are Chosen. To Explain this Ænigma is, that a great many of the prophane, have the happiness to divest themselves of that name to see and obtain the Entrance into our sanctuary, but very few are constant, zealous, and fervent to merit the happiness of coming to the height and knowledge of the sublime Truth. If you ask me what are the requisite qualities that a Mason must be possessed of, to come the Center of Truth? I answer you, that you must crush the head of the serpent of Ignorance, you must shake off the yoke of Infant prejudice, concerning the Mysteries of the reigning Religion, which worship has been Imaginary and only founded on the spirit of Pride which envies to command and to be distinguished at the head of the vulgar, in

[293]

affecting an Exterior purity, which Characterizes a false piety, Joined to a desire of acquiring that which is not its own, and is always the subject of this exterior pride, and unalterable source of many disorders, which being Joined to gluttonness is the daughter of Hypocrasy, and employs every matter to satisfy Carnal desires, and raises to those predominant passions, Altars, upon which he maintains without ceasing, the light of Iniquity, and sacrifices continually offerings to Luxury, Voluptuousness, Hatred, Envy, and perjury. Behold my Brother <what> you must fight against and destroy before you can come to the Knowledge of the true, good and sovereign happiness. Behold this monster under the figure of a Serpent that you must conquer: A serpent which we detest as an Idol, which is adored by the Ideot and Vulgar under the name of Religion. In the Degree of Elected of 15, Illustrious Knights, Grand

Master Architect, and the Royal Arch, you have seen many things, which if mentioned here would be only a repetition of what you are already acquainted with, you will always find in those Degrees, Initial letters Inclosed in different Triangles or Deltha: you have also seen the Planet mercury, the Chamber called mount *Gabaon*, or the 3^{d} heaven, the winding stair Case, Ark of Alliance, The Tomb of Hiram

[294]

Abiff facing the Ark and the Urn, the precious Treasure found by the assiduous Travellers, the 3 zealous brethren Masons, the punishment of the haughty Master Masons in being buried under the Antient ruins of Enoch, and finally you have seen the figures of Solomon and Hiram King of Tyre, and Saint John the Baptist.

3: J^{s} By the 3, J: J: J:^{s} you know the 3 sacred names of the Eternal, and mount Gabaon, where you come to, by 7 degrees which compose a winding stair Case.

7 STEPS. The 7 Steps represent the 7 principal and different Degrees to which you must come, to attain the height of Glory represented by the mount, where they formerly sacrificed to the most High; When you arrive to that, you are to subdue yourself in your passions, and <not> do any thing which is contrary to our Laws.

PLANET MERCURY} By the Planet Mercury you are taught continually to mistrust, shun and run away from those who by a false practice maintain commerce with people of a vicious life, who seem to despise the most sacred Mysteries, that is to depart from those who by the vulgar fear or a bad understanding should be ready to deny the solemn Engagement they have contracted amongst us. When you come at the foot of our Arch, you are to apprehend that you are come to the Sanctum Sanctorum, you are

[295]

not to return, but rather persist to sustain the Glory of our Order, and the Truth of our laws, principles and Mysteries, in like manner as our respectable father Hiram Abiff, who deserved to have been buried there for his Constancy and fidelity. We have also another Example in the firmness of *Galaad* the Son of *Sophinia* Chief of the Levites under *Surinan* the High Priest, as mentioned in the History of Perfection. Learn in this moment My dear brother what you are to understand by the figures of Solomon Hiram of Tyre and Saint John the Baptist. The two first Exhorts you by their zeal in the Royal art to follow the Sublime Road, of which Solomon was the Institutor and Hiram of Tyre the supporter, a Title Legitimately due to that King, who not only protected the order but contributed with all his might to the construction of the Temple, (furnishing Stone from Tyre and the Cedars from Lebanus) which Solomon built to the honor of the Almighty. The 3d or Saint John the Baptist teaches you to preach marvellous of this order, which is as much as to say you are to make secret missions among men which you believe to be in a state of entering the road of Truth, that they might be able one day to see her *virtuous* Visage uncovered. Hiram Abiff was the symbol of Truth on Earth; Jubulum

[296]

Akirop was accursed by the Serpent of Ignorance which to this day raises altars in the hearts of the prophane and fearfull; this prophaneness backed by a fanatick zeal, becomes an instrument to the monasterial and religious Reign which struck the first stroke in the heart of our Dear father Hiram Abiff, which is as much as to say undermined the foundation of the Celestial Temple which the Eternal himself had ordered to be raised to the sublime Truth and his Glory. The first stage of the world has been witness to what I have advanced, the simple natural law rendered our first Fathers the most uninterrupted happiness; they were in those times more virtuous, but as soon as the monster of Pride started up in the Air, and disclosed herself to those unhappy mortals, she promised to them every sort of happiness, and stole on them by her soft and bewitching speeches, Vizt. that they must render to the eternal Creator of all things, an Adoration with more Testimony and more extensive than they had hitherto done &c. This Hydra with her hundred heads at that time mislead, (and continues to this day to do,) men who are so weak as to submit to *her* Empire; and this Error will subsist untill the moment that the true Elected shall appear and destroy her entirely. The Degree of Sublime

[297]

Elected that you have passed, gives you the knowledge of those things which conducts you to the time and sole Good: this is the Grand Circle figured here which represents the Immensity of the Eternal supreme, which has neither beginning nor End. The triangular Delta figured here is the mysterious figure of the Eternal: the 3 letters which you see, first the G, at the top signifies Grandeur of the Masons, the S, submission of the <said> Order, and the *U*, Union that ought to reign among the brethren, which altogether make but one body or equal figure in all its parts, thus is the Triangle called Equilateral, the great letter G, placed in the Center of the Triangle signifies great Architect of the Universe, which is God; and in this Ineffable name is found all the Divine Attributes: this letter being placed in the middle of the Triangle, is for us to understand, that every true Mason must have it profoundly in his heart. There is another Triangle repeated, in which is Inclosed these Letters of which you have had an Explanation in the 6th Degree this Triangle designs the connection of the brethren in virtue, the solemn promises that they have made to love each other, to help, succour and keep Inviolably secret the Mysteries of the Perfection

[298]

proposed in all their Enterprizes: It is said that in that Degree you are Entered the 3d heaven, that is to say, you have entered in the place where pure Truth resides, since she abandoned the Earth to monsters who persecuted her. The end of the degree of perfection is a preparation to come more clearly to the knowledge of True happiness, in becoming a good mason Enlightened by the Celestial luminary of Truth in renouncing voluntarily all adorations, but those that are made only to one God the Creator of heaven and Earth great good and merciful. The Knights of the East or sword, the Princes of Jerusalem, Knights of the East and West, are known to us, in our days to be Masonry renewed, and all of them leads us to the same end of the Celestial Truth, which is to say finished. The Knights of the Black and White Eagle, and the sublime Princes of the Royal secret and Grand Commanders, are the Chief of the Grand Enterprizes of the Order in General.—Here ends Brother Truths Harangue.—Then says father Adam to the Candidate "My Dear Son, what you have heard from the mouth of Truth, is an Abridgment of all the Ceremonies which you have gone through, in the different degrees you have passed in Order to come to the knowledge of the holy Truth, contracted in your last engagements: Do you persist in your demand of coming to the holy Truth, and do you desire it with a clear heart," Answer me? The Candidate answers, I persist. Then father Adam, says, "Brother Truth, as the

[299]

brother persists, approach with him to the sanctuary in order that he may take a solemn Obligation to follow our laws, principles and Morals, to attach himself to us for ever." Then the Candidate falls on his knees, and Father Adam takes his hands between his own, and the Candidate repeats the following Obligation 3 times.

Obligation.

"I: A:B: Promise in the Face of God, and between the hands of my Sovereign and in the presence of all the Brethren here present, never to take arms against my King, directly or Indirectly, in any Conspiracy against him. I promise never to reveal any of the Mysteries of this sublime Degree of Knights of the sun, which is now on the point of being entrusted to me, to any person or persons whatsoever, without their being duly qualified to receive the same, and never to give my Consent for any one to be admitted into our Mysteries, only after the most scrupulous Circumspection and full knowledge of his life and conversation, and who has given at all times proof of his zeal and fervent attachment for the order, and a submission at all times to the Tribunal of the Sovereign princes of the Royal Secret. I promise never to confer this Degree of Knight of the sun without having a permission in writing from the Grand Council of Princes of the Royal secret, from the Grand Inspector or his Deputy, known by their Titles and Authority.

[300]

"I promise and swear to redouble my zeal for all my Brethren Knights and Princes, that are present and absent, and If I fail in this my Obligation, I consent for all my Brethren, (when convinced of my Infidelity,) to seize me and thrust my Tounge through with a red hot Iron: to pluck out both my Eyes and deprive me of smelling and hearing; to cut off both my hands, and Expose me in that Condition in the field to be devoured by the Voracious animals, and if none can be found I wish the Lightning of heaven might execute on me the same Vengeance. Oh! God! maintain me in Right and Equity, Amen, Amen, Amen."

After this Obligation is 3 times repeated, Father Adam raises the Candidate, and gives him one kiss on his forehead, being the Seat of the soul; he then decorates him with the Collar and Jewell of of [*sic*] the Order, and gives him the following signs, Token and Words.

SIGN. The sign is to Clap the right hand on the left breast which the other answers, by putting up the first finger of his right hand, (the others clinched,) above his head to show that there is but one God, which is the true source of real Truth, consequently there can be, but one and true religion, and that same which Adam received from God.

PASS–WORDS} The first says *Stebium*, which signifies, Prima Materia, or the principal Cooperator of all things the Answer to this, is *Albra–ert*, which signifies

[301]

a King full of Glory and without blot.

SACRED–WORD} The Sacred Word is *Adonai*, which signifies Sovereign Creator of all things.

SIGN. The Sign to know a Knight of the Sun is, to ask him to give his hands, which he will put together and put between yours, you kiss his forehead and say *Alpha*, the other answers *Omega*.

Then the Candidate goes round and gives the Sign, Token, and Word, to every one, which he brings back to Father Adam, and he then sits down with the rest of the Brethren; then brother Truth gives the following Explanation of the Philosophical Lodge.

SUN. The Sun represents the Unity of the Eternal supreme, the only Grand work of philosophy

S:S:S. The 3 S[s] signifies, *Stellato, Sedet, Solo*, or the residence of the sovereign matter of all things.

3 CANDLESTICKS} The 3 Candlesticks shews is the 3 Degrees of fire.

4 TRIANGLES} The 4 Triangles represent the four Elements.

7 CHERUBIMS} The Seven Cherubims represent the 7 metals Viz[t]. Gold, Silver, Copper, Iron, Lead, Tin and quicksilver.

CONCEP[on] IN THE MOON} The Conception or woman rising in the moon demonstrates the purity that matter must subsist of, in Order to remain in its pure state unmixed with any other Body, from which must come a new King, and a Revolution in

[302]

fulness of Time, filled with Glory whose name is *Albra–ert*.

HOLY SPIRIT The holy Spirit under the symbol of a Dove, is the Image of the Universal spirit, that gives light to all, in the three states of nature, and are the *Animal, Vegetal* and *Mineral*.

ENTRANCE OF THE TEMPLE} The Entrance of the Temple is represented to you by a body; because the Grand work of nature is compleat as Gold, potable and fixed.

GLOBE. The Globe represents the matter in its Original state, that is to say compleat.

CADUCES. The Caduces represents the double mercury that you must extract from the matter, that is to say, the Mercury fixed; and from thence is extracted Gold and silver.

The word Stibium is the password of the philosophical Lodge, and signifies the Antimony from whence (by the Philisophic fire) is taken an *Alkali* which we employ in our Grand works.

THE END OF THE PHILOSOPHICAL EXPLANATION

Then father Adam Explains the Moral Lodge.

SUN. The sun represents the Divinity of the Eternal for as there is but one sun to light and Invigorate the Earth; so there is but one God to whom we ought to pay our greatest Adoration.

S.S.S. The 3 S[s] Teacheth you that science adorned with Wisdom, creates a holy man.

3 CANDLESTICKS} The 3 Candlesticks are the Image of the life of

[303]

man, considered by Youth, Manhood and Old Age, and happy are those that have been Enlightened in those ages, by the light of Truth.

4 TRIANGLES} The 4 Triangles shew us the 4 principal duties that create our Tranquil life, Viz[t] 1st Fraternal Love among men in general and particularly among Brethren in the same Degree with us. 2[d] In not having any thing, but for the use and advantage of your brother. 3[d] Doubting of every matter that cannot be demonstrated to you clearly, by which an attempt might be Insinuated as mysteries in matters of Religion, and thereby lead you away from the holy Truth, and 4th Never to do any thing to another, that you would not have done to you this last precept well used, understood and followed on all Occasions is the true happiness of philosophy.

7 PLANETS} The 7 planets represent the 7 Principal passions of men.

7 CHERUBIMS} The 7 Cherubims are the delights of this life, namely, seeing, hearing, Tasteing, smelling, feeling, Tranquility and health.

CONCEPTION} The Conception in the moon, shows the purity of matter, and that nothing can be unpure in the Eyes of the Eternal supreme.

HOLY SPIRIT} The holy spirit is the figure of our Soul, which is only the breath of the Eternal, and which cannot be soiled by the works of the body.

[304]

TEMPLE. The Temple represents our Body, which we are obliged to preserve our natural feeling.

FIGURE OF A MAN. The figure in the Entrance of the Temple which bears a Lamb in his arms, Teaches us to be attentive to our wants, as a shepherd takes care of his sheep: to be charitable, and never to let slip the present Oppertunity of doing good; to labor honestly, and to live in this day, as if it was to be our last.

COLUMNS OF B. & J.} The Columns of Boaz and Jachin are the symbols of the strength of our souls, in bearing equally misfortunes, as well as success in our life.

7 STEPS OF THE TEMPLE} The 7 steps of the Temple are the figures of the 7 degrees which we must pass before we arrive to the knowledge of the True God.

GLOBE. The Globe represents the world we Inhabit.

LUX EX TENEBRIS} The device of Lux Ex Tenebris, teacheth, that when man is Enlightened by reason, he is able to penetrate the darkness and obscurity, which Ignorance and superstition spreads abroad.

RIVER. The River across the Globe, represents the utility of the Passions, that are as necessary to man in the Course of his life, as water is requisite to the earth, In order to replenish the plants thereof.

CROSS. The Cross surrounded by 2 serpents, signifies that we must watch the vulgar prejudices to be very prudent in giving to any, our knowledge and secrets in matters Especially of Religion.

END OF THE MORAL EXPLANATION.

[305]

TO CLOSE THE COUNCIL.

Q: – (by father Adam). Brother Truth what progress have men made on Earth, to come to true happiness?

A: – (by Broth[r] Truth)—Men have always fallen on the vulgar prejudices, which is full of nothing but fraud and falseness—very few have struggled, and less have knocked at the door of this holy place, to attain the full light of real Truth which we all ought to acquire.

Then father Adam says, "My dear Children, depart, and go among men, Endeavour to inspire them with the desire of knowing holy Truth the pure source of all perfection." Father Adam then makes the Sign, by putting his right hand on his left breast, and all the Brethren put up (in answer,) the first finger of their right hand, and the Council of Knights of the Sun is closed by 7 knocks.

Here follows a Philosophical Explanation.
In manner of Lecture.

Q: – 1st Are you a Knight of the Sun?

A: – I have mounted the 7 principal Steps of Masonry: I have penetrated into the bowels of the earth, and among the Antient ruins of Enoch found the most Grand and precious treasure of the Masons; I have seen, contemplated and admired the great Mysterious and Tremendable

[306]

name engraved on the Deltha △: I have broke the pillar of beauty, and thrown down the two Columns that supported it.

Q: – 2[d] Pray tell me what is that Mysterious and formidable name?

A: – I cannot unfold the sacred Characters in this manner, but the one substituted in its place is the Grand word of *Adonai.*

Q: – 3^d What do you understand by throwing down the columns that sustained the pillar of Beauty?

A: – Two reasons: 1st When the Temple was destroyed by Nebuzaradan, general of the army of Nebuchadnezer. I was one that helped to deface the Deltha on which was engraved the Ineffable name, and broke down the Column of beauty in order that it should not be prophaned by the Infidels, and 2^d as I have deserved by my Travel and labor the bounty of the great *Adonai,* the mysteries of Masonry in passing the 7 principal Degrees.

Q: – 4th What signifies the 7 planets?

A: – The lights of the Celestial Globe, and also their Influence, by which every matter exists on the surface of the Earth or Globe.

Q: – 5th From what is the Terrestrial Globe formed?

A: – From the matter which is formed by the concord of the 4 Elements, designed by the 4 Triangles that are in regard to them, as the four greater planets.

[307]

Q: – 6th What are the names of the 7 planets?

A: – The sun, Moon, Mars, Jupiter, Venus, Mercury and Saturn.

Q: – 7th Which are the 4 Elements?

A: – Air, Fire, Earth and Water.

Q: – 8. What Influence have the 7 planets on the four Elements?

A: – Three General Matters, of which all bodies are composed, namely, Life, Spirit and Body, otherwise Salt, Sulphur and Mercury.

Q: – 9th What is life or Salt?

A: – The Life given by the Eternal supreme, or the planets, the agents of Nature.

Q: – 10. What is the spirit or Sulphur?

A: – Fixed matter, subject to several productions.

Q: – 11. What is the body or Mercury?

A: – Matter conducted or ripened to its form by the Union of salt and sulphur, or the agreement of the three Governors of nature.

Q: – 12. What are these three Governors of Nature?

A: – Animal, Vegetal and Mineral.

Q: – 13. What is the Animal?

A: – We understand in this, life, all that is Divine and Amiable.

Q: – 14. Which of the 4 Elements serve for its Production?

A: – All the 4 are necessary, among which nevertheless Air and fire are predominant: It is these that render the Animal, the perfection of the 3 Govern-

[308]

-ments which man is Elevated to, by the breath of the divine spirit, when he receives his soul.

Q: – 15th What is the Vegetal?

A: – All that seems attached to the Earth and reigns on its surface.

Q: – 16th Of what is it composed?

A: – Of a generative fire, formed into a body whilst it remains in the Earth, and is purified by its moisture and becomes Vegitable, receives life by air and water, whereby the 4 Elements though different Co–operate Jointly or seperately.

Q: – 17th What is the Mineral?

A: – All that is generated and secreted in the Earth.

Q: – 18. What do we understand by this name?

A: – That which we call Metals, Demi metals and Minerals.

Q: – 19. What is it that composes the Mineral?

A: – The air penetrating by the Celestial Influence into the Earth, meets with a body which by its softness, fixes, congeals, and renders the mineral matter more or less perfect.

Q: – 20. Which are the perfect metals?

A: – Gold and Silver.

Q: – 21st Which are the Imperfect metals?

A: – Brass, Lead, Tin, iron and quick silver.

Q: – 22d How came we by the knowledge of these things?

A: – By frequent observations and the Experiments made in natural Philosophy, which has brought

[309]

to a certainty, that nature give a perfection to all things, if she has time to compleat her Operations.

Q: – 23d Can art bring metal to perfection as much as by nature?

A: – Yes, but you must have an Exact knowledge of nature: her Operations, the Quint Essence of the Elements and the fire of Philosophers.

Q: – 24th What will assist you to bring forth this knowledge

A: – A matter brought to perfection, and rendered an Universal Medicine: this matter is that which has been sought for under the name of the philosophers Stone.

Q: – 25. What does the Globe represent?

A: – An Information of Philosophers for the Conduct of the art in their work?

Q: – 26. What signifies the words, "Lux ex Tenebris,"?

A: – That is the depth of darkness, you ought to retire from, in Order to gain the true Light.

Q: – 27. What signifies the Cross on the Globe?

A: – The Cross is the health of the true Elected.

Q: – 28. What does the 3 Candlesticks represent?

A: – The 3 degrees of fire, which the Artist must have knowledge to give, in order to procure the matter, from which it proceeds.

Q: – 29. What signifies the word Stibium?

A: – It is the password of the Philosophers, and signifies Antimony or the first matter of all things.

[310]

Q: – 30th What signifies the 7 degrees?

A: – The different Essential Degrees of Masonry which you must pass, to come to the sublime degree of Knight of the Sun.

Q: – 31st What signifies the divers attributes in those Degrees?

A: – 1st: The Bible, or Gods law, which we ought to follow, 2d: The Compass teaches us to do nothing unjust, 3d: The square conducts us Equal to the same end, 4th: The Level demonstrates to us, all that is just and Equitable, 5th: The perpendicular, to be upright and subdue the vice of prejudging, 6th: The thressel board is the Image of our reason where the functions are combined to reflect, compare and think, 7th: The rough stone is a resemblance of our vices that we ought to reform, 8th: The Cubic stone, is our passions that we ought to surmount, 9th: The Columns signifies strength in all things, 10th: The flaming Star teacheth, that our hearts ought to be as a clear sun, among those that are troubled with things of this life, 11th: The key teaches us, to have a watchful eye over those who are contrary to reason, 12th: The box teaches us to keep our secrets Inviolable, 13th: The Urn teaches us, that we ought to be as delicious perfume, 14th: The brazen sea teaches us, that we ought to purifie ourselves and destroy vice, 15th: The Circles in the Triangle,

[311]

demonstrates the Immensity of the Divinity under the symbol of Truth, 16th, The Poinard teacheth the Step of the Elected, "many are called but few are chosen" to the sublime knowledge of pure Truth, 17th: The word *Albra–ert*, signifies, "a King full of Glory and without blot." 18th Adonai, "Signifies sovereign Creator of all things," 19th: The 7 Cherubims are the symbols of the delights of life, known by seeing, hearing, Tasteing, feeling, smelling, Tranquility and thought.

Q: – 32. What is represented by the Sun?

A: – It is an Emblem of the Divinity which we ought to regard as the Image of God: This Immense body represents (as I say) the Infinity of God, wonderfully well, as the only source of light and good; the heat of the sun, produces the rule of Seasons; recruits Nature, takes darkness from the winter, in order that the deliciousness of Spring might succeed.—END OF PHILOSOPHICAL LECTURE.

ANOTHER GENERAL LECTURE.

Q: – 1st From whence came you?

A: – From the Center of the Earth.

Q: – 2d How have you come from thence?

A: – By reflection and Study of Nature.

Q: – 3d Who has taught you this?

A: – Men in general are blind, and lead others in their blindness.

Q: – 4th What do you understand by this blindness?

[312]

A: – I do not understand to be privy to their Mysteries, but I apprehend under the name of blindness those, who cease to be ardent, after they have been privy to the light of reason.

Q: – 5th Who are those?

A: – Those who the prejudice of superstition and fanatiscism renders slaves to Ignorance.

Q: – 6th What do you understand by fanatiscism?

A: – The zeal of all particular sects, which are spread over the Earth, in believing themselves to be Inspired, and yet commiting precisely the crime of offering to fraud and falsehood.

Q: – 7th And do you desire to be raised from this darkness?

A: – My desire is to come to the Center of the Celestial Truth, and to travel by the brilliant light of the sun.

Q: – 8. What represents that Body?

A: – It is the figure of an only God, to whom we ought to pay our adoration and Admiration: The sun being the Emblem of God, we ought to regard it as the Image of Divinity, for that Immense body represents wonderfully well the Infinity of God, and is the only source of light, consequently of God, he Invigorates and produces the seasons and replenishes nature entirely, in takeing the horrors from the winter and produces the delights of the Spring.

Q: – 9. What does the Triangle with the Sun in its Center represent?
A: – It represents the Immensity of the supreme
Q: – 10. What signifies the 3 S^s^?

[313]

A: – Sanctitas, Scientiæ, and Sapientia, which signifies that science accompanied with wisdom makes men holy.
Q: – 11. What signifies the 3 Candlesticks?
A: – They represent the Courses of life, by Youth, Manhood and Old age.
Q: – 12. Has it any other meaning?
A: – Yes. The Tripple light that shines among us, in order to take a man out of darkness and Ignorance into which he is plunged and to bring him to *Virtue, Truth* and *Holiness*, a symbol of our perfection.
Q: – 13. What signifies the 4 Triangles that are in the great Circle?
A: – They are the Emblems of the 4 principal views of the life of Tranquility, Viz^t^ 1st: fraternal Love for all mankind in general, more in particular for brethren who are certainly more attached to us and who with horror have seen the wretchedness of the Vulgar. 2^d^: To be cautious among us, of things and not to demonstrate them clearly to any, who are not qualified to receive them, and to be likewise cautious in giving Credit to any matter however artfully it might be disguised without a self conviction in the heart. 3^d^: To cast from us every matter, where we perceive that we may ever repent the doing thereof, takeing care of this moral precept, to do to everyone of your fellow Creatures no more, than you would

[314]

choose to be done to you, and 4th: We ought always to confide in our Creators bounty and to pray without ceasing, that all our Necessities may be relieved, as it seemeth best to him for our advantage:—to wait for his blessings patiently in this life; to be persuaded of his sublime Decrees, that whatever might fall out contrary to our wishes will be attended in this end with good Consequences: to take his Chastisement patiently, and be assured that the end of every thing as proposed by him is the best, and certainly will lead us to Eternal happiness hereafter.
Q: – 14. Give me the signification of the 7 planets, which are Inclosed in a Triangle, which form the rays of the Exterior Circle, and us inclosed in the Grand Triangle?
A: – The 7 planets according to philosophy represents the 7 Principal passions of the life of man: these passions are very useful when they are

used with moderation, for which the Almighty gave them to us, but grow fatal and destroy the body when let loose; therefore it is our particular duty to subdue them.

Q: – 15th Explain these 7 passions to us?

A: – 1st: The propagation of our species, 2^{d}: A desire of acquiring Riches, 3^{d}: Ambition to acquire Glory in the Arts and sciences, and among men in General, 4th: superiority in Civil Life, 5th: Joys and pleasure of

[315]

Society, 6th: Amusement and gaity of Life, and 7th: Religion.

Q: – 16th Which is the greatest sins of all, that man can commit and which renders him odious both to God and Man?

A: – Suicide, Homicide and Sodomy.

Q: – 17. What signifies the 7 Cherubims, where their names are wrote in the Circle called the first heaven.

A: – They represent the Corporeal delights of this life, which the Eternal gave to Man when he created him, and are seeing, hearing, smelling, Tasteing, feeling, Tranquility, and Thought.

Q: – 18. What signifies the figure in the moon, that we regard as the figure or Image of the Conception?

A: – The purity of nature which procure the holiness of the body, and there is nothing Imperfect in the Eyes of the supreme.

Q: – 19. What is represented by the figures of the Columns

A: – They are Emblems of our Souls, which is the breath of life, proceeding from the all puissant which ought not to be soiled by the works of the body, but to be as firm as Columns.

Q: – 20th What is represented by the figure in the porch which carries a Lamb in his arms?

A: – The Porch ornamented with the Columns of B and J, and surmounted with the Grand J repre-

[316]

-sents our body, and we ought to have a particular care in watching our Conversation, as it is a secret deposit, which we ought to confide in our Creator, and also to watch our need as the shepherd his flock.

Q: – 21st What signifies the 2 Letters *J* and *B*, at the porch?

A: – They represent our Entrance in the Order of masonry, also the firmness of Soul which we ought to possess from the moment of our Initiation: This we ought to merit before we come to the sublime Degree of knowing holy Truth and we ought to persevere, and be firm in whatever situation we might be in, not knowing whether it may turn to our good or Evil, in the passage of this Life.

Q: – 22d What signifies the large *J* in the Triangle on the Crown of the Portico?

A: – That large *J*, is the Initial of the Mysterious name of the great Architect of the Universe, whose greatness we always should have in our mind, and that our Labours ought to <be> employed to please him, which we should always have in our view as the sure and only source of our actions.

Q: – 23. What signifies the 7 steps, that leads to the Entry of the porch?

A: – They mark the 7 Degrees of masonry, which are the principal we ought to endeavour to arrive at, in order to come to the knowledge of holy Truth.

Q: – 24. What is represented by the Terrestrial Globe?

[317]

A: – The world which we inhabit, and wherein true Masonry is its principal ornament.

Q: – 25. Give me the Explanation of the great word *Adonai*

A: – It is the word which God gave to Adam, for him to pray by, a word our common father never pronounced without trembling.

Q: – 26. What signifies *Lux, Ex, Tenebris?*

A: – Man made clear by the light of reason, penetrates through the obscurity of Ignorance and superstition.

Q: – 27. What signifies the river across the Globe?

A: – It represents the utility of our passions which are necessary to man in the course of his life as water is necessary to render the Earth fertile as the Sun draws up the water, which being purified falls on the Earth and gives Verdure.

Q: – 28. What signifies the Cross, surrounded by two serpents on the Top of the Globe?

A: – It represents to us, not to respect the vulgar prejudices; to be prudent and to know the bottom of the heart in matters of Religion; to be always prepared not to be of the sentiments with sots, Ideots and Lovers of the Mysteries of Religion; to avoid such, and not to hold the least conversation with them.

Q: – 29. What does the book with the word *Biblia* on it represent?

A: – As the Bible is differently Interpretted by the different sects, who divide the different parts of the Earth; thus the true sons of Light or

[318]

Children of Truth, ought to doubt of every thing at present as Mysteries or Metaphysicks thus all the decisions of Theology and philosophy teach, not to admit that which is not demonstrated as clearly as that two and two makes four. And on the whole to adore God and him only, to love him better than yourself, and always to have a Confidence on the bounties and promises of our Creator. Amen! Amen! Amen!

The final End of the Degree of
Knights of the Sun.

[319]

Apare et Legi, Dice et Tace.
The Neplus ultra of Masonry.

Chapter of the Grand Inspector of Lodges Grand Elected Knights of Kadoch, or of the White and Black Eagle.

The chief is the thrice Illustrious Frederick King of Prussia, under the Title of thrice Illustrious Knight, Grand Commander.

Form of the Chapter.

The Chapter of the Grand Elected, must be composed of 5 brothers, every one vested in this degree; they must be all in black with white gloves.

Ribbon and Jewel} The Order is a broad black ribbon, worn from the left shoulder to the right hip, to which hangs the attribute of the Order, which is a red Cross, the same as the Teutonic Knights used to wear, in the middle of two swords across like a Saint Andrews Cross. No Aprons are Worn.

There are no decorations, nor any Emblem in this Chapter, as the Curtain is Intirely drawn. There is only figured on the ground the Mysterious Ladder, which must be covered untill the Candidate has taken his Obligation. *Observe this well;* you are never to admit a person to this eminent Degree, unless you have a full proof of his fidelity. Of the 5 brothers who compose this Chapter, two must be with the Candidate, in another apartment, untill he is Introduced. The other

[320]

Three remain in the Chapter to assist the reception. In a distant place, a Knight of Kadoch or of the white and black Eagle cannot Initiate another Brother in this

Eminent degree unless he has a proper power or patent from an Inspector General or a Deputy Grand Inspector under his hand and seal; and when a reception is made the Grand Commander remains alone in the Chapter with the Candidate and must be so situated that the Candidate cannot see him; as he is not to know who Initiated him.

Form of Opening the Chapter.

Q: – Illustrious Knight are you Elected?
A: – Yes, Thrice Illustrious Knight Grand Commander I am.
Q: – How came you to be Elected?
A: – Fortune decided for me.
Q: – What proof can you give me of your Reception?
A: – A Cavern has been witness of it.
Q: – What did you in the Cavern?
A: – I executed my Commission.
Q: – Have you penetrated further?
A: – Yes, thrice Illustrious Grand Commander.
Q: – How shall I believe you?
A: – My name is Knight of K....h, you understand me.
Q: – What is the Clock?
A: – The hour of Silence.
Q: – As it is so, give me the sign, to convince me of

[321]

your knowledge against surprize; on which they all draw their swords, when the Grand Commander knocks once very hard on the table before him and says, "Illustrious Knights, the Chapter is Open";—As soon as the Knights with the Candidate in the Anti Chamber have heard the one blow in the Chapter, by which they know that the Chapter is open, one of them comes and knocks at the Door one stroke, one of them in the Chapter goes and opens the Door and asks what he wants he replies, that a servant Knight demands to come to the degree of Grand Elected, as he has all the requisite Degrees and qualifications of masonry, which are necessary. Which being reported to the Thrice Illustrious Grand Commander he says, "Illustrious Knights can we admit this free Mason among us without running any risk of Indiscretion from him?" The two other Knights then answer, "We swear and promise for him." Then the thrice Illustrious Grand Commander approaches, and they take one another by the hand, and take the following Obligation to each other.

The Obligation.

"We Promise and swear by the living God, always supreme, to revenge the death of our Ancestors: and which ever of us who should in any manner commit the most light Indiscretion touching the secret of our order, shall have his Body buried under the throne of this Illustrious

[322]

"Assembly, So God protect us in our design and maintain us in Equity and right Amen.

Form of the Reception.

A little while after the two Knights with the Candidate have heard the great knock of the Grand Commanders to open the Chapter, they both take their swords in their hands, and after one of them has been at the door, and when they think that the Grand Commander has finished the necessary business, they Introduce the Candidate, and leave him in the hands of the Grand Commander and all four retire, to guard the door of the Entrance and every other door of the adjacent rooms if any: The reason of their going out of the Chapter is, that never any person assisted at the reception of a Knight Templar. When the Candidate enters the Chapter he prostrates his face to the Ground: The Grand Commander behind the Curtain, reminds him of the principal points of Masonry, from its beginning to the Epocha of the Assassination of Hiram Abiff. Solomons desire of punishing the Traitors in the most exemplary manner; the method he took in disposing the matters relative to them who went in search of the 3 Villains, in Order to execute <his> Vengeance. He repeats to him the zeal, Constancy and fervency of *Joabert, Stolkin,* and *Gibulum,* who after their painful search (by Solomons order) had the happiness of finding among the ruins of Enochs Temple in the 9th arch, the precious Treasure of

[323]

the perfect Masons. He continues to remind him of the firmness of the Grand Elect and perfect Masons at the time of the Temples destruction, when they rushed at all risks through the Enemys untill they obtained an Entrance into the sacred vault to find the pillar of Beauty and hinder, (by Effacing the Ineffable word) that it should be exposed to the prophane. Then he reminds them of the 72 years Captivity and the clemency of Cyrus King of Persia, who by the request of Zerubabel not only gave the Israalites their freedom, but ordered that all the Treasure of the Temple taken by Nebuchadnezer, should be restored them in order to decorate the new Temple, which he ordered them to build, to the Infinite god, and created them Knights. Then he repeats the Clemency of Darius to Zerubabel (at the head of the Embassy from Jerusalem to Babylon) with their complaints against the Samaritans who refused to contribute to the sacrifices of the new Temple, according to the proclamation of his predecessor Cyrus, in favor of the Knights of the East, when they received Darius's Letters to all the Governors of Samaria &ca., And how the Ambassadors were received on their return to Jerusalem, and Elected princes by the people. Then he reminds him after this 2d Temple being destroyed, how the most zealous masons united under a Chief, and worked to the reformation

[324]

of manners, and elevated in their hearts some spiritual Edifice and rendered themselves worthy by their works; they were more particularly esteemed and distinguished in the time of *Manchin*, who was the most remarkable among them; a great many others embraced Christianity, and communicated their secrets to those Christians whom they found had the good Qualities for it living in common, and forming themselves as one family, which shews how the brilliant order of Masons sustained themselves untill the 6th Age and how it fell into a Lethargy after that; notwithstanding which there have always been found some faithful masons, which is clearly proved by the Brilliant manner in which the order of Masonry revived in the year 1118, when 11 Grand Elect and perfect Masons the most zealous, presented themselves to *Garinous*, Prince of Jerusalem, Patriarch and Knight Mason, and pronounced their promises between his hands; they taught him the succession of the times and progress to the time that the Princes went to conquer the holy Land. The Alliance and Obligation that were formed between those Princes, was, that they would spill the last drop of their blood, in order to Establish in Jerusalem the worship of the most high. He informs him that the peace that came after these wars, hindered them to accomplish their design, and therefore they have continued by theory what they had

[325]

sworn to do practically, never admitting in their order by only those who had given proofs of friendship, constancy and discretion. In fine, the Illustrious Grand Commander makes a General history in genealogy of the Masonic Order, its progress its decline, and the manner how it was sustained untill the Epocha of the Crusades, and untill the historical Circumstances that has given Occasion to the Degree which the Candidate expects. A Degree that will give him a perfect knowledge of the preceeding Degrees, and manner how Masonry has come to us.

After which the Candidate takes the following Obligation, his right hand on the Bible, and his left hand between those of the Grand Commander, Viz^{t}.

The Obligation

"I, A: B: Promise and swear, never to reveal the secrets of the Grand Elected Knights of Kadoch or white and black Eagle, to any person; to revenge Masonry on the Traitors, and never to receive in this Degree, but only a Brother who has come to the Degree of Prince of Jerusalem and Knight of the Sun, and then only by an Authority given to me by a Grand Commander or Deputy Inspector under his hand and seal. I promise to be ready at all times to conquer the holy Land, when I shall be summoned to appear; To pay due obedience at all times to the Princes of the Royal secret, and if I fail in this my Obligation, I desire that all the penal-

[326]

-ties of my former Obligations may be Inflicted on me Amen!"—he kisses the Bible and rises.

Then the Grand Commander proceeds and says "My dear brother, he, who has bestowed this degree on you which you have now aspired to, and who is described in this place as Grand Commander and Grand Inspector of all Lodges and grand Elected, is sensible of the Importance of the secret already confided in you; It is therefore necessary to recommend a Circumspection, and also to observe to those who take the name of Knights of the white and black Eagle of Kadoch to be always attentive not to give the least suspicion relative to our mysteries, Orders, progress and end of Masonry. The Imprudence and Indiscretion of many Brothers has given a knowledge to the world of many of our Emblems, by which Masonry has suffered greatly and will be repaired with difficulty: their Indiscretion has caused the loss and retreat of many Puissant Brothers, who would have been an Ornament and support to our Lodge. Such Indiscretion my Dear Brother in this Degree would be without any recovery, as there are no more Emblems, when every matter shall be discovered and disclosed to you; that will leave room for some events, of which you will see the Consequences, when you shall have heard all my Instructions. The words which our Brothers place at their Obligations Viz^{t}. Amen! Signifies

[327]

"because there is no more; that shall be no more, if this shall be against." This ought to be no longer a secret to you, who is going to have the Explanation of the Origin of Masonry, and what has occasioned the society. Truth penetrates the Clouds and the shade, which we can leave to come to the knowledge of what we was before, we were in quality of Knights of Kadoch, white and black Eagle, and what we are as symbolick Masons, and what we can be, by the destruction of our Enemies. Let us Pray. O! most Eternal, beneficial and all gracious, great Architect of the Universe; We from the secret depths of our hearts offer thee a living sacrifice: We humbly beseech thee to Inspire our Enemies with a just sense of the evils they have done us, and from their having a conviction of their wrongs, they might atone for their manifold Injuries, which doth not belong to us they servants to redress ourselves; but by their eyes being opened we might be reconciled, and by a hearty union take possession of those blessed Lands, where the Original Temple was first established, where we might be gathered into one band, there to celebrate thy holy praises once more on the holy mount, in whose bowels were deposited the ever glorious, respectable, ever blessed and awfull name. Amen! Then the viel is taken off the floor, and the Grand Commander proceeds as follows, "Learn that the slightest Indiscretion will Infallibly undermine us, and throw us into an horrible abyss,

[328]

where we should see buried, the whole order of masonry, the remains of an Illustrious and glorious Order, by its Heroism in favor of the unfortunate, how great it has been in the time, when its power, authority and Riches were arrived to the highest pitch, when the distinguishing Birth of those who were members of it, celebrated its Glory: It was not less so, in its unjust and tragick end when by a noble firmness, Knights appeared in Irons, in the middle of the flames and Torments. What can we think of the prophecy of James Demolay, which was verified according to his prediction? What respect ought we not to have for the couragious zeal of those, who have kept the precious remains of an Order, which the blackest Treason, Envy and the most atrocious Malignity has not been able to Extinguish? What hatred should we not have to those Usurpers who occupy the wealth and Dignity of this Order? They cannot be regarded but only as a powerful Enemy, the ashes of whom ought to renew <in our minds> that unfortunate period, when the number of the Knights shall be encreased to be able under the auspicious conduct of a Grand and able powerful Commander, and under the Establishment of that Order; retake the possessions of all the wealth and Dignity, which did belong to them formerly, and is now held by those, who have no other title this day, but Injustice and Malignity. This my dear brother be not said to Intimidate

[329]

those, who have as well as you aspired to this Degree, which we are going to confer on you, but to Inspire them with an ardor and discreet zeal that they ought every one, to wait the time in silence to become Essential: And as this Trust is the most Authentick mark of a sincere friendship, they ought to wish to augment the number of the Knights, and fear to confer this Degree with too much confidence on an Ordinary friend, least his discretion should not be as assured as yours. You must remember my dear brother the Obligation you have taken between my hands, at the beginning of the Ceremony, and render the Justice that you deserve. I have too good an opinion of you, to fear the least Indiscretion in you concerning the first notions I have given you, of this last Degree in Masonry. If in this discourse you have made any remark, that might have taken you off, to pronounce that vow that we are obliged to take from you (before we can give you any greater knowledge of the Degree of the Grand Elected Knights of Kadoch;) Consult yourself and see if you are disposed to penetrate further and fulfill Exactly all the points of the Obligations that you are going to pronounce with me; in Order to link you to us forever, (here is a pause for some time.) N:B. If the Candidate is afraid to engage, or hesitates to pronounce the further Obli-

[330]

-gations; the Illustrious Grand Commander without going further sends him our and Closes the Chapter. In regard to the notions which the Candidate might have already got, the Obligation which he has already taken will assure us of his discretion; if on the Contrary he persists in going further, and will take the 2^{d} Obligation the Grand Commander continues the Ceremony in the following manner. Then the Candidate kneels at the feet of the Grand Commander, puts his right hand on the Bible, and his left hand between the hands of the Grand Commander: When in that posture, the Grand Commander says, "You swear and promise to me on that you hold the most dear and sacred, 1st To practice the works of Corporal Mercy; to live and die in your religion, and never declare to any man, who received you, or assisted at your Reception in this sublime Degree." The Candidate answers, "I promise and swear." Then the Grand Commander says, "say with me, *T'sed Halaad,* which he repeats.

"2dly You Promise and swear, to have Candour in all your actions, In consequence of which never to receive into this Degree any brother who is not your most Intimate friend, and then by consent of Two Grand Elected Inspectors, if to be met with or by a patent given you for that purpose." The Candidate answers, "I promise and swear," then he repeats *Scharlabac.*

[331]

"3^{rdly} You promise and swear at all times a sweetness of mind, as much as you are Capable, to love and cherish your brothers as yourself, to help them in their necessities, to visit and assist them when they are sick, and never to draw arms against them on any pretence whatsoever," he answers "I promise and swear." The Grand Commander says, "say with me," *Moteck.*

"4thly You promise ands swear to regulate your discourse by truth, and to keep with great Circumspection and regard the Degree of the white and black Eagle or Kadoch"; he answers, "I promise and swear," "say with me," *Emunah.*

"5thly You promise and swear, that you will travel for the advantage of heaven, and to follow at all times and in all points every matter that you are ordered and that is prescribed by the Illustrious Knights and Grand Commanders, whose Orders you swear submission and obedience to, on all Occasions, without any restrictions," he answers "I promise and swear." The Grand Commander says, "say with me," *Hamach, Sciata.*

"6thly You promise and swear to me, to have patience in Adversity, and you swear never to receive a Brother to this Degree on any pretence whatsover whose will is not free, as Religious Monks and all those who have made vows without restrictions to Supervisors, he answers, "I promise and swear," say with me, *Sabael.*

[332]

7thly You promise in the end and swear, to keep Inviolably secret, what I am going to confide in you, to sacrifice the Traitors of Masonry, and to loop upon the Knights of Malta as our Enemies: To renounce for ever to be in that order, and regard them as the unjust usurpers of the rights, Titles and Dignities of the Knights Templars in whose possession you hope to enter with the help of the Almighty," he answers, "I promise and swear," then say with me, *Choemel, Binah, Tabinah.*

After the Candidate has pronounced the last words the Grand Commander relieves him and says, "By the 7 Conditions, and by the power that is transmitted to me, And which I have acquired by my discretion, my untired Travels, zeal, fervor and Constancy I receive you Grand Inspector of all Lodges, Grand Elect Knight Templar, and take rank before the Knights of Kadoch white and black Eagle which we bear the name of. I desire you not to forget it: It is Indispensible for you my brother to mount the Mysterious Ladder which you see there; it will serve to Instruct you in the Mysteries of our Order, which is absolutely necessary, that you may have a true knowledge of it. Then the Candidate mounts the Ladder, and pronounces each step he rises, the name or the word belonging to it; when he is on the 7th or highest step, and has pronounced the 3 last words, the Ladder is lowered down, in order that the Candidate may pass

[333]

over, because he cannot retire the same way, as he would be obliged to go back, against which he has taken his Obligation, not to retire, by the views and Interest of the Order, which is the reason that the Ladder is lowered, and he passes over it, then he reads the words at the bottom of the Ladder, *Neplus Ultra.*

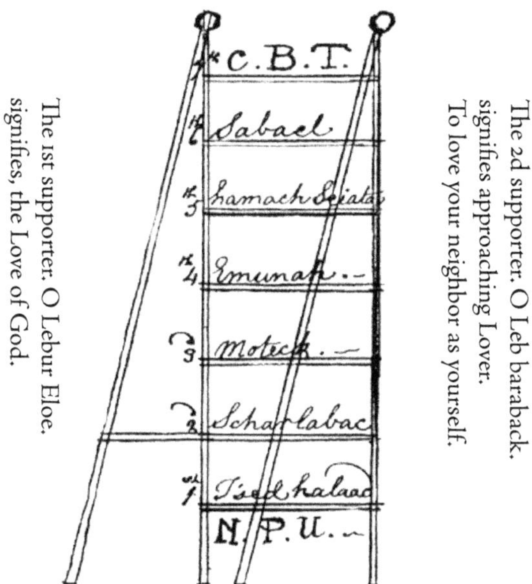

Then the Grand Commander Embraces the Candidate and says to him, "My dear brother I am going to give you the sign, Token and Word, with the pass word of the Grand Elected and Grand Inspectors, after I have given you the Explanation of the Mysterious Ladder, which you have ascended and passed over, without knowing the reason thereof. This Ladder is, my dear brother the most

[334]

Essential and Analogous to the History, which I shall recite to you. Like a ladder it is composed of 2 supporters, which will give you a just Idea of the strength of *Phillip Le Belle* (or the fair) King of France, in his Union with the Pope *Clement* the fifth. The re–union of the 2 supporters by the 7 steps, gives you a just Idea of the 7 Conditions that *Phillip* the fair imposed on the Arch–bishop *Bertrandgot,* to make him Pope, and the 2 supporters being united by the 7 steps, or Conditions are the base of the Union between the King and this Pope Elect. The 7 steps are also a resemblance of the 7 points of your Obligation which you have contracted; and also of that which *Phillip* the fair made *Bertrand Got* take; by the 7th Article of which he swore the final destruction of the Knights Templars, and in the same manner by the 7th point of your Obligation you swear to bear an Implacable hatred to the Knights of Malta, and engage yourself to endeavour their total destruction, in order to recover the rights and dignities of what they possess. Lastly, this moment my Brother is the time to Instruct <you> fully in this Degree of Grand Elected, and give you a true knowledge how Masonry has come to us. If you pay attention to the principal fate of that Story, you will easily make the application yourself, the more you are Instructed therein.

The History

Vide Vertots History of Malta Vol: 2d Page 31 & 32} After the Death of *Benoit* the 11th who died July the

[335]

13th:—1304: the Candidates met for the Election of a new Pope, and found themselves in two factions, French and Italians. Phillip the fair King of france had then several views, which could not be accomplished without the assistance of the Pope to be Elected; and as his party in the Conclave fomented these Divisions to favor Phillips design (who taking advantage of these Circumstances,) sent for *Bertrand Got*, then Archbishop of Bourdeaux, (son of Bertrand, Lord of Villandrau, in the same Diocess) and in the conference which he had with him at a pleasant Country seat near St John of Angels; he there Informed him of his Designs, and the divisions in the Conclave, which put it in his power to Elect a Pope, and that he was disposed to prefer him provided he would swear to perform 7 Articles, the 7th of which was even to be a secret to him untill the time for the Execution thereof was ripe; accordingly he revealed the 6 first Articles which are foreign to our history, but to the 7th, for the exact performance of which they both took the sacrament to each others promise, and *Phillip* the fair took the Brother and Nephew of *Bertrand Le Got* as hostages for the performance of the 7th Article. This King having found a man fit for his purpose to be the agent of his Revenge caused him to be Elected Pope, and promoted to St Peters Chair in the year 1305 under the name of Clement the 5th this Pope after his Election established his See, at the City of *Lyons*, where his

[336]

first care was to execute the first 6 conditions which Phillip had Imposed on him. The time of declaring the 7th being arrived, Phillip did not delay declaring to the Pope that by his oath he was to Injoyn him to Intirely destroy and exterminate the Knights Templar, to the extent of Christendom. Here is what, that attracted the hatred of *Phillip* the fair, and what made him take the barbarous resolution of destroying them all: Some time before the death of Benoit the 11th there happened a sedition in Paris occasioned by Phillip; who had coined some money which was light, mixed and base metal:

Vide Vertots History Vol: 2d page 65} On which the populace were mutinous, they plundered and demolished the house of *Stephen Barbet*, Master of the Mint; they went afterwards to the Kings dwelling and committed a great deal of Indecencies insomuch that every matter conspired an Innsurrection.

Vide Peter Dupoys Collectn} The Knights Templars (against whom Envy had raised many powerfull Enemies) were suspected to have been at the bottom of these outrages, and was the cause (although without any foundation,) that their ruin was determined on by the King, for which purpose he sought the means of getting Assistance, when the most favorable Opportunity offered itself by the death of Benoit the 11th in order to put in his stead a *Pope* on certain Conditions that should be imposed on him. Nothing was now wanting but a pretence (for when force and Authority is in

[337]

hand every matter becomes easy,) for which purpose they prevailed on two abandoned men, with money, whose names were *Gerard Labé*, And *Benoit Mehuy*; they promised to them to get Admission among the Knights Templars and when admitted into their Mysteries to accuse the whole order of the greatest crimes: which these two Villians executed Exactly. They desired to be received into the order, which was easily attained as they had seemingly honest Exterior Titles and apparent good qualities, besides a supposed Credit at Court. Every thing conspired in their favor and they were received, but it lasted not long before the Templars repented heartily of having lighted the fire brand, which was the cause of the deplorable and Tragic scene, when most all of the Templars were Involved in one common destruction. For these 2 Wretches soon after their admission accused the whole order of the most dreadfull and Execrable crimes; demanding to be seperated from them, for the reason of the unheard of terrible things suggested to them. The treason is good but the traitor is detestable, thus did they suffer the same lot that was intended for the Templars; for they by their Treachery went through the most dismal Torments and not suffered to live although they had been the Instruments of Vengeance to the Templars by their false accusations. Upon their reports the King (who had lately had an Interview with the Pope

[338]

at Poetier;) took the most secret measure to arrest all the Templars in his dominions in one day; This was done on the 13th of October 1307, two years after the Accusation of these Villians was made. They seized on all their papers Titles and Treasures, and generally all their wealth over which was placed Overseers and Stewards. King Charles of Naples in the like manner ordered all the Templars to be arrested in *Provence*: those taken in France were looked up in the Castle of *Melun*, in order to take their Trials. The Pope at the same time sent for their Grand Master *James De Molay* as Native of Burgundy, (who was then at war with the Turks in the island of Cyprus,) who as soon as he received the Orders of the *Pope*, came to *Paris* with 60 Knights of the order; among whom was one *Guy*, brother of the Dauphin *Devenois*, *Huges de peraldes*, and *Theodore Bazille, de Manancoun* they were all arrested, and made to suffer the most dreadful torments in order to draw from them a Confession of the crimes they were accused of, though without effect; as they dared bravely all and every Torment, rather than accuse themselves of things they were Innocent of. So that on no other proof but that of the two Infamous subborners, their Tryals were concluded, (being impossible to procure the least Evidence against them, as never any person assisted at the making of a Templar.) They executed & burnt alive 57 in one day, and the...

[**Pages 339–40 are missing.** *The following text is from a similar copy of the ritual in the Archives of the Supreme Council, 33°.*]*

[They were executed & burnt alive, to the number of 57 in one day & 59 the next day & so on until they had completed almost their total destruction. They pardoned none, not even those that served them, in accusing the whole order. For as Templars, they were included in the general sentence & burnt alive, with others. Let the end of those unhappy wretches serve as a lesson to us, that we are not in future, to be seduced, by fine promises & initiate any, but those, who have given by a long train of services, proofs of the most solid worthiness. Least we might be, by their indiscretion, dragged once more with all the Knts of the W & B eagle or K—H in a common fate. The grand master of the 4 above mentioned brethren nevertheless, were not were not comprehended in the first execution. The Pope for reasons (see Vertot history of Maltha) kept the judgment to himself. Most all the Templars, at the time of this persecution (which lasted till 1314) were arrested in all the christian states, but were not all put to death. Philip was continually hurrying the Pope to make an end of James De Molay, the grand master

* *Knight of Kadosh or White & Black Eagle Inspector of all lodges Grand Elect 24th. 29th degree Grd Elected Knt of Kadosh.* (c.1800), pp. 37–40. Archives of the Supreme Council, 33°, S.J. The cover of the Ms. bears the name C[harles] W. Moore.

of his companions. After having groaned 7 years in prison, overloaded with irons, which was done at last. They were burnt alive the 11th of March 1314 in the Isle of Paris, moveing to pitty & tears, the numerous spectators who were present, for their steadyness, heroically & constancy and solemn vows of their innocence which was afterwards apparent. Supported by an event extremely memorable. James De Molay the Gd Mr seeing himself ready to end his life, in the flames (after having languished in Irons for several years & which was now become a relief to him, to end his life in any manner, rather than undergo a longer lingering life in this uncertain world) with great composure turned himself & directed to god in prayer. Oh almighty & everlasting God, who knows the innocence of the victims, which have been sacrificed for several years, permit us to reflect on the reproach and infamous torments, which you permitted J:C: to be covered with at his death, to redeem from the slavery & our sins. To give an example to the innocent, by teaching them by his mildness to suffer without murmuring the persecutions & torments which injustice & blindness prepared for him & them. Forgive O God the false accusations & imputations which has caused the ~~whole~~ destruction of the whole order, of which your divine providence had established the chief & if thou art pleased to accept the prayer, which we now humbly offer to the. Permit oh God that one day, this abused people, might know the innocence of those who have endeavored to live, in thy holy fear & love. We wait from thy bounty & compassion, the rewards of the torments & death we suffer, which we offer to thee, in order to enjoy thy divine presence in everlasting happiness.]

[341]

Then addressing himself to the people he said "Good people, who see us ready to perish in the flames, you will be able to Judge of our Innocence For now I summons *Pope Clement* the 5th in 40 days and *Phillip* the fair in twelve months, to appear before the awful and tremendous Throne of the ever living God to render an Account of the blood they have wickedly shed." After which they were hurried to Execution fearing a Rescue from the populace. The Prediction of *James De Molay* was accomplished, as Pope Clement the 5th died the 19th of April in the same year at *Rocquemour* on the Throne, and *Phillip* the fair within a twelvemonth at *Fontainbleau*. The news of the Persecution of the Knights Templars, had already reached the Knights which were left in *Cyprus* who in the absence of their Grand Master had been overpowered by the Turks, when they lost *Acre* with several other strong places in that Island, and were obliged to retire to the Isle of Rhodes and the adjacent Islands. The persecutions were carried against them into Open Council at *Vienna* the first of October 1311, when their order were banished, their Estates confiscated and left at the Popes disposal, who in the year 1312 gave a part to the Knights of Saint John of Jerusalem who yet at this day possess the greatest part of their Estates. This a–version makes to this day a part of the Obligations of the Grand Elected Knights Templars as the number of them who escaped

[342]

was very small, rendered that adversion more powerfull, they sought to renew and Increase their Order, in admitting persons, in whom they believed their behaviour and quality indisputable, those in short whom they thought worthy of keeping the most Important secret. Instructed them of the wonders that had operated at different times among the good and virtuous Masons, Heirs worthy of those whom Solomon had distinguished and favoured after the Construction of the Temple; knowing their Candour and Intrepidity which appeared among them in the greatest dangers: their Wisdom, Union, Charity, Love, Impartiality firmness, discretion and Zeal; they thought they could do no better, than endeavor to unite themselves to those Masons, their fathers, protectors, support and help; sought the favor to be admitted into their society and Initiated into their Mysteries. Those new Initiated in the Mysteries, were informed by the Masons who they were, the barbarious events which they had escaped, and the resolutions they had secretly taken to Increase their number, to be able one day to reclaim their rights, re–establish their Order and take possession again of their Estates. They offered their Brethren the Masons their assistance in takeing their revenge, and as a common cause to accept the Tribute from them of the most Just Gratitude and thankfulness. The Grand Elected Knights and Princes Masons

[343]

approved their designs, accepted their offers and agreed among themselves, instead of the Characters of the Order which was a Cross to use the Sign Token and Word of Masons; and by the conformity of several analogous events to their History, persuaded them that the different Signs of Masons would put them Intirely under cover, against the Maliciousness of those as *Gerard Labé*, or *Benoit Mehuy*, should such endeavour to be admitted into the order of which they should undertake in vain to put us under the danger of a like Event; that they should not trust the true secret of the order but to those, whom they had perfectly tried, and of whom they were as sure as of themselves, after having made them pass through the different Degrees, which we know in Masonry, having taken their birth from the Construction of the Temple of Solomon, since its Origin until the destruction of the same Temple and Characterized witnesses of the most remarkable events, by the event entirely Analogous to the destruction of the Knights Templars, whom as Elects of Masonry crieth only to revenge the death of their Illustrious Grand Master and retake their possessions. My dear Brother from the Degree of Master Mason that you have received, and when you have learnt to shed Tears at the Tomb of Hiram Abiff, have you not been disposed in other degrees to Vengeance? Did they not show you the

[344]

Traitor Jubulum Akirop (or Abyram) in the most dreadfull Colours? Would it be Exaggerated in comparing the Conduct of *Phillip* the fair to his? And compare the 2 Infamous Villians *Gerard Labé*, and *Benoit Mehuy* to the two villians who joined *Akirop* to murder Hiram Abiff? Do they not kindle in your heart the same Revenge, which those unhappy fellow Crafts deserved, and was executed on them? These Tryals that you have gone through to learn the Historical facts of the holy Bible, do they not serve you to understand and sound your heart to make a Just application of the death of Hiram Abiff in comparing it with that of *James de Molay*? By the Degree of 9 elected where your heart was disposed to revenge, you have been prepared to the Implacable hatred that you have sworn to the Knights of Malta, on whom you ought to revenge the death of James De Molay. As a Grand Elected you have acquired by your proved discretion in symbolic Masonry the light which leaves nothing more for you to desire, than your submission to the Degree of the sublime Princes of the Royal secret, our Chief and Grand Elected of the Order, who have bestowed on you this singular favor. This is my Most Illustrious brother how and by whom Masonry is derived, and has been transmitted down to us. You ought to see what it is to enter into our lawfull rights, that we seek to Asociate

[345]

with men whom merit, braveness and good manners gives them Titles, which only birth–right grants to the Ancestors of the Templars. You are now a Knight and on the Level with them. You have the same events to run, as much from the side of Envy as persecution, which you may escape by keeping carefully your Obligation and secreting from the Vulgar your Estate and what you are. Having attained to this Degree of Light, which your merit only, and the knowledge that we have of your manners, hath brought you to: We are prepared and persuaded that our Confidence towards you will be sufficient to make you apprehend how Important it is to you, not to be the cause of our not repenting in your Innitiation: We know you perfectly to have the least doubt of you, thus we did not hesitate to light you in the true Interest of the Order, that by your uniting yourself to us with a sincere submission, you will labor to acquire that perfection, your zeal deserves. You are now in the rank of those who shall be elected to the Grand work once your name is in the urn of your Election, the delicious perfumes of your actions, will bring you to the true happiness of your desire, which I wish you. Amen! Amen! Amen! After this discourse the Grand Commander knocks 1 great blow on the Table, in order to call the 4 Knights into the Chapter who were out, after which the Grand Commander finishes the reception and gives the new Knight

[346]

the Sign, Token and Word, he arms him, and decorates him with the attributes, and communicates to him the name he must take in future, which is uncommon to all others, and is Knight of Kadoch or Knight of the white and black Eagle, instead of Knight Templar.

JEWEL AND RIBBON The Jewel is a red Cross as before described, but in the room of that, now it is a black spread Eagle with 2 heads, suspended by a broad ribbon of a fiery Colour from the left shoulder to the right hip; The Eagle as if going to fly, with a naked sword in his Claws.

SIGN. The Sign is seting your right hand on your heart the fingers extended, and then let your hand fall on your right knee the fingers extended.

TOKEN. The Token is the same as that of the nine Elected 8 and 1.

PASSWORD. The pass word is *Necum* or *Nikah* (meaning revenge) otherwise *Manchen*.

GR[d] WORDS. The Grand words are, one says, *Nichamaka, Bulion,* [BLANK SPACE], the other answers, *Bagul–kal pharaxal,* then they both Embrace and say *Adonai!*† N:B: The brothers who desire to be better acquainted with the foregoing Interesting history of the Knights Templars may consult the following Authors Viz[t] Villanius's History. History of all Orders by Mathei, (in Paris,) History of Malta by Vertot, and Essay on Paris by Saint Foix.

LECTURE OF THIS DEGREE

Q: – 1st Are you a Grand Elected?
A: – I am thrice Illustrious Knight.

[347]

Q: – 2[d] Who received you in this Degree?
A: – A Worthy Deputy Grand Inspector by the Consent of 2 others.
Q: – 3[d] What was done with you?

† *The Knight of Kadosh or White & Black Eagle Inspector of all lodges Grand Elect 24th. 29th degree Grd Elected Knt of Kadosh.* (ca.1800) in the Archives of the Supreme Council, 33°, S.J., reads, "... one says MICHA–MOCHA BAELIM, the other answers BAGULHAL, PHARAXEL. Then they both embrace & say ADONAI." (In the original, however, the words are reversed; e.g., IANODA = ADONAI, etc.)

A: – He created me Knight.
Q: – 4th How can I believe you?
A: – My name which I bear will convince you.
Q: – 5th What is your name?
A: – Kadoch or Knight of the black Eagle.
Q: – 6th Was any thing else done to you?
A: – The Deputy Inspector adorned me with habit ribbon and Jewel of the Order.
Q: – 7th Where have you received the prize of your Elect^{n}
A: – I have received it in a very deep Grotto and in the silence of the Night.
Q: – 8. To what do you apply to?
A: – I work with all my might and strength to raise an Edifice worthy my brothers.
Q: – 9. What progress have you made?
A: – I have acquired the knowledge of the Mysterious Ladder.
Q: – 10. Of what is that Ladder Composed?
A: – Two supporters and 7 Steps.
Q: – 11. What are the names of the two supporters?
A: – *O Lebur Eloe!, Oleb Barabac.*
Q: – 12. What design have these two supporters?
A: – The 1st is the love of God and the other the love of our Neighbour.
Q: – 13. What are the 7 steps of the Mysterious Ladder?
A: – The virtues which I must practice conformable

[348]

to by Obligations.
Q: – 14. Name them to me?
A: – 1st *T'sed Halaad*, practice or works of mercy, 2^{d} *Scarlabac*, Candor of our Actions, 3^{d} Motteck sweetness of Character which all brethren must follow, 4th *Emmunah*, Truth in discourse, 5th *Hamach Serata* advancement to the practice of Heaven, 6th *Sabiel* patience in advancement, 7th *Schoemel, Binah, Tabinah* signifies that we must be prudent to keep secret every matter that is Confided to us.
Q: – 15. What is your Ordinary pass–word?
A: – *Manchen*, a name of the grand Master most renowned among the salitaries, known by the name of Kadoch.
Q: – 16th What signifies that name?
A: – Solitary or separate.
Q: – 17. What was the answer of the salitaries, when they were asked to what they pretended?

A: – *Averecha Recolgit Adonai; Klamid tellesake Sophy,* which is I will bless God at all times, and I will praise him with my mouth.

Q: – 18. Do they never say any thing Else?

A: – Yes, they say also, *Begaherard, Stibium hemuy,* which is, I will assist the poor always, and sustain them with all my might and power.

Q: – 19th How comes the Cross surmounted with the Eagle and the sword?

A: – That is, that I shall remember to employ my sword in fulness of time, under the banner of the black Eagle to support the order.

Q: – 20th Where did you work?

A: – In a place of security to re–establish secretly the

[349]

Edifice ruined by the Traitors.

Q: – 21st What success do you expect for it?

A: – The reign of Virtue; accord of brothers, and the possessions of our fore fathers, and everlasting happiness.

Q: – 22d Have you shed Tears?

A: – Yes! I have.

Q: – 23d Have you wore mourning?

A: – Yes, and I wear it still.

Q: – 24th Why do you wear it?

A: – Because Virtue is despised; and as long as vice reigns, Innocence will be Oppressed, and crimes will be left unpunished.

Q: – 25th Who is it that will punish vice and reward Virtue

A: – The Great Architect of the Universe alone.

Q: – 26. How so?

A: – To favor our design and desire, (here every brother says, three times) God favor our designs.

Q: – 27. Have you any other name than Kadoch, or Knight of the black Eagle?

A: – I have still the name of *Adama,* that from the most *low,* I must go to the most *High*!

Q: – 28th Give me the signs of knowledge against surprize

A: – Here it is, (and he gives it in the following manner) he puts his hand on the heart of a brother in the same manner as with the poinard in the Degree of 9 Elected, then give the Token of the Grand Elected, then give the Token of the Grand Elected, and then both strike the right knee

Q: – 29th How came you to carry your fingers extended on your heart?

[350]

A: – To show that my trust is in God.
Q: – 30th How came you after that to extend your hand?
A: – To shew to my brother that he is welcome to all in my power, and to encourage him to Vengeance
Q: – 31st How came you to let your hand fall on your right knee?
A: – To show, that we must bend our knees to adore God! Amen!

End of Lecture.

To Close

Q: – What is the Clock?
A: – The break of day demonstrates.
Grd Comr If the break of day demonstrates, Let us depart for revenge; after which the Grand Commander puts his hand on his heart, and then lets it fall on his right knee: which is answered by all. Then the Grand Commander embraces each brother and they each other all round, and then the Chapter is Closed.

The End.

Note. The Grand Inspector Stephin Morin, founder of the Lodge of Perfection &ca in a Consistory of Princes of the Royal Secret held at Kingston in Jamaica, In the year of masonry 7769, Advertized the Princes Masons, that lately a Commotion had been at Paris, and that Enquiry had been made, whether those masons who styled themselves Knights of *Kadoch* were not in reality Knights Templars. It was therefore resolved in the Grand Communication of Berlin and Paris, that said Degree should be stiled Knights of the white and black Eagle, and the Jewel of the order should be a black Eagle as mentioned in the 24th Degree.

[351]

The 25th Degree

or Prince of the Royal Secret, or Knights of Saint Andrew faithful Guardians of the sacred Treasure.

Ne plus Ultra.

To Open.

The grand commander knocks with his scepter or sword 1, and 4, which is repeated by the two Lieutenant Commanders (who act as Wardens,) the Grand Commander then pronounces the word *Salix*; the Wardens reply *Nonis*, Upon which all the Brethren say *Tengu*. The Grand Commander then orders the Candidate in, and delivers to him the following Obligation.

The Obligation

I: A: Z: Do of my own free will and accord in the presence of the Grand Architect of the Universe and this Consistory of the sovereign Princes of the Royal secret or Knights of Saint Andrew, faithful Guardians of the sacred Treasure, most solemnly vow and swear under all the different penalties of my former Obligations that I never will directly or Indirectly reveal or make known to any person or persons whatsoever any or the least part of this Royal Degree unless to one duly qualified, or in the body of a regulated Constitutional Consistory of the same; him or them whom I shall find such, after strict and due trial. I furthermore vow and swear under the above penalties, to always abide and regulate myself agreeably to the statutes and Regulations now before me, and when in a Consistory to behave and demean myself as one worthy of being honored with so high a Degree, that no part of my Conduct may in the least reflect discredit on this Royal Con-

[352]

-sistory or disgrace to myself. So may God maintain me in Justice and Equity to make a due performance thereof. Amen! Amen! Amen! Amen! Amen! Amen!

N:B: The Candidate who receives this Degree must be examined in the preceeding Degrees of Kadoch prior to Entry; when by the Introductor he will be made acquainted with the pass word, which is *Polcal*, and which he must give to the Two Lieutenant Commanders and then by the Introductor he is led to the Grand Commander or sovereign, and takes the foregoing Obligation.

Then the Grand Commander says, "My Dear Brother the preparations necessary to be observed in holding a Grand Chapter or Council of the sovereign Princes of the Royal secret, are as follow, to wit,

The Grand Chapter or Consistory ought to be held in a Building two stories in heigth; to be situate on a small Eminence, in an open Country: In the second Story there must be three apartments, and must be held in the day. The Tylers are placed on the first floor. The first Chamber in the upper Story is for the Guards. The Second is for prepareing. The third is where the Grand Chapter is held.

This apartment must be hung with black Sattin strewed with silver Tears, Cross bones and Skulls.

2dly A Throne is placed in the East, under which a chair of State is placed for the sovereign of Sovereigns and Grand Illustrious Prince and Grand Commander in Chief: The throne is to be ascended by 7 steps, covered with black sattin, strewed with flames; before the Sovereign is a Table covered with black Sattin strewed with tears; On the fore part of which is to be a Skull

[353]

and cross ones, with the Initials I.M. The I, over the head, and the M, under the Bones.

3dly The Grand Commander, Sovereign of Sovereigns is to be armed with a Buckler and named sword, his Scepter and ballance on the Table before him, and the Laws only.

4thly In the West are the two Wardens; their Titles are "Lieutenants Commanders," they wear bucklers, their naked swords are laid across on the Table before them which is covered with Crimson sattin, bordered with black, strewed with Tears: on the front part of the Table, the Initials N.K.—M.K. embroidered with Golden Letters.

5ly The Minister of State stands on the right hand of the Sovereign, and acts as Grand Orator.

6ly The Grand Chancellor stands on the left.

7ly Next to the Minister of State stands the Secretary.

8ly Near the Chancellor stands the Grand Treasurer.

9[ly] Below them on each side the Engineer or Grand Master Architect, and the Captain of the Guards.

10[ly] Six Brethren stand before them, dressed in red without Aprons: All wear the Jewel of the Order on their breast suspended to a black ribbon in a Triangular form.

The Royal Secret or rendezvous of the Sublime Princes.

Instructions for the Re Union of the Brethren Knights princes and Commanders of the Royal secret or Kadoch, which signifies the holy brothers seperated. Frederick the 3[d] King of Prussia Grand Master and Commander in Chief, Sovereign of Sovereign at

[354]

the head of an Army composed of the Knights of the black and white Eagle, including the Prussians, English and French, as well as other Christian Brethren, joined by the Princes of Lebanon or the Royal Axe, the Knights of Saint Andrew or Rose Cross; the Knights of the East and West, the Princes of Jerusalem; the Knights of the East; the Grand Elect Perfect Masters and sublime, the Knights of the Royal Arch, and Knights sublime Elected.

The Equilateral triangle in the Center of the Draft, represents the center of the army, and shews where the Knights of Malta are to be placed, that is those who have been admitted into our Mysteries, having agreed to surrender their rights to us, and have shewed themselves faithful Guardians, they are to join the Knights of Kadoch.

The Corps in the Center is to be commanded by five princes, who are to take the Command by rotation according to their Degrees; they are to receive their orders from the Sovereign of Sovereigns, Grand Master and Commander in Chief, these five Princes are to fix their standards in the five Angles of the pentagon, as represented in the Draft, to wit,

1st The Standard T bearing their Arms. A Golden Lion holding in his mouth a key of Gold, with these letters S.Q.S. engraved in it: The field azure, at the bottom of the flag are these words, "Ad majoram Dei, Gloriam."

2[d] The standard E bearing an Inflamed heart with Gules sable, winged and covered with Laurel, field

[355]

argent.

3[d] The Standard N, bearing, a spread Eagle with a crown connecting both heads, in the form of a Collar, holding a sword in his right claw with the point downwards, and a bloody heart in the left Claw field light green.

4th The standard or flag G. the arms an Ox sable field Orr.

5th The standard U, bearing, The Ark of the Covenant with two light coloured green palm trees, in a purple field with these words, "Laus Deo."

A FIGURE OF 7 SIDES & 7 ANGLES} The Heptagon represented in the Draft, points out the Incampment of the Princes of Jerusalem and the Princes of Lebanon, these are to receive Orders from the above mentioned five Princes.

A FIGURE OF 11 SIDES & 11 ANGLES} The Hendecagon represented in the draft represents the Incampments of the brethren of all denominations as shall hereafter be explained. It is to be observed that every Tent represents a whole camp and the flags and pendants, points out the different Degrees in the Craft, each letter that distinguishes the flags, are taken from three words in this sublime Degree. Thus the degree of Knights of the Rose Cross or of Saint Andrew and the white Eagle, will be distinguished by a white flag and pendant slightly stained with red and is represented by the Tent S.

Tent E called Malachia, and shews the Court of the Knights of the East and West and Prince of Jerusalem

Tent A called Zerobabel has a light green flag

[356]

and pendant, and shews the camp of the Knight of the East or the Sword.

Tent L called Nehemiah, has a red flag and pendant, and represents the Camp of the Grand Elect, Perfect Mason and Sublime.

Tent I called Homen has a black and red flag and represents the Camp of the Royal Arch.

Tent X called Phaleg, has a black flag and pendant and shews the Camp of Elected of Nine, Illustrious of 15 and sublime Knight Elected.

Tent N called Joyada, has a red, and red and black flag and pendant and shews the Camp of Prevost & Judges

Tent O called Eliab has a green and red flag and pendant and shews the camp of the Intendant of the building and Intimate secretary.

Tent N called Joshua, has a green flag and pendant and shews the Camp of perfect Master.

Tent S, called Esdras has a blue flag and pendant and shews the Camp of the symbolick masons and Volunteers.

The hour fixed on, shall be 5 after sunset and shall be made known by 5 great guns, one fired with a pause and the other 4 briskly.

1st Rendezvous, at the port of Nantzs, from Nantzs to the port of Rhodes, from that to Cyprus and Malta where the several Naval forces of all Nations are to Assemble.

2d At Cyprus &c.
3. At Joppa, and to proceed to Jerusalem where they will be joined by our faithful Guardians there.

[357]

Standard bearers names. Bezaleel, Eliab, Monchen, Garinous and Emerk.

The watch word for every day in the week are as follows, Vizt they are not to be changed but by express Orders from the King of Prussia.

Sunday	Cyrus	Answer	Ezekiel
Monday	Darius	do	Daniel
Tuesday	Xerxes	do	Habakuk
Wednesday	Alexander	do	Sophonias
Thursday	Philadelphus	do	Haggai
Friday	Herod	do	Zecharias
Saturday	Hezekias	do	Malachi
	names of the protectors of the orders		names of the prophets

Explanation of the Tents and their Letters.

You begin from the letter S, which is the Tent of the Knights of the East and West, at the top of the Draft then follow the letters against the sun and you will find Vizt S.E.A.L.I.X. N.O.N.I.S. In the Camp of the Pentagon, you will likewise find the Initials, to be read in the aforesaid manner, T.E.N.G.U. which compose together the words Vizt Sealix, Nonis, Tengu, the latter signifies the rallying of the wise brethren, who have hitherto been seperated.

These letters when followed in due order, form the Initials of each word, which composes a prophecy in the french language Vizt Souterons, Apresent L'Invincible Xerxes, Nous Offre Notre Incomparible Sacre, Tresor Et Nous, Gaignerous, Victorieusement.

The sublime Princes will have the possession of our

[358]

Treasure, they being the Antient Treasurers of the order and the Knights of Malta who shall join us shall have and enjoy the same honors and priviledges. The Princes of Jerusalem shall with the degrees of the black and white Eagle, and will command the Knights of the East, with all the lower Degrees, their pass word thrice pronounced Elchadia which signifies Deltha.

1st SIGN. The sovereign of Sovereigns puts his right hand on his heart, and stretches it forth perpendicularly with the fingers extended, which is repeated by the Wardens and others.

PASSWORD. "*Polcal*," which signifies, "separate."

ANSWER. "*Phusaskal*," meaning, "Reunited to accomplish." Then both together say, "*Nika, Mika*," that is, "I will be revenged."

WORD. The Sovereign of Sovereigns then says, "*Sealix*"; the Wardens reply, "*Nonix*," and then all the Brethren say "*Tengu*."

The Sovereign of sovereigns then says, "My Dear brethren let us imitate our Grand Master James de Molay who to his death, placed his hope in the Grand Architect, and pronounced the following words at the Instant he departed this Transitory world, for Eternal bliss, "*Spes mea in Deo est*,"

The Grand Consistory is closed by 1 and 4, in the same manner as it was opened.

A General Recapitulation to be read only in this Degree. "My dear Brethren, The saracens having taken possession of the holy Land, those who

[359]

were in the Crusade, not being able to expel them determined with Godfrey de Bouillon the Conductor and Chief to viel the Mystery of Religion, under emblematical figures, by which they would be able to maintain the devotion of the Soldiers and protect themselves from the curious of those who were their Enemies, in similitude to the Example of the Bible the Style of which is parabolick.

Those zealous brothers chose Solomon's Temple for their mark, which has strong allusion to the Christian Church, and have been since known by the name of, "*Master Architect*," and since which time they have employed themselves to Improve the Law of that admirable Master. From hence it appears that the Mystery of the Craft are the Mysterys of religion; those brethren were scrupulously careful not to entrust this important secret to any whose discretion was not proved, this is the reason why they invented different Degrees to try those who entered among them, and only gave them symbolick secrets without explanation, to prevent being betrayed, and only to know themselves to each other; for this purpose it was resolved to use different Signs, Words and Tokens in every Degree, by which method they would be secure against Cowans and Saracens

These different degrees were fixed first to the number of Seven, by the Example of the Grand Architect, who built the Universe in Six days and rested on the Seventh, which is designed by the seven points of Reception in the Masters Degree.

[360]

Enoch employed Six years to construct the Arches and in the seventh, after having deposited the sacred treasure, disappeared and was transported to the abode of the blessed. Solomon employed Six years to construct his Temple, and Celebrated to dedication on the seventh with all the solemnity worthy the Divinity and himself, tis this sacred place we choose to make the basis of figurative Masonry, in the first Degree, there are three symbolicks to be applied

1st The first day of the Creation which in its beginning was only Chaos, is figurated to us by the Candidates comeing out of the back Chamber, neither naked or Cloathed, deprived of the light, which the master gives to him, and in short after haveing suffered the painful tryal at his reception and his Obligation.

The Candidate sees nothing before his is brought to light, and all his powers of Imagination (relative to what he is to go through) are suspended, which alludes to the figure of the Creation of the vast Luminous body confused among the other parts of the Creation, before he was extricated from darkness and fixed by the Almighty Fiat.

2ndly The Candidate approaches to the footstool of the Master and there he renounces all Cowans; he promises to subdue his passions, by which means he is united to virtue and by his regularity of life demonstrates what he professes; this is figurated to him by the steps that he takes in approaching the Altar, the symbolick meaning of which is, the seperation of the firmament from the Earth and water, the second

[361]

days Creation.

3dly The Master gives to the Candidate the first masonick light, Explains the first symbols, gives him the Sign, Word and Token which characterizes a Mason, by which means he is known by his brethren on all occasions, and in the midst of all who are not Masons, from whom Virtue has seperated him. These are the three symbols of the first Degree which distinguishes the apprentice from the other Degrees. The second Degree has two symbols applicable thereto, which joined with the 3 first creates the number five, which distinguishes the fellow Craft.

4thly The fourth day the Grand Architect produced fruits to the Earth, which was seperated from the water, and is figured by the reception of the brother to the 2d Degree, that is seperated him from the Apprentice that he might learn the use of the square, Level and plumb; by which means he renders himself able and useful in working to improve in knowledge of the Society which is the fruits of his reception.

5thly The Grand Architect embellished his work the fifth day in filling the earth with Animals, waters with fish and the air with birds is figurative to the fellow Crafts employing themselves to polish and cut stones, by the beauty of the brilliant star. To the third Degree there are two symbols which added to the five former creates the number seven which is the Master Mason.

6thly In the Degree of Master you are taught to pass from

[362]

the square to the Compass, which shews you are to pass from one virtue to another untill you have obtained the whole. Hiram Abiffs death at your reception, teaches you what you *ought to do*, what you *have been*, what *you are*, and where you *will be*, which is compared to the sixth day when God created man from the dust, gave him life and distilled into him a soul, and prescribed laws to him for his Government.

7thly We lead the generality of Masons to these three Degrees where they are to rest under the shade of the sprig of Cassia (happy Tree) which the Master of Masters who passed seven days in tranquility, dedicated to Divine use, untill the Globe is dissolved.

You are taught in the first and second Degrees to labor by example of the Masons, who built Solomons Temple in order to improve and raise in our hearts an Edifice proper to render homage to the Grand Architect of the Universe, of which we ought to be the living Temple which ought to be ornamented only with Virtue. We are taught to polish Stones, which teaches us to correct our manners, to regulate ourselves by the Compass, to square our actions which will conduct us to good works, which every virtuous man would seek. We have the two Columns Jachin and Boaz as the symbols of virtue and prudence which prove to us that man is made for society where he ought to display his virtues and be an Ornament of humanity. The three pillars (supporters of the Temple) demonstrate that every brother indued

[363]

with virtue becomes Essentially a supporter to the Craft. In the Masters Degree is represented Hiram assassinated by false brethren, this ought to put us in mind of the fate of Adam occasioned by perverseness in disobeying his great and awful Creator.

The symbolic Mysteries of the death of Hiram Abiff conveys to us that of the Messiah, for the three knocks which was given to Hiram at the three Gates of the

Temple, alludes to the three points of Condemnation against Christ, at the high Priests Caiphas, Herod, and Pilate it was from this last he was conducted to that most violent, Ignominious and Excrutiating death.

The said three knocks with the square, 24 inch Guage and setting Beetle, are also symbols of his three sufferings, Viz[t] the box on the Ear, the flagellation and the Crown of thorns. The Brethren Assembled round the Tomb of Hiram Abiff, are the representation of the disciples lamenting the death of Christ on the Cross, the Masters word which is said to be lost, since the death of Hiram Abiff is the same that Jesus Christ pronounced on the Cross, and which the Jews did not comprehend. *Eli! Eli! Lamasabacthani*, which is my God! my God! have pity on me, and forgive my Enemies, instead of which are used Mahabon which in Arabian signifies, the son of the widow is dead, which is now a substitute for the other.

The false Brethren represent Judas Iscariot who sold Christ, the red Colour of the Grand Elect perfect Master calls to remembrance the loss of the blood of Christ, the sprig of Cassia is the figure of the Cross, because with this wood was his Cross made.

[364]

The Captivity of the Grand Elect, Perfect Master and sublime shews us the persecution of the Christian religion under the Roman Emperors, and its liberty under Constantine the Great; it also calls to our remembrance the persecution of the Templars and the unhappy life that James de Molay led, in Irons, near seven years, at the end of which our worthy Grand Master was executed, and burnt alive with his four Companions the 11th of March 1314 In the Isle of Paris, exciteing pity and Tears in the people, and who saw them die with a firmness and heroick Constancy, sealing their Innocence with their blood. My dear Brother from the Degree of Master in which you shed tears at the Tomb of Hiram Abiff and in some other Degrees, has not your heart been led to revenge, has not the crime of Jubulum Akirop been represented in the most hedious light, would it be unjust to compare the conduct of Phillip the fair to his, and the Infamous accusers of the Templars, to the two ruffians who were accomplices with Akirop, with Gerard Labe, and Benedict Mehuy, do they not kindle in your heart an equal aversion. The different stages you have travelled, and the time you have taken in learning these historical Events, no doubt will lead you to make the proper application, and by the degrees of Master, Nine Elected, and Kadoch you are properly disposed to fulfill all your engagements, and to bear an Implacable hatred to the Knights of Malta and to revenge the death of James de Molay, and

[365]

by your extensive experience in symbolic Masonry which you have attained by your discretion leaves you nothing more to desire here; You see here my dear brother, how and by whom Masonry is come to us and to endeavour by every just means to regain our just rights, and that we are joined to a society of men whose Merit, Courage and good behaviour held to us the rank, that birth alone gave to our Ancestors.

You now are on the same level with them, the same events to run as much from the side of envy as from persecution; avoid every evil by carefully keeping your Obligations, and carefully conceal from the Vulgar what you are, and wait that happy moment when we shall all be re–united under the same sovereign in the Mansions of Eternal bliss.

Soutenons a present L'Invincible Xerxes, nous offrons notre incomparable sacre tresor et nous Gaignerons victorieusement.

Let is Imitate the Example of our Grand Master James de Molay who to the end put his hope in God and at his last dying moments ended his life with these words, Spes mea in Deo est.

The End

[367]

The following three Degrees are not Included in those of Stephen Morins, but were first Introduced into the Island of Jamaica by Moses Cohen, from North America, as Deputy Inspector.

Select Master of 27. N° 1.

Form of the Lodge.

A representation of king solomons private Chamber King Solomon is seated under a rich Canopy in the East, before a triangular Table, covered with crimson and Gold, a Crown on his head, and a scepter in his hand. Hiram King of Tyre on his right hand, and Hiram Abiff on his left, with a hammer or Hiram in his hand, and a Trowel before him on a Triangular table (as Conductor of this work) In the West is placed the Captain of the Guards with a drawn sword, and decorated with a Crimson ribbon round his neck, at the end of which hangs a trowel. The Conductor is placed in the South of the Chapter with a hammer in his hand and the Grand secretary in the North.

To Open

Solo^{n} – "My dear Brother of Tyre, shall we finish the secret work we have so happily begun?

H^{m} of T. – Thrice Illustrious brother, it is my ardent wish to see the same finished, and secreted, as well in our hearts as in the bowels of the earth; that I may return home with the satisfaction of having discharged my duty to the Craft, in depositing

[368]

and securing their most precious treasure.

Solo^{n} – Dear Brother Hiram Abiff ask the Captain of the Guards is the secret vault is well secured?

H:A: – Brother Captain are we well guarded and is every thing in security?

Captn – Thrice Puissant and Illustrious Grand Master we are well guarded and every thing is in perfect security

N:B: the Captain previous to his answer strikes on the door 4 and then 1 which is answered without in the same manner.

Solo^{n} – Brother Conductor are all our select brethren here?
Cond^{r} – Thrice Illustrious, I find the number of 3 times 9.
Solo^{n} – Brother Conductor what is it O Clock?
Cond^{r} – Thrice Illustrious, It is 9 O Clock when the prying eyes of mankind are closed in sleep.
Solo^{n} – Since it is 9 O Clock, it is time to resume our work, give the brethren notice by the mysterious number of 9, that the hour of work is at hand, and that every one repair to his station.

Then Hiram Abiff strikes 8 quick and 1 slow which is repeated by Hiram King of Tyre and then by King Solomon.

Cond^{r} – Brethren, since it is our thrice Illustrious Grand Masters orders, that the Chapter of select Masons should be opened, and every one repair to their station it is to be accordingly done; Then he strikes 8 quick and 1 slow, which is repeated by all the brethren clapping with their hands 8 and 1. Then the Grand Master and all the brethren give the sign of silence by putting their right fore finger on the lips, and

[369]

covering their Eyes with the left hand.

Solo^{n} – I declare this Chapter of select Masons open, and every Brother will take care and behave accordingly.

There must be a narrow and dark passage from the door to the west end of the Lodge, supported by 8 unfinished Arches, at the bottom or end a 9th Arch finished and covered with a thick Curtain, where none but the 3 Grand Masters are allowed to enter, to execute their secret works: The rest of the select Masons are distributed among the 8 unfinished Arches, at work with their Trowels &c.

Order of Reception

The Candidate is to be Conducted to the Antichamber which is Solomons most retired and private room and there left alone, with these Orders; that whenever he finds the the [*sic*] entrance to the vault open, and not being hindered from approaching it by the Grand steward (whose care it is to guard the entrance) that he may then enter. The Grand Steward opens the door of the vault on a Jar, and sists down with his face turned from the door: The Candidate then enters according to his Instructions; and is stopped by the Captain of the guards, who asks, "Who comes there?" The Candidate answers, "A zealous brother who comes to partake of your labour." The Captain then demands the Sign, Token and Word, for his entrance, but not being able to satisfy him, he seizes the Candidate by the throat and puts the naked sword to his breast, and cries our, "Brethren, there is an Intruder," on which the Brethren make a noise

[370]

with their tools, and all of them cry out, "An Intruder, and Intruder," which alarms the 3 Grand Masters, who come out of the 9th Arch with their swords drawn, and demand; "What is the matter?" on being informed by the Captain of the guards, that one had intruded into their most secret works, they Cry out, "put him to death immediately"! The Captain of the Guards on going to execute the orders, finds the Criminal to be no less, than the Kings most Intimate and fast friend Izobad; he and they fall on their knees, and beg the King to consider on whom his orders were to be executed. King Solomon finding who the Criminal is, in a great passion commits him to the Captain of the of the Guards saying, "take care of this guilty man, and bring him forth when called for, or thou must answer it with thy Life." The 3 Grand Masters after a short consultation come forth, Solomon gives a loud knock as a signal for the Criminal, whom the Captain brings in, tied with a rope, and surrounded by the guards.

Solon – What hast thou done, O! miserable *Izobad*, thy disobedience and curiosity, has made thee forfeit thy life: my 2 Colleauges are Implacable, and my Obligation will not permit me to pardon thee.

Izobad falls on his *knees* and says, "Thrice Illustrious King and Grand Master, you may remember how great my zeal was always for your sacred person; I was at all times the happy sharer of your favors, and always the first Intrusted with your Royal

[371]

secrets and Mysteries, untill of late finding some secret works carried on, of which I was not trusted with. I long greived in secret thereat, and at last took the Liberty of complaining to you of your want of Confidence in me; to which you answered several times, be Contented *Izobad*, thou wilt find in time the passage of this secret place open to thee which contended me. This Evening as I came to your retired room to look for you, I found the door of this vault open, and the Grand Steward, not hindering me from approaching as he used to do, I took it for granted that your promise of finding the passage open to me one time or other was now fulfilled, as I have never found the door of the Vault open before now, I was sure it was done for my reception, but far be it from me, that either Curiosity or disobedience should have led me to it."

The 3 Masters seem much surprized and lift up their hands and eyes in Admiration, which is repeated by all the Brethren. The 3 Grand Masters then consult together in a very low voice, after which Solomon addresses the 2 Grand Masters, as follows

Solon – "My Brother Colleagues, what shall we do with *Izobad*; I find he is not so guilty as we had thought him to have been."

H. of Tyre – As he was misled by your inconsiderate promise my Dear Illustrious brother; I think we must admit him one of our select number.

Solo^{n} – My dear Brother, our number is already accomplished and we can admit of no more.

[372]

H:A. – Illustrious Brothers, our brother *Ahishar*, the Grand steward, as he has neglected his duty of guarding the entrance of this Royal secret vault, he is no longer qualified to be one of the select, and therefore let *Izobad* be put in his place.

Solo^{n} & H: of T:} We thank you Brother for you good advice, *Ahishar* is unworthy to be any longer one of our Select.

Solo^{n} – Izobad, will you take a solemn Obligation to keep inviolably secret, that there is such a secret vault as this?

Izobad.– I will most Cordially.

Solo^{n} – Free him from his bondage: (he is then unbound) He kneels on both his knees, his hands across on the Bible, and takes the following Obligation.

Obligation.

I: A:B: in the presence of the Grand Architect of the Universe and before this Illustrious Assembly dedicated to the most puissant, most terrible and most merciful Creator, do most solemnly swear, that I will never discover, the signs, Tokens and Words, belonging to a Select Mason, to any below me, now will I discover to any one living, the secret of this Royal vault, either by speaking, writeing, Engraving, marking, cutting, carveing, staining or painting, or by any dumb sign or motion, whereby the least hint might be taken, that in this place exists a secret work, or that any secrets are deposited there. I furthermore swear, that I will never penetrate into the secrets of the 9th Arch, unless legally authorized by our thrice Illustrious

[373]

Grand Masters. All this I swear with a firm and steady resolution to keep, without any hesetation equivocation, mental reservation, or self evasion of mind in me whatsoever; and besides all my former penalties to have my hands chopped off, my eyes pulled out of their socketts, my body cut into pieces and thrown among the rubbish of the Temple, that there might remain, no more the resemblance of such a vile wretch, was I to violate this my solemn Obligation: So help me God, and keep me steadfast in the same: Amen! Amen! Amen! Amen! Amen! and kisses the book 5 times.

Solo^{n} – I raise thee select Mason of this Royal vault, you must be blind and dumb to every thing you have seen and heard. After which the Grand Master Conductor, gives him the Signs, Token and Words.

1st SIGN. must be given on entering the Royal vault or a Chapter of Select Masons, is that of a Master with his fingers clinched.

TOKEN. The token is to take each other by the past Masters Grip, then advance reciprocally, slowly up to the Elbows, then pass over with your left hands 5 times.

PASS W^{d}. The pass word is *O! Giblim*.

2^{d} SIGN. Is by stretching out your hands cross ways, lift up your eyes to heaven, and say *Hesed*, signifying Mercy, then drop your hands on the sword side (the sign alludes to the situation he was in, when sentenced to death, and the sword alludes to the Mercy shewn him afterwards.)

3^{d} SIGN. The 3^{d} sign is that of silence and blindness, by putting

[374]

the forefinger of your right hand to your lips, and the left hand over your eyes (alluding to the Obligation of being blind and dumb to every thing he has seen or heard)

4th SIGN. Is that of Admiration.

2^{d} TOKEN. Clap your right hand on the others left breast who Answers, the same.

GR^{d} W^{d} The Person who gives the Token says *Ish Soudy*, signifying a man of my secret or trust.

THE HISTORY

King Solomon, Hiram King of Tyre and Hiram Abiff at the building of the Temple, having agreed most solemnly among themselves, not to confer the Degree of a Master Mason, to anyone, untill the Temple was finished, and to give it to none, but who were really deserving of it; they likewise entered into a solemn Obligation, not to give the Degree of a Master Mason, except there should be 3 Master Masons present, for fear that one or two alone might be partial to his or their friend, and confer on him that Degree though not worthy of it: at the same time they considered the strictness of their Obligation, and in case anyone of them should be snatched away by death (as it really happened) before they had conferred it on others, that the Masters word must be lost forever as the 2 remaining brothers could not give it: To remedy this evil they resolved to build a secret vault, from Solomons most private room to reach under the Sanctum Sanctorum, and that to be supported by 9 arches, and in the 9 arch the 3 Grand

[375]

Masters to deposit a pedestal, with the Initial letters of the grand word thereon, that in Case it should be lost, it may be found in future Ages by some skilful Masons, and the lost word be again recovered. they likewise deposited several other things, for the good of the Nation in General and the Craft in particular

This work was intrusted to 27 select Masons, chosen out of the most skilfull Masons from *Gebul* a City in *Phenicia* famous for the arts and sciences, particularly that of Sculpture. Those 27 select were put under a solemn Obligation not to discover to any in the world, that such a secret vault had been built: As soon as the sacred vault was finished, they erected at the further end of the vault, which was under the sanctum Sanctorum a stately Arch, wherein the 3 Grand Masters retired as soon as it was finished, to deposit there, their secrets &c. Whilst the select worked on the outside on the other 8 Arches which supported the vault; they went commonly to work at 9 at night and left off at 12. *Ahishar*, the Grand Steward guarded the entrance of the secret vault, in the Kings private appartment and let none pass without giving him first the Sign, Token and Word. *Izobad*, the Kings favorite and most Intimate friend, finding some private work carried on his being privy to it, complained to the King most bitterly for the want of his Confidence; The King willing to oblige him, but not having it in his power to him then, as the number of 27 was already accomplished, told him, Do no grieve my

[376]

Izobad; thou wilt one time or other find the passage open to you (meaning whenever he should receive the Degree of Master Mason.) The rest of the History you have heard in the reception.

The Lecture.

Q: – 1st Brother Conductor, are you a select Mason?
A: – My Brethren know me as such; I have seen the Royal Vault and worked in Company with my Brethren therein.
Q: – 2d How did you enter the Royal Vault?
A: – Through zeal and fervor for the Royal art, which was mistaken for curiosity and disobedience, and almost cost me my life.
Q: – 3d How was you admitted a Select Mason?
A: – By mercy and Justice.
Q: – 4. Explain yourself my Brother?
A: – My zeal led me to a place, through a misconstruction of King Solomons promise, by which I had forfeited my life, but mercy prevailed and they did Justice to my zeal and Constancy.
Q: – 5th What do you mean by a select Mason?

A: – The 3 Grand Masters willing to carry on a secret work they selected out of all the Masons, the most able Architects and Sculpturs, and them the most virtuous, and such as was fit to be trusted with the secret.

Q: – 6. How many did they select?

A: – 27 in number.

Q: – 7. Why 27 and no more?

A: – For erecting of 9 Arches in the Royal Vault, 3 for every arch, which makes the number 27.

Q: – 8. Why did they appoint 3 only for every arch?

[377]

A: – This is a secret not known to me as yet.

Q: – 9. Where was this Royal Vault begun?

A: – From Solomons most private room, a subteraneous vault was dug under ground which reached under the Sanctum Sanctorum.

Q: – 10. After this Royal Vault was made what did you do there?

A: – We erected a superb Arch under the Sanctum Sanctorum and supported the same with 8 other Arches towards the entrance.

Q: – 11. After the 9th Arch was finished what as done there

A: – I cannot tell, as it was carefully covered from our sight and none but the 3 Grand Masters were permitted to enter therein on pain of Death.

Q: – 12. Was you never promised to be made acquainted with the secrets it contained?

A: – Yes, we were promised, that in due time we should be intrusted with the secrets it contained.

Q: – 13. Was that promise ever fulfilled to you?

A: – No, the death of our respectable Master Hiram Abiff which happened at the finishing thereof, put a stop to all that work, the 9th Arch as well as the entrance of the Royal vault, was carefully closed up, and the secret buried in our hearts.

Q: – 14. Why did Solomon erect 9 Arches?

A: – As the 9th Arch contained the most holy secrets therefore he chose 9 which is the number of the attributes of the Almighty.

Q: – 15. Why are they only 9 Attributes to the Almighty? When every thing that is great and Good, is to be attributed to him?

[378]

A: – It is to shew that the Divinity is unchangeable and can neither receive addition or dimunition, like the number 9 which is not the Case with

the other numbers.
Q: – 16. What Countryman are you?
A: – A Phenecian, thrice Illustrious.
Q: – 17. From what place in Phenicia?
A: – From the City of *Gebul.*
Q: – 18. What is you name?
A: – *Giblim* is my name.
Q: – 19. How old are you?
A: – 3 time 9 accomplished, makes 27.
Q: – 20. What is the Clock?
A: – It is high 12.
Q: – 21. If it is high 12, what remains to be done?
A: – To practice virtue, fly vice and remain in silence.

Then the thrice Illustrious says

Since there remains no more to do than to practice virtue and fly vice, Let us enter into silence.

On which he makes the sign of silence, by putting the fore finger of the left hand on his lips and says, *Ish Soudy,* which is repeated by all the brethren

After which the Conductor strikes 8 and 1, which is repeated by all the brethren clapping 8 & 1.

Gr^d^ Mr Brethren this Lodge is Closed.

THE END.

[379]

Knight of the Royal Arch
N° 2.

Form of the Chapter.

The grand master, with his senior and Junior Deputy Grand Masters. (The Grand Master representing *Zerobabel*; and his Deputies *Ezra* and *Nehemiah*,) are seated in the *East*, under a rich Canopy of Crimson with Gold; before them is a triangular Altar or table covered with the same Colour as the Canopy; on the Altar is placed a Bible, a △ plate of Gold, and in the middle thereof, a five pointed star, on which is engraved the letter [BLANK SPACE] and the Letters I ^{B} L on the three Angles of the plate, with a dagger laying across. The Grand Master is decorated with a Golden or yellow coloured ribbon around his neck, to which is suspended a gold Compass extended to 90 degrees; in the middle or Center whereof is a △. The 2 deputy Grand Masters are decorated in the same manner, except, that their Compasses are extended to 60 Degrees only, and no Initial in the △. In the *West* are seated before a Table, the Grand Master Conductor and the Captain of the Guards; The Grand Master Conductor is decorated with a Golden Triangle, appended to a yellow Collar, with a dagger and Mallet across: The captain of the Guards with a like Collar, to which is appended a Golden Triangle with 2 cross daggers, and holding a drawn sword in his hand. The Scribe or Grand secretary sits before a small Table △, a little distance from the Grand Master, decorated with his Jewell through

[380]

a △. A small distance from the Grand secretary are seated before a small table, the Grand Treasurer and Grand Master of the Ceremonies:—The Grand Master of the Ceremony who is seated in the south is decorated with a Collar like the others, to which is appended, a hovering Angel, holding in one hand a dagger, and in the other a Trowel. The Grand Treasurer also is decorated with the Jewel of his Office through a △; The Grand Senior Deacon is placed on the right hand of the senior Deputy Grand Master, and the Junior Grand Deacon at the left hand of the Junior Deputy Grand Master; each of them with a drawn dagger in his hand and decorated like other Deacons, except the addition of a dagger through the Jewel which is a △.

To Open

The Grand Master gives a loud knock and says, "Brother Junior Deputy Grand Master, your deacons place in this Chapter,"?

A: – At my left hand, Hail Puissant.*

Gr^d^ M^r^ (To the Junior Grand Deacon) Your Business there my Brother?

A: – To Carry orders to the Captain of the Guards; to place the Centinels; and see the Chapter perfectly secured

Gr^d^ Mr Brother Junior Deputy Grand Master, let him perform his duty, and Immediately go with my Orders to the Captain of the Guards, to have the Centinels fixed, and the Chapter well secured.

The Junior Grand Deacon carries those orders to the Captain of the Guards, who knocks 9 times at the door, which is answered by the Grand Tyler who is

[381]

without, by 9; The Junior Grand Deacon returns and saluteing the Grand Master, he says, "Hail Puissant Grand Master, the Centinels are all placed and the Chapter is in perfect security."

Gr^d^ Mr Brother Senior Deputy Grand Master, are you a Knight of the Royal Arch?

A: – I am, and Glory therein; I have passed from the Compass to the Triangle; I have descended into the Abyss of the 9th Arch, and returned from thence by the help of 2 zealous brethren, loaded with precious treasures, for which we have been amply and gloriously rewarded, by being created Knight of the Royal Arch, and made a Grand Elect and perfect Mason.

Gr^d^ Mr Brother Junior Deputy Grand Master, are you a sublime and Perfect Mason?

A: – I am. I have seen the precious Triangle, with the divine Letters engraved thereon; the explanation whereof was given me, by which means I attained the just title of sublime and perfect Mason.

Gr^d^ Mr Brother Senior Grand Master, your Deacons place in this Chapter?

A: – At my left hand, Hail Puissant.

Gr^d^ M^r^ (To the senior Grand Deacon,) Your business there my Brother?

A: – To carry the Grand Masters Orders to the Conductor that his will and pleasure may be made known through the Chapter; and especially when their Assistance is required.

Gr^d^ Mr What is it O Clock, Brother senior Deputy Grand

* The words "Hail Puissant" are a phonetic error for "All Puissant."

[382]

Master?

A: – The sun has already passed its Meridian.

Gr[d] M[r] Send Notice to the Grand Conductor, that I am going to open this Chapter, and that the Assistance of the Brethren are required.

The Senior Grand Deacon, Carries those Orders to the grand Master Conductor in the West; on which the Conductor gives a loud knock, and the Conductor says, "To Order Brethren,".

The Senior Grand Deacon returns, and informs the Grand Master, that he has delivered his orders. Then the Conductor gives 3 knocks, which are repeated by the Grand Master of Ceremonies in the south and by the Captain of the Guards in the West. The Conductor then reports to the following effect. "Brethren, Take notice that the Hail Puissant and Grand Master is going to open this Royal Chapter and requires your Assistance," on which all the brethren rise, and join their hands cross ways all round the Chapter.

The Grand Master gives the first part of the sacred word J.....h in a whisper to the Senior Deputy Grand Master; he whispers the 2[d] part to the next, and the brother adjoining him, the 3d part or syllable to the brother next to him, and so round the Chapter 3 times, in such a manner that the whole sacred word is given by each brother; after which the Junior Deputy Grand Master strikes 9 times, the Senior Deputy Grand Master strikes 9 times, and then the

[383]

Grand Master strikes 9 times and says, "I declare this Royal Chapter duly opened; and I trust and sincerely hope that every brother will demean himself accordingly":—Then the Conductor gives one blow and says, "Brethren take Notice; this Royal Chapter is opened, and it is expected that every brother will behave himself with propriety accordingly." On this the Brethren clap their hands 9 times, which is counted by the Master of the Ceremonies; and then all the brethren in the Chapter salute the Grand Master with the hailing sign

Order of Reception.

The Candidate is divested of his upper garments and blindfolded, with a rope round his waist; he is attended by the Master Conductor, who knocks on the door 3, 5, 7 and 9 which is answered within, by the Chapter of the Guards on the Table before him; Then the Captain of the Guards, addressing himself to the Grand Master says, "Hail Puissant, there is an alarm; I believe some person wishes for admittance. On which the Grand Master orders the Grand Master of Ceremonies, "to see who knocks, and what is wanted?" The Grand Master of Ceremonies Answers, "A Zealous Judamite, who has regularly and faithfully served his time to all the Antient Degrees of Masonry and is now come to help his brethren in forwarding the works of the new Temple." After the Grand Master of Ceremonies has made the Grand Master acquainted the same,

[384]

He demands, "Is he perfect in all those Degrees; can you Answer for him?

A: – I can.

Grd Mr Do you really believe he is a Judamite and no Imposter?

A: – I do, by his seeming zeal.

Grd Mr That might be; but we must not trust to mere appearances, for they too often and alas! too fatally deceive: We have had the sad experience of many Imposters, therefore let him be Introduced according to Antient form; Let his capacity be duly tried and his sincerity strictly examined, before we admit him into the Temple

The Grand Master and his Deputies leave their seats, and place themselves, *East, South* and *North* all the members standing round in a Circle; the Candidate is then received at the door by the Grand Master of Ceremonies on the 5 points of fellowship; He is then led 4 times round the Lodge, the Master of the Ceremonies walking before him, and the Captain of the Guards behind him with his sword drawn; the first round he gives the Entered Apprentice's sign, and he is saluted in the south by all the Brethren with 3 Claps; the second round he gives the fellow Craft's sign, and he is again saluted with 5 Claps; at the third round he gives the Masters sign and is saluted with 7 Claps, and at the 4th and last round he gives the select Masons sign and is saluted with 9 Claps; Then he is led by the Conductor to the Junior Deputy Grand Master, who he taps 9 times on his left shoulder, who demands

[385]

"Who come there?"

Grd Mr of Ceremonies Answers, "A zealous brother who wants admittance into the Temple.

Junr Depty Grand Master. What Qualifications have you which entitle you to it?

The Candidate, Answers, "This," (and gives the Past Masters Sign, Token and Word.

Junr Depty Grand Master, then says, "pass him to the Senior Deputy Grand Master for further examination. He then taps 9 times on the Senior Deputy Grand Masters shoulder, who demands as follows.

Senr Dpty Grand Master, Who comes there?

Masr of the Ceremonies. A zealous Brother who has proved himself one of the superior Masons, wishes for admittance into the Temple.

Senr Dept^{y} Gr^{d} M^{r} – Have you no further qualifications to entitle you to that favour?

The Candidate answers, "I have."

Senr Dept^{y} Gr^{d} M^{r} – Given them to me?

The Candidate – Gives the sign, Token and word of a Select Mason.

Senr Dept^{y} Gr^{d} M^{r} – O! God!—pass him to the Grand Master in the East for further Examination. He then taps 9 times on the Puissant Grand Masters shoulder, who says as follows.

Gr^{d} Mr Who comes there, and what do you want?

M^{r} of Ceremonies. – A Zealous Brother who has proved himself an expert and true Giblimite, and wishes for admittance into the Temple.

Gr^{d} Mr What is he?

[386]

M^{r} of Ceremonies. – A Judamite who is very zealous to help his brethren in forwarding the sacred works.

Gr^{d} Mr How am I to be convinced of that? perhaps you are a samaritan, and only come to Obstruct our works, as many of your people have done before?

The Candidate says, "I am a true Judamite and nothing but zeal brings me here.

Gr^{d} Mr Have you no other proofs but your own bare assertion?

The Candidate answers, I have a most sacred word; properly pronounced and revered, and known to none but a true Judamite—I have also a solemn sign.

Gr^{d} Mr Give them to me?

The Candidate. (lifting up his hands and Eyes to heaven pronounces J.....h!

Gr^{d} M^{r} I heartily greet you my dear Brother; I am fully convinced of your sincerity and zeal; I will freely admit you into the Temple on this Condition, that you will very carefully search among the ruinous foundation for discoveries; say my brother will you promise me this?

The Candidate answers, "I do most Cordially."

The Grand Master then orders two Brethren to conduct him to the ruinous Arches already discovered; the members from themselves into two lines, joining their hands, their Elbows downwards like a broken Arch.—the Candidate is carried through them, they pressing their elbows on his back, as if forceing himself through a long passage, which is repeated three times; After which

[387]

the Conductor says, "Hail Puissant, the Candidate can penetrate no further." On which the Grand Master says, to the Candidate, "Dear Brother, I am now going to reward your zeal in admitting you into the most sacred place of the temple;

will you take a most solemn Obligation? Will you swear to us an Inviolable fidelity and Constancy? The Candidate answers, "I will readily and chearfully.

The Grand Master then seats himself under the Arch which represents the 9th Arch; over the top is an Artificial Sun at full meridian.

The Candidate kneels down on both knees, his hands on the holy Bible; the dagger and the Triangle, his thumbs and fingers forming a Triangle and takes the following Obligation.

The Obligation.

I: A:B: of my own free will and accord, and in the presence of the Grand Architect of the Universe, and also before this Royal Chapter dedicated to the most high, most just, most terrible and most beneficient Creator; and to *Zerobabel, Ezra* and *Nehemiah*: Do hereby and hereon most solemnly and sincerely swear, that I will always hail, conceal and never reveal, the part of the Royal Arch Mason (now in delivery to me) to any one below me; but only to him or them whom I shall find justly and truly so after a due and strict examination, or in a regular constituted Chapter of Knights of the Royal Arch; I further swear that I will not suffer a

[388]

Royal Arch Brother to be wronged by any one in his property; defamed in his Character, or dishonored in his family, if in my power to prevent it; and more particularly that I will not be the cause of those Injuries being done to him myself. I further swear that I will keep my Brother Royal Arch Masons secrets as my own, even those of murder and Treason not excepted†; and that I will endeavor to rescue him from all dangers which may come to my knowledge, although the same should be attended with some risque of my life: I further swear that I will pay due obedience to the Grand Master and Grand Officers of this Royal Arch Chapter during my being a member thereof and be a strict observer of all the bye laws, rules and Regulations of this Chapter; and that I will duly attend and answer all the summonses of this Royal Chapter, if within the distance of 40 miles, and I am not prevented by any unavoidable Casualties. I furthermore swear, that I will never Assist or be present, in entering and raiseing one of this order out of a regularly constituted Chapter; and that I will erect or give my consent to the erecting of a royal Arch Chapter within 25 leagues distance of a regularly constituted Chapter of this Degree, unless being duly authorized by power, patent or dispensation from a regular Constituted Royal Arch Chapter. I furthermore swear that I will never be concerned in any plot or Conspiracy against the state wherein I reside, and that I will be a good

† This is a phonetic mistake of *excepted* for *accepted*. See p. ?? of the Introduction for a full explanation.

subject, and pay due Obedience to the Laws and Constitutions during my residence in the place where such laws and

[389]

Constitutions are in force and Effect. All this I swear with a firm and steady resolution to perform the same, without any hesitation, Equivocation mental reservation, or self evasion of mind in me whatsoever, Under no less penalty (besides suffering my former penalties in their full tenor,) Then to have my skull trepanned, my brains laid open to the Scorching sun at high Meridian; my body Quartered, and those Quarters exposed on the high roads, that there may remain no more remembrance of such a vile wretch as myself, should I violate this my sacred Obligation. So God help me and keep me stedfast in the same. Amen! Amen Amen!" (The Candidate then kisses the holy bible 3 times.) The Members form an Arch over the new admitted Brother's head and the Grand Master demands—"What do you now desire?"

The Candidate Answers. "Light,"—and is brought to light by the Conductor who orders him to look upwards and then asks him, "What do you see my Brother?

The Candidate says, "A fleshy Arch under an Artificial one;

1st Sign. Then he orders him to look at the representation of the full sun over the Arch, at the same time clapping his right hand over his Eyes, to prevent the rays of the sun darting upon them—this is the first sign. Alludeing likewise to the penalty of his Obligation.

2d Sign. The second Sign is to join the two thumbs and forefingers together, forming a Triangle △. Then the Grand Master strikes the Candidate with a dagger on both shoulders, and

[390]

raising him he says, "Rise my brother, let your future services merit more favour," After which The Grand Master and Officers return to their respective places, whilst the last Initiated brother is let down into the Arch by the help of 2 other brethren where he finds a Pedestal with a Gold △ plate; On it a Copy of the law, and a book of the arts and sciences: Also a Considerable Treasure, which he hands up to his 2 Companions by means of a rope, retaining only the pedestal with the gold plate affixed to it, after which he is hauled up by them who let him down, having the pedestal and gold plate in his arms. The 3 zealous brethren then acquaint the Captain of the Guards, that they have found something: The Captain of the Guards Introduces them to the Grand Master saying (after hailing him), "Hail Puissant Grand Master; these 3 fortunate brethren who were working in the house of the Lord without fee or reward meeting with a secret vault; after removing the key stone two of them let the third brother down by a Rope, and they have found therein those things which are now presented to you": The Grand Master and his Deputies receive them, and the roll is opened by the Grand Master who says, "This is the written Law, which a Draft of the Arts and Sciences," and (opening the box after considering very earnestly the golden Triangular plate) he holds a private Consultation with his 2 Deputies for some time, he and they get up from their seats, and lifting up their hands and Eyes to heaven with admiration Exclaim,

GRAND WORDS} "Glory be to the Great J.....h! we have now found that which has been so long lost and

[391]

in vain searched for. Then each taking a white wand and hanging to it a garland, or a Crimson Collar, to which a golden Trowel is hung, and reaching them to the 3 zealous brethren, the Grand Master says, "My dear brethren, receive this each of you as the first reward for your zeal and fidelity; you have restored to us that which has been so long lost; Take your seats and we will consider what further reward you deserve for the ample service you have rendered the nation in General and the Craft in particular."

The 3 brethren are seated at some distance opposite the Grand Master. After some consultation with his Deputies, the Grand Master addressed the 3 zealous brethren thus, "Dear brethren, among things you have found, is the real and true Grand Masters word, which was lost by the death of our Respectable Grand Master Hiram Abiff and has providentially been deposited in the Arch by our former 3 Grand Masters as the Initials engraved on the Pedestal plainly shews: To reward you fully and amply for your service, zeal and fidelity; we have agreed to invest you with that sublime word which you have found, and to raise you to the degree of a Grand Elect, sublime and perfect Mason, provided you will swear to us an Inviolable fidelity and Constancy to what you have undertaken: are you therefore willing to take a Solemn Obligation?"

The Candidates Answer, "We are, most Cordially."

Grd Mr Then approach here and receive a full reward for your zeal, fervor and Constancy: (here the Candidates approach,) You are now arrived to the utmost

[392]

limits of Masonry," (here the Candidates kneel down in a Trianglular form; their hands joined crossways, before them a cloth wherein is painted the Arch, the names of our 3 Grand Masters, or the Initials of them are formed in 3 lines of the base, with silver or Tin Letters, and the Grand Word in a Circle. In this position they take the Obligation.

The Obligation.

We A:B. C:D. and E:F. do solemnly swear, that we will redouble our zeal in forwarding this work; and that we will to the utmost of our power protect our work and workmen from all Intruders and the Enemies of this our sacred work; We furthermore do swear that we will never give the Grand sacred word we are now to receive, except in the same manner as we shall now receive it: And that we will never invest any man with the same unless authorized for that purpose, or in the Body of a Regularly constituted Chapter of Sublime and Perfect Masters, and that the person to whom this Order of Masonry shall be given, must first be found duly qualified, by having previously regularly passed through all the former Degrees necessary to his Qualification: All this we swear with a firm and steadfast resolution to keep with exactness the same, without any hesitation Equivocation; Mental reservation or self evasion of mind of any nature whatsoever, and in failure besides our former penalties in their full Tenor, to be dishonored and our memories to be made shameful in future ages of Masons, like those of the 3 Ruffians

[393]

who murdered our Respectable Grand Master Hiram Abiff. So help us God and keep us stedfast in this our solemn Obligation.—They kiss the holy Bible 5 times, saying afterwards Amen! Amen! Amen! Amen! Amen!. They also kiss the Daggers (which are reached them by the Grand Master and his Deputies) 5 times: Then the word is given them One is instructed to say I___; the other B___ and the third L___ and so alternately untill every one has compleated the same: Then the Grand Master strikes them with their swords upon their shoulders saying, "We Invest you with a dagger, that you may defend and protect with one hand that which ye have undertaken to perform with the other." The Grand Master then gives the Token

Token. He takes each of them, first by the Masters Grip then by the past Masters Grip, from thence with a sudden Jerk unto the pit of his arm, and raises him: (the brother doing the same reciprocally,) as if out of the Arch; pronouncing at the same time

Grand Word.} O! J.....h!. The Grand Master says, "We raise you my dear Brethren sublime and perfect Masters, and may you, as full reward for your fidelity, zeal, fervor and Constancy, ever prove yourselves worthy of the high Honor confered on, and sacred Trust now reposed in you."

The History.

When *Artaxerxes*, King of the Medes, who is called in Scripture *Darius* the Mede; (the Uncle and father in Law of *Cyrus* the great) died: *Cyrus* ascended the throne of the Persian Empire as sole

[394]

Monarch, which was 536 years before the Christian Æra, and ended the seventy years, Babilonish Captivity. *Cyrus* Issued a proclamation through all his Dominion, saying, "The Lord God of heaven and Earth, has given me all the Kingdoms of the Earth, and has charged me to build him a House at Jerusalem in Judea; who is there among you of all his people, his God be with him, and let him go up to Jerusalem, and he shall be furnished out of the Kings Treasury with every thing necessary." Upon this proclamation, they gathered together about 42,000 of the people of Israel, who went up under the direction of *Zerobabel* as their Governor, and *Ezra*, and *Nehemiah* his Deputies. Cyrus delivered unto *Shashbazar*, whom he appointed Treasurer, all the holy Vessels belonging to the Temple of Jerusalem which *Nebuchadnezer* took out of the Temple of Jerusalem: he also furnished *Zerobabel* with letters to his Governors and Lieutenants in *Syria*, to furnish them with every thing necessary on their Journey and one in particular to *Savalt*, the Horite, Governor of *Samaria*, ordering him to pay the tribute of his province into the hands of *Shashbazar* the treasurer for the use of the building of the Temple. The *Samaritans* were a mixture of *Judaism* and Heathenism, and implacable Enemies of the Jews: Who when they arrived at Jerusalem, many of the *Samaritans* came to them saying, "We worship the same God you do, therefore we will assist you in Building of his Temple," which offer was accepted by them; but instead of forwarding the works

[395]

they did every thing to obstruct them; And *Cyrus* being then employed in the Egyptian and Cytherian Wars, they found means to corrupt his Ministers in Lebanon, and they never paid those Tributes which *Cyrus* ordered: though very little was done in *Cyru's* Reign. *Cyrus* died 529 years before the Birth of *Christ*; when he was succeeded by his son *Cambyses* (who in the book of Daniel is called *Ahasueras*) who was of a cruel Temper, and then engaged in the Egyptian and Etheopian wars: during the 8 years and 5 months of his Reign, the Enemies of Judah takeing advantage of those disorders in the Persian Court, and still more corrupting the Ministers of Cambyse's they almost put an entire stop to the works at Jerusalem, as well of the City as of the Temple; by not paying in the first place, the tribute which was allotted them by *Cyrus*, and still more by insulting them even in their private works; which obliged the masons to provide themselves with arms of defence as well as with working tools. The Jews were then in a low and miserable Condition; such was the state of affairs when *Cambyses* died on his return to Persia to punish the Usurper *Smyrdas* the Magre, who is called in scripture *Atachshastra* or *Axtaxeres* who looked like the true *smyrdas* the second son of *Cyrus*, whom *Cambyses* caused to be murdered; Smyrda's brother a Chief of the Magre and Governor of *Persepolis*, finding the Persians much displeased with *Cambyses* for his

[396]

Cruelties, gave out that *smyrdas* the son of *Cyrus* was still alive, and presenting in publick his Brother *Smyrdas*, who looked very much like the true *Smyrdas*, dressed in Royal robes and proclaimed him King of Persia. As soon as the Enemies of the Jews heard of the Death of Cambyses and the action, or the Usurpation of *Smyrdas*, they Immediately forbid the works going on at Jerusalem, and he willing to oblige the Governor in order to Establish himself firmly on the Persian throne, readily granted them their request and a full stop was put to the work, during his Usurpation, and it was not properly resumed, untill the 2d year of the reign of *Darius*. *Smyrdas* having reigned only 8 months after the death of *Cambyses* he being found out as an Imposter was murdered by a Conspiracy formed by the Chief Lords of *Persia*; and the above mentioned *Darius* the son of *Hystaspes* was promoted to the throne, by the other 6 Lords according to their agreement. At the news of the advancement of *Darius* to the Persian throne, Nehemiah who was very Intimate with him, and a great favorite of that Monarch, Immediately set out for the Persian Court in Order to solicit of *Darius* the full permission of continuing and finishing the rebuilding of the Temple. The hope of Nehemiah's success gave the Jews that were at Jerusalem great spirits, and they immediately resumed their works, though very slowly, and with such

[397]

secrecy, that they would admit no stranger into the Temple under any pretence whatsoever: It was with them a Custom on such Occasions to blindfold every person, that the works might not be seen; which were carried on at that time, fearing greatly Imposters, and their being by that means betrayed. In the situation of being hoodwinked every person was brought to the Grand Master and Intendant of the Buildings for an Examination and if he could prove himself a true Judamite, he was admitted amongst the workmen, otherwise he was obliged to depart without perceiving any thing: In the mean time *Nehemiah* arrived at the Persian Court, and being graciously received by *Darius*, was immediately appointed Cup bearer to that great King. *Darius* was at this period of his reign so much taken up in Establishing himself firmly on the Throne of *Persia*, That *Nehemiah* could get not proper Oppertunity to solicit him in behalf of his nation and the finishing of the Temple untill the beginning of the 2d year of his Reign; whereon *Hanania* came from Jerusalem and told him the deplorable state of the Temple and City which made him exceedingly melancholy: *Darius* perceiving him in that situation as he served him with the Cup at his Royal Table, and that he was in great affliction, hastily, but through a zeal of sincere friendship, taxed *Nehemiah* with Insin-

[398]

-cerity and a doubt of his Princely regard for him: But the Cup bearer conscious of no crime or disposition to offend the King, or disaffection to his Royal person, humbly told him the cause of his melancholy proceeded from the deplorable Condition which his brethren at Jerusalem and the Temple of the living God were in: And then solicited for the Confirmation of the Decree given in favor of the Jews by his predecessor *Cyrus*. On being made acquainted with these particulars, *Darius* immediately granted his Petition; and appointed him Lieutenant Governor under Zerobabel: Upon attaining this favor, *Ne–hemiah* directly returned with his Companion to Jerusalem. At his arrival there they again began their works publickly; When *Savalt* and his Adherents heard of it, they tried to repel it by main force but the Jews being so well on their guard, they could make no impression on them: finding all their efforts ineffectual they applied to *Tatnai*, the Governor of Assyria, and to *Shatherbuznai* of lesser Syria, who made it their business to come to Jerusalem and demanded by what authority they had continued the Building of the Temple, they were shewed the decree of *Cyrus* on which the Governors transmitted a Copy of it to *Darius*, for the purpose of being informed if such a Decree had ever been granted to the Jews. As soon as *Darius* received the letter containing the Copy of the Decree, he caused search to be made

[399]

among the Archives at *Ecbatane*; when the Decree which Cyrus had caused to be made in favour of the Jews and the Temple was found. On which Darius not only gave a full Confirmation of the same to the Governor of Assyria but also to the commander *Satherbuznai* of lesser Syria, and directed them strictly to pay their respective tributes unto the hands of the Grand Treasurer at Jerusalem for the use of the Building of the Temple, and sacrifices for the welfare of the King and his family, with a promise of punishing the disturbers or Interrupters of the work in future. One day as 3 zealous Masons were cleaning the foundation over which the sanctum sanctorum used to be, they came to a hollow place and after some search they discovered an Arch covered, and with great labour they moved the keystone thereof with their pick axes; which when they had done, there appeared to them an opening wide Enough for a man to descend, they accordingly agreed among themselves, that one of them should be tied with a rope round the waist and that the other 3 brethren should carefully let him down. It was then high noon, the sun in its meridian and its rays darting perpendicularly down, so that the Brother who had descended could plainly distinguish the objects which were about him: In the first place he discovered a large square box, on one side were those three names in large golden letters S:K:I. H:K:T. and H:A. On the top stood a

[400]

Triangular Pedestal, on the upper part of which was placed a Golden triangular polished plate, with the Letters I^{B}L engraved thereon: on which he called to his 2 Companions who were above, and told them of the Occurrence which had recently happened, and of the previous treasures which he had found; they being amazed at what they had heard, desired him to send them up, which he did, by tying them to the end of the rope, and they were drawn up with great safety, except the pedestal with the golden triangular plate affixed to it which he held in his arms: He then on the return of the rope, tied it round his waist, and his 2 Companions hauled him up together with the triangular pedestal and Golden plate which he still held in his Arms. As soon as he came near the opening, they found it very difficult to lift him up by the aid of the rope alone; therefore one of the brethren took him by the wrist after the manner of the Master's Grip, in order to help him out, but that failing to effect the purpose of raising him up; he advanced further to the Grip of the past Master, and that also proving insufficient, he again Essayed a further hold by passing up to the Elbow; and not finding even that to be equal to the purpose of bringing his Companion to the surface of the Earth, he griped him under his arm pit, and with a sudden jerk lifted him out of the Arch; on which happening to look at the same time upwards, the rays of the sun striking perpendicularly in his Eyes, and not being possibly able to bear them, he clapped his right hand over his eyes, and then viewing the

[401]

pedestal, he perceived the 3 letters engraved thereon which filled him with great admiration and Joy and he cried out, "Oh! J.....h," as soon as he had been taken out of the Arch. The immediately reported to the Captain of the Guards the whole of their fortunate Adventure, and he went with them to *Zerobabel*, the Grand Master; and *Ezra* and Nehemiah his Deputies, who were then with him: after hailing them, he said, "Hail Puissant Grand Master! these 3 Zealous brethren were working in the house of the Lord, without fee or reward, they accidentally met with a key stone, and after much toil and trouble in removing it, they found an opening, when by the means of a rope, 2 of the brethren, let this their brother down, and these are the things which they have there found." The different articles were then delivered to the Grand Master and his two Deputies, who after having examined them very attentively consulted some time; when they arose in a kind of Extasy, lifted up their hands and eyes to heaven and with Admiration and cried out, "Glory be to the great J.....h, we have now found that which has been so long lost and in vain searched for." The Grand Master then addressing them said "Dear Brethren take this as the first reward of your fidelity, zeal, fervor and Constancy (and gave each of them a Garland or Crimson Collar, with a Golden

Trowel suspended to it, and a white wand or Staff) as a Token of freedom and to have an easy access at all times in every part of the Temple": We will

[402]

further consider in what manner to reward you more amply: After the Grand Master had again consulted some time together with his Deputies: He spoke to them thus, "My dear Brethren I must acquaint you, that you have found a most precious Treasure, besides a true Copy of the Law, and a direction to the arts and sciences; you have also found a large Quantity of precious stones and other Articles: but the greatest is this gold triangular plate, on which is engraved the Initial letters of the true Masters word, which has been lost by the death of our respectable Grand Master Hiram Abiff who was trecherously murdered by the ruffian fellow Crafts, and now found and restored by you my respectable Brethren and Zealous Masons: Happy for yourselves and us, ye have now fulfilled the prophecy of the prophet Haggai, who says, "The Glory of the second Temple, shall be far greater than that of the first." I give you therefore that which you have found, and raise you to the Degree of a sublime and perfect Master," which they accordingly did, after creating them Knights of the Royal Arch and investing them with a Dagger, and Trowel, that they may defend with one hand, that which they began with the other. In this manner the Masters word was found, after it had been lost 488 years, since the death of our Grand Master Hiram Abiff. This Restoration happened in the second year of Dariu's Reign, which was five hundred and Eighteen years before the Christian Æra.

The End of History.

[403]

The Lecture

Q: – 1st Brother Conductor are you a Grand Elect, perfect and Sublime Mason?

A: – I am hail Puissant.‡ I have seen the golden triangular plate, with the Letters engraved thereon, and I know their explanation.

Q: – 2d By what means did you obtain the favour of being raised a sublime and perfect Master?

A: – By my zeal; fervor and Constancy, and the great services I rendered the nation in General and the Craft in particular. I had been recently created Knight of the Royal Arch, and as a full reward for my Labour and fidelity, I was immediately afterwards raised to the sublime Degree of perfection.

‡ As before, the words "hail Puissant" are a phonetic error for "All Puissant."

Q: – 3d What were those services you rendered the Nation in General and the Craft in particular?

A: – In discovering the Royal Arch and the precious treasure therein.

Q: – 4th How did you discover them and at what time?

A: – By the direction of providence at high 12 O Clock at noon: when in Company with 2 Zealous Brethren we were removing the rubbish from the ruinous foundation, under which the Sanctum sanctorum formerly stood, throwing down our pick axes with Intent to go and refresh ourselves, we perceived a hollow sound under us, and being curious to know from whence it proceeded, we applied ourselves to a search, and takeing up our working Tools, after some time carefully looking about, we discovered a ring which led to a vaulted place, closed with 3 large

[404]

key stones, which with considerable labour and Difficulty we removed and found a deep Arch underneath.

Q: – 5th How did you descend into the Arch?

A: – I was let down by my Companions, by the help of a long rope tied round my waist.

Q: – 6th How came you to see in that subteraneous dark Arch?

A: – The sun being at its meridian, darted down its refulgent rays, and enabled me to distinguish the objects around me.

Q: – 7th What did you find there?

A: – A large square marble Base, on which lay a roll of parchment; a Considerable Treasure of Gold, a quantity of precious stones, and a triangular pedestal, with a gold triangular plate thereon.

Q: – 8th How did you dispose of these things?

A: – I tied every thing I could remove to the rope in a proper and secure manner, (except the pedestal) and my 2 Companions above, drew them up, and the pedestal I brought up with me.

Q: – 9th Why did you not send up the pedestal with the rest of the things?

A: – Because there was something on the golden plate animating, which made me loth to part with it.

Q: – 10. Did you know then what was on the Golden plate?

A: – No; only the letters engraved thereon were so brilliant that it convinced me there was something in, or about it, which made me unwilling to part with it.

Q: – 11. How did you ascend out of the Arch?

A: – After every thing had been hauled up, I tied the rope

[405]

again round my waist, and takeing the pedestal with the golden triangular plate thereon, in my arms, I was drawn up by my two Companions.

Q: – 12. Did you find it as easy to ascend as to descend?

A: – No; for after they brought me up to the head of the vault, the lift was too heavy for them; therefore one of my Companions took me by the wrist after the manner of the Masters Grip, in Order to help me out, but that failing to effect the purpose <of> raising me up; he advanced further to the Grip of the Past Master and that also proving insufficient, he again Essayed a further hold by passing up to the Elbow, and not finding even that to be equal to the purpose of bringing me up to the surface of the Earth, he griped me under my arm pit, and with a sudden Jerk lifted me out of the Arch.

Q: – 13. What did you see when you cam out of the Vault?

A: – I lifted up my Eyes to heaven, humbly and with a grateful heart, to return thanks to the Almighty: When the rays of the sun struck so forcibly in my eyes that I was forced to clap my hands over them, and cried out O! Jehovah!

Q: – 14. What made you mention this most sacred name?

A: – Because having cast my eyes on the golden Triangular plate which rested on the top of the Pedestal, I perceived the Letters which compose that holy and divine name engraved thereupon. This naturally filled my heart with Joy and veneration, and the letter J, inspired me with being the Initial of that sacred word, and I could not in the rapture of heart

[406]

I was in, forbear invoking it.

Q: – 15th After you returned out of the Arch what do you do then?

A: – We reported every thing we had met with, had seen and done, to the Captain of the Guards, who conducted my two Companions and myself to the Grand Master Zerobabel and his Deputies, to whom we related all that happened, and delivered all we had found.

Q: – 16. What did the Grand Master and his Deputies do, and what did they say on that Occasion?

A: – They seemed to be greatly surprized, and after examining every thing very attentively, but more particularly the Triangular golden plate on the pedestal, they arose in an extasy of Joy, lifting up their hands and Eyes to heaven, in devout Admiration exclaiming "Glory be to the Great J.....h, we have found that which has been so long lost, and in vain searched for."

Q: – 17. Did the Grand Master do anything else?

A: – He presented each of us with a Garland or Crimson Collar with a Golden trowel appended thereto and a white wand as the first reward for our fidelity and zeal, and promised to consider how to reward us more amply.

Q: – 18. And did you ever receive any other reward?

A: – Yes; the most glorious one, for we were recently afterwards created Knights of the Royal Arch and raised to the Degree of Grand Elect and perfect Masters.

Q: – 19. Why do you call it the Royal Arch?

A: – Because the Arch was erected by our two Royal Grand Masters Solomon King of Israael and Hiram

[407]

King of Tyre assisted by Hiram Abiff our respectable but unfortunate Grand Master.

Q: – 20. How can you prove this?

A: – By the Inscription on one side of the marble base found in the Arch, on which were wrote in gold the following letters, S:K:I.—H:K:T. and HA.

Q: – 21. When was that Arch built?

A: – At the time of the Building of the first Temple, and finished a little before the Completion thereof.

Q: – 22. How came you to know of that Circumstance?

A: – By the Inscription on the second side of the marble base.

Q: – 23. By whom was it built?

A: – By 27 select Masons, chosen by the 3 Grand selected Masters, from among the Giblimites, the most expert and virtuous masons amongst all the different workmen, as appears by the Inscription on the third side of the marble base.

Q: – 24. Explain to me on what account it was built?

A: – As a repository for the greatest secrets of Masonry in case there should be a doubt of their safety or any apprehension of their being either lost or in danger by the death of any of the 3 Grand Masters before they were bestowed on any others, (as it really happened;) Or when they should return to their Country, from captivity, if such a melancholy event should happen, to find a true Copy of their Law, which would certainly be corrupted during such

[408]

an unfortunate period; also a direction and knowledge of the arts and Sciences, which if in a like perilous situation would certainly be prejudiced or lost. And in the last place to deposit a treasure to forward any after Establishment

Q: – 25. How was you admitted into this Royal Chapter?

A: – By 3, 5, 7 and 9, which gained me admittance.

Q: 26. How was you received?

A: – By the 5 points of fellowship.

Q: – 27. Why so my brother?

A: – To signify that I will go hand in hand with my Brethren in forwarding their works; to stand by them in dangers, and support them in adversity; to keep their secrets, but more particularly those of the Royal arch, and be the same to them behind their backs as before their faces: this being the good conduct which every brother should display one to the other.

Q: – 28. How did you proceed further?

A: – I was strictly Examined by the Deputy Grand Masters towards my qualifications, and when they found me qualified, they sent me to the Grand Master for further examination and Instruction: to him I proved myself a true Judamite, on which I was conducted through 8 of the covered Arches, and then received a solemn Obligation in the 9th or last Arch.

Q: – 29. When you first was received in this Chapter had you the free enjoyment of your five senses?

A: – No; I was hoodwinked and continued in that situation untill I had forced myself with some difficulty through a certain narrow place.

Q: – 30. What did you see when you was brought to the Light?

A: – A fleshy Arch, beneath an Artificial one, with the

[409]

representation of the Sun at high Meridian over it.

Q: – 31. What did all that signify?

A: – It serves emblimatically to Instruct us, that we are all flesh; that we are frail and weak; that we must one day or the other yield to nature, and drop into the silent grave; and lastly that we must (or ought) to qualify ourselves whilst living, to enable us to receive the great light of the Divinity after our death, by purity of heart virtuous deeds and good works.

Q: – 32^{d} What signifies the Trowel appended to your Collar?

A: – We are by that badge or Jewel of our order Instructed that as the Trowel conveys mortar and Cements many thousand Individual stones into a solid or lasting body, so are we in like manner to convey good deeds and services to each other, in Order to cement mankind, but particularly brother Masons together.

Q: – 33^{d} What signifies the Dagger?

A: – It represents the Idea or situation which the Royal Arch Masons were in, at the building of the second Temple, who were necessitated at the same time they were pursuing their work with one hand to hold this Instrument of defence in the other, in order to repel those who attempted to give them disturbance: In a moral sense it furnishes us with this useful lesson of Instruction; that we should punish those who would wish to interrupt the cement and Union we have formed amongst ourselves by the emblem of the Trowel.

Q: – 34th How old are you?

[410]

A: – Two, Six, Twelve and Thirteen.

Q: – 35. Explain them to me?

A: – In the second year of the Reign of King Darius was the Royal Arch discovered; In the sixth year of that King was the Temple finished, and Consecrated in the Twelfth month called Adar and on the thirteenth day of that month: In commemoration of which we annually keep that day solemn.

Q: – 36. What O Clock is it?

A: – It is night and time for refreshment and rest

Gr^{d} Mr Since it is night and time for refreshment and rest, Give the brethren due notice, that I am going to close this Chapter, and request their Assistance.

Conductor. Strikes three times.

Junior Deputy Grand Master, strikes five times.

Senior Deputy Grand Master strikes seven times.

Hail Puissant Grand Master strikes Twelve times, in all twenty seven times.

The Conductor then says, "Brethren take notice that the Grand Master, Hail Puissant is going to close this Chapter, and requests your assistance."

Then all the brethren join their hands as at the Opening of this Chapter, and it is Closed in the same manner.

Gr^{d} M^{r} says, "I declare this Royal Arch Chapter closed and it accordingly stands closed untill our next regular or Ordinary meeting"—and strikes 1 blow—which is answered by the Senior Deputy Grand Master, Junior Deputy Grand Master, and the

[411]

Conductor, All the brethren clap with their hands 3, 5, 7 and 12. And then salute the Grand Master with the hailing sign, and then the

Lodge is Closed.

Apron. The Apron is to [be] lined with deep red and bordered with yellow and red, (the flap red,) in the middle thereof a Triangle with these Letters ⸸ B L on the Æra of the Apron an Arch, open at the Top with the Meridian sun over it, darting its rays down into the Arch, at the bottom of the Arch a base with the pedestal, and a roll on it, on each side of the Arch a hand out of a Cloud, in one a Trowel in the other a defensive Dagger.

Order. The ribbon is a dark red, watered about 4 inches broad, bordered with yellow, and to be worn from the right shoulder to the left hip, to which must be suspended a Trowel and Dagger.

Gloves. The Gloves red, bordered with yellow.

The End.

[412]

Grand Master Ecose. N° 3.

Reception of a Scottish Elder Master.

First a blue lodge of a Master is Opened, the Candidate is then proposed and vouched for, after which the Lodge is closed and the Candidate is led out of it.

Form of the Lodge.

The high and Exalted Grand Master in the Chair the Grand Officers and all the Knights is seated round a Table covered with green cloth: The Grand Master from the Chair addresses the brethren in the following manner. "Most honorable Knights and Brethren; I have resolved to open this day in the name of the Almighty Grand Architect of heaven and earth: this our high Exalted Lodge, that we may propose, consider and undertake one thing or another for the good of mankind in general and this our honorable Order in particular. But the present Exalted scottish Knights, and my Dear brethren, arm yourselves with fortitude towards the scottish Chair, to enable this our Assembly to consider strictly with me, everything: that we might never resolve or undertake anything of which we should have cause to repent; at first, let your Knightly steadiness assist me in the opening of this Lodge.

To Open.

Q: – What is the Duty of the Grand Senior Warden in Opening the scottish Lodge?

The Senior Warden rises from his seat with his hat on, draws his sword and Answers, "To see that this Grand Lodge is utmostly secured, that it may so remain."

[413]

Then the high Exalted Grand Master orders the Grand Senior Warden to do his duty in every point The Senior Warden then goes out to examine if every thing is in security; after which he returns, stands by the chair with his sword drawn and makes his report to the Grand Master.

Then the Grand Master asks the Junior Warden (who likewise stands up and draws his sword,)

Q: – How much is the number of our Exalted scottish Lodge?
A: – It is four.
Q: – How much does 3 and 4 make?
A: – It makes 7 compleat.
Q: – What signifies the number 7?
A: – Because it is the noblest and most compleat number.
Q: – How does the wind blow?
A: – From the 4 Quarters of the Globe.

Then the High Exalted Grand Master, asks the Grand secretary (who likewise stands up and draws his sword)

Q: – Is every thing in readiness belonging to the opening of our Grand scottish Lodge?
A: – Yes most Exalted Grand Master every thing requisite to this Grand and solemn undertaking is in readiness.

Then all the Knights submissively beg, that the Lodge may then be opened.

Q: – What weather is it?

[414]

A: – (By all the Knights) A most glittering starred sky.
Q: – What is it O Clock?
A: – It is high midnight.

Upon which the most Exalted says, "My Grand scotch Masters, Exalted Knights and Brethren: I declare this Lodge to be opened, and every brother will conduct himself accordingly."

Then the Grand Senior Warden says, "Noble Knights and brethren Assembled, Let us not forget the duty we owe towards the most Exalted Grand Master." Upon which all the Knights rises up draw their swords, holding them in their left hands take off their hats with their right hand and saluting the Grand Master, the whole body at one motion, takeing the time from the Grand Master of Ceremonies, by lowering the points of their swords at the same time bowing their heads very low, then putting their hats again, sheathing their swords and giving the common Scotch Sign, then every one returns to his place.

Order of Reception.

The Grand Master of Ceremonies goes out, orders the Candidates hands to be washed, his shoes taken off and blindfolds his eyes, gives 4 knocks at the door which is opened to him by the Junior Warden who at the Entering of the Candidate, throws a golden coloured rope with 4 knots in it, round his Neck. N:B: The knots must be made in such a manner that in one pull they must be opened, and during the opening of the Lodge, the Candidate must lay in the Anti Chamber on the Ground.

[415]

After the Candidate is entered with the preceding Ceremonies, he is placed between Boaz and Jachin. Then the most Exalted speaks to him as follows.

Gr^{d} M^{r} My worshipful Brother, you desire to become a Grand Scottish Master?

A: – I do most Cordially.

Gr^{d} M^{r} I must inform you my brother that your desire is of a very high nature. Are you perfect in the common Blue Masters Degree?

A: – Yes I am.

Gr^{d} Mr Then give the Signs Tokens and words to the Grand Senior Warden. (he gives them)

Gr^{d} Mr Dear brother, since you have proved your knowledge of the duties in the blue Masters part, to our satisfaction, I will now instruct you in the Mysteries and duties of the Scottish Master provided you have confidence to go through the same. An Elder scottish Master is a high, priestly Order my brother, through the great Circumspection of his dutys, his works, and his knowledge is heavens high priest: different from the Blue Master or Mason of the 3 lower Degrees, wherein your title now was but a common matter, by which you was only taught to venerate the Godhead, under the name of the most Great, most wise, and Almighty Architect. But an Elder scottish Master must pay a more deep and feeling veneration to the Almighty God. That due veneration we are taught by the great teacher and declarer of our holy Order

[416]

(where he says) "The true worshiper will worship him in spirit and in truth," further he saith, "And they shall be unto me a people and I will be unto them their God." The first mentioned veneration is in common to all men and brethren as directed by common sense; but the latter belongs only to them who wholly dedicates their hearts, for the dwelling place of the great and merciful God the Grand Architect of the Universe, which is only practised amongst the true Scotch Masters. Will you my dear brother remain by your former way of worshiping, or are you resolved to begin your veneration in spirit and truth, and henceforward to be Instructed and directed by the System and practice of the scottish Masters." The Candidate says, "Yes, I will most Cordially."

Gr^{d} Mr Have you during the time of your blue Mastership duly and faithfully observed the following Articles.

1st Have you paid due veneration to the most Great most wise and mighty Architect?

Candidate answers, Yes, I always have.

2^{ndly} Have you Improved yourself by flying from vice and practising Virtue?

Candidate answers, Yes, I have.

3dly Did you study the Industrious labours and ~~the~~ the useful precepts of the wise?

Candidate answers, I did most carefully.

4^{thly} Did you always live peaceably amongst the Masters, and did you at all times defend their rights from the rebellious Crafts?

[417]

Candidate answers, I did to the utmost of my power.

Gr^{d} Mr Well my Dear brother I am happy to find, that you are worthy of being received among the Elder Masters But I must first ask whether you have resolution and fortitude, to undertake the holy work of the 4 Masters? As this work is more Exalted and greatly differs from the work you have hitherto been used to; for untill now you used the square and Compass only for Mathematicks, Geometry and Exact Drafts of Architecture. But in the scottish Masonry the square and Compass, is quite to another piece of work Employed; for as hitherto You have only worked on single and outward building, and make but an Imperfect Draft of the world: but by the scottish work you will bring forth the most shining and brilliant materials (yea sufficient for raising a whole world.) Will you most sacredly and solemnly swear and promise to keep the mysteries of Scotch Masonry in everlasting silence? And for ever conceal, nor directly or Indirectly deliver or Communicate them, or any part thereof, to the brethren of the blue Order, or to any in the world besides?

The Candidate answers, I do most cordially consent to all the preceeding Injunctions, and do most solemnly promise to observe them.

Then the Grand Master, Orders the Grand Junior Warden to lead the Candidate out of the porch, into the out Court of the Temple, from thence into the Temple, or sanctuary, and then into the sanctum

[418]

Sactorum, and from thence to conduct him unto the three Golden Basons.

The Grand Junior Warden leads the Candidate 4 times round the Lodge, and as often as the Candidate comes before the Altar or Pedestal; The Grand Master from the Chair, gives 4 scottish knocks, and gives the common scotch sign, which Sign is repeated by all the brethren standing round: Then the Grand Master says, "Oh! how great and glorious is the presence of the Almighty God! which gloriously shines from between the Cherubims;" after the second 4 knocks he says, "We adore thee—Oh! Great and might J.....h! whose Existance is from the beginning to Eternity; Glorious be his great and mighty name for ever and ever!" at the third 4 knocks he says, "How adorable and astonishing are the rays of that great and glorious light, which sent forth its brilliant beams, from the holy Ark of Alliance and Covenant." At the fourth and last 4 knocks, The Grand Master says, "Let us with the deepest reverence and duty adore the fountain of the glorious spirit, who is the most merciful and beneficient ruler of the Universe and all the Creatures it contains." After this the Candidate is led to the Altar where he kneels down on both knees and takes the following Obligation.

The Obligation.

I: A:B: of my own free will and accord, do most solemnly and sincerely swear in this most sacred and holy Temple; In the presence of the most

[419]

brilliant and glorious rays infused by the presence of the most Terrible most Puissant, and merciful and Almighty God, the Grand Architect of the Universe, and before this Right Worshipful and Exalted Chapter, Assembled of Grand Scotch Masters and Valliant Knights of Saint Andrews: that I will always hail for ever conceal and never reveal, any part or parts of the Mysteries of the Scotch Masonry which I am to receive just now or shall be Instructed in any time hereafter, to any of the brethren of the blue Order of Saint Johns Lodge, more the less to any prophane person in the world besides. I furthermore swear, that I will never give this Degree and order of Grand Scotch Master and its Mysteries to a brother of the blue Order, singly by himself, unless properly and duly authorized for the same, and the brother to whom it is, so given being duly qualified to receive it, by having gone regularly and duly through the preceeding high Degrees of sublime Masonry, and at least having regularly served as a Master in the Chair of a Regular Constituted Lodge of the Order of Saint John. All this I solemnly and sincerely promise with a steady resolution to keep, and in failure thereof, I invoke that all the Curses may be fastened on my soul, and that I might be an everlasting example of a Cursed wretch to all mankind in future ages. I promise farther, to redouble my zeal and friendship towards my brethren, more particularly towards

[420]

my brethren scotch Masters; that I will heartily and sincerely love them, that I will assist them with my Counsel and support them with my power, even it should be attended with a probability of the loss of my property, my honor, or my life, as far as lies in my power, and Consistant with my own preservation. So help me Oh God! and keep me stedfast in this my most solemn and sacred Obligation, Amen! Amen! Amen! Amen! the Candidate kisses the book four times.

The Candidate is then carried back into the west where he is placed between the two Grand Wardens when the Grand Master from the Chair speaks to him as follows. "My dear brother, Do you desire now to see that great and Glorious light of our Temple." The Candidate answers, "Yes; I am desirous. Upon which the Junior Grand Warden unfolds the bandage from his Eyes, when he beholds the Glory of Solomons Temple; and more particularly he then perceives the rays of the flaming Star which is suspended over the head of the Grand Master of Solomons Chair. Then the Grand Master speaks to him as follows "Do you see my dear brother the glorious light which so brilliantly shines, between the Cherubims, from the Ark the seat of Mercy? The Candidate Answers "I see with Joy the most glorious light.

The Grand Master then advances to the new admitted brother with his drawn sword in his hand which all the brethren likewise do. The Grand

[421]

Master then speaks to him as follows, "My dear Brother this, and all the swords of the Scottish Knights shall deprive you of your life in any part of the Globe, in case you should be so Unconscionable a wretch as to disclose or discover the least of the secret Mysteries of the Scottish Knights. But I can Assure you as long as you are true and Constant to your promise and Obligations, that all the valiant Knights will stand by you, protect and rescue you out of all Impending Dangers, even at the risque of their honor, property and life, and their swords must defend you as long as you remain virtuous, true and Stedfast to your trust and Obligations, and prove yourself a true, as well as Valiant Knight. And they will finish you whenever you prove otherwise. I wish you a great deal of Joy in this your Exalted station and the honorable Degree you have arrived at; May the great J.....h assist you to persevere in these most solemn and sacred Engagements, that you may fulfill them in every particular point. After which the new Initiated brother is taught to make the 4 scottish Steps Viz^{t} from the West to the South, from thence to the East and then to the North, and to the West again, which is fully explained to him afterwards in the Draft. The Grand Master of the Ceremonies gives him the signs Tokens and Words.

1st SIGN Is called the Common Scotch sign, and which is to carry your right hand half clinched to your left

[422]

thigh, as if you was going to draw a sword or dagger, then in that position draw up your hand to your throat, as if you would rip open your belly.

2d SIGN. Is to bring your hands across your forehead, in the form of a Saint Andrews Cross, the right hand uppermost, your fingers extended and forming a square with your thumbs, then bring them in that position under your Chin, at the same time clinching your fingers, this sign performed after this manner represents a death's head and Cross bones.

TOKEN. Is to put your right hand on a brothers neck, the left hand to his arm pit, and then do, or act as if you endeavored to raise each other.

PASS WORD. Is *Gabaon*, signifying a River.

GRAND WORD, Is J.....h!

A Knight of saint Andrew, who wishes to make himself known to another, takes his sword or dagger in the left hand in such a manner as if he was going to give a back stroke, crossing at the same time his right hand over the left in the form of a Saint Andrews Cross the fingers clinched, holding them upwards as if he would hold some working tools in his hand N:B: the first part of the second Sign alludes to the Priests in the Temple, who always put their hands to their foreheads, with their fingers and thumbs extended as to keep off the rays, whenever they gave their Benediction; this Ceremony is still observed in the Synagouges. Then the Grand Master Invests him with the Apron, at the same time explains to him the meaning of the green Colour Vizt That a scottish Master in all his works and undertakings must put

[423]

his Trust in Almighty God, and only from him alone success can be hoped. He gives him then a naked sword in his left hand and a Trowel in his right: fixing his hands in the form of a Saint Andrews Cross holding the sword from his right in such a position as if he was going to give a back thrust which signifies by this Sign that the Knight of Saint Andrew having carried on their works, and wars against the Saracens, with the swords in their hands, they have forwarded and protected the workmen, as always having the working tool in one hand and the sword in the other. The Grand Master puts up his sword to his side, and the new Initiated brother is then placed between the 2 Grand Wardens; Then the Grand Master gives him the following Explanation of the Draft before him. "It is well known to you my Dear brother, that to the High Priest in Solomons Temple, the Temple the porch, with its out Court, the sanctuary, and Sanctum Sanctorum was open to him, and since you are a Grand Scottish Master, and of course in high Priestly order my brother, We must all have free access not only into the Porch, the out Court and the sanctuary, but even to the sanctum Sanctorum as a secret place for your works: you see also the whole Temple before your eyes, consider the consecrated out Court, and the 2 pillars, but they are now shortened and broken, the signification whereof you shall now know. Now behold the sanctuary; you must know my brother

[424]

that in the Sanctum Sanctorum of Solomons Temple, there was nothing else but the Ark of Alliance and Covenant wherein were the two tables and the ten Commandments, also the blossomed rod of Aaron laid on the outside before it. The Ark of Alliance which was the mercy seat, was Incircled by two Cherubims, the godhead discovered himself to the high Priest in a stream of fire under a thick Cloud; the form of the ark which you see painted before you, serves a Knight of Saint Andrew, as an Emblem to adore the Invincible and Eternal J.....h! and sometime signifies that a Knight of Saint Andrew ought not alone to have the law of the Eternal God always engraved on his heart, but never should Contemplate, undertake or do any thing contrary to those laws and precepts. You have now my Dear brother as a Grand Scottish Master under the great and holy name of J.....h, to adore the Godhead in the bottom of your heart, and mind that such adoration and spiritual veneration surpasses greatly the common adoration of *Adonai*. The brazen sea and flaming star, are Emblems you meet here, but are not found in the Temple, but they are Hieroglyphic emblems of the Scotish works: The seven dots you see here does not signifie the seven fold arrangements of our Order as it does in the lower Degrees of the blue Order of Saint John, but they signify in the physical works of the different kind of metals

[425]

and when you find otherwise the seven planets, besides other stars marked, it signifies the other mineral matters as well as the seven planets which should only be the real Solomonish; out of this you can conclude that the secret knowledge of the Grand scottish Master points to the mixing and Changing the different materials: that you may conceive a notion and understanding of this matter, you must mind that every thing in this world subsists out of 3 substances; the three substancial Mixtures are Salt [symbol], sulphur [symbol], and spirit [symbol]; the first Occasioned the firmness; the second the softness, and the third mixture the spiritual and vaporous particles: these 3 mixtures work together so forcibly, that in it Consists the true cause of its Changeing the different Metals: Out of the remarks of the three mixtures is to understood, the 3 golden basons; in the first was engraved an *M*, in the second a G, and in the third was not any engraving. The Initial Letters in the 2 first Basons, signifies in the hebrew language (alluding to the *M*,) *Milach*—which is in Hebrew Salt, and the G, *Gopherith*, which in hebrew signifies sulphur, and there being no engraving in the third bason, is from the cause or reason that the vaporous and flowing spirit has no Character of Letter to express it: from this Cause therefore none was there to be found. These three basons were in the time of the Crusades found by four elder Masters of Scotland in the ruins of the Temple in a

[426]

square hollow Corner stone, and in memory of those four Elder Masons from Scotland, all the Elder Masons are called Elder Scottish Masters to this day. The before mentioned three headed substantial Matters by which you can facilitate the changing of the Metals, must be done through the five points or rules of the Scottish Mastership. The first master point shews us the brazen sea, wherein must always be, rain water, and out of this rain water the scotch Masters Extracted the first matter which is the Salt 🜔, which salt must afterwards undergo a seven fold overhauling and Clarifying before it is properly prepared: this sevenfold Clarifying by which we must understand the steps of Solomon Temple and the brazen sea; the first point and rule of the scotch Masters serves us for an Emblem. So have you my brother likewise been ordered to put your foot on the same, after having prepared the first: The Second sunstantial matter namely Sulphur 🜍 must be out of the purest of Gold, to this must be added, purified and heavenly Salt 🜔, and this must be mixed as the heart directs; all this must be put in a vessel in the form of a ship, in which the mixture must remain like the ark of Noah 150 days, and to be brought into the first damp, warm degree of fire, that it may rot therein, in order to bring forth the mineral fermentation. This is the 2^{d} point and rule of the scottish Master, therefore you must for the 2^{d} time Set your foot on the Ark of Noah. The 3^{d} work consist in multiplying the said matter, by adding to them

[427]

quick flying spirit which is done through the water of the heavenly salt 🜔 as well as the salt 🜔 which must be daily put into it, and very carefully and strictly observed, not put too much or too little, for if you put too much to it, it will destroy that growing and multiplying substance, and if too little is put to it, the work will consume, and destroy itself and dwindle away, as not being of sufficient substance to preserve it. The third point and rule of the Scotch Master, gives us the Emblem of the Building of the Tower of Babel; this Emblem is represented thus by our Scotch brethren to shew us that by the Irregular and unproportionable Mixture, the work was stopped and the workmen could not proceed any further; therefore my Brother you must put for the third time your foot on this Tower, as this is the third point and work of the scotch Master: Now follows a fourth work which this Cubical Stone represents, and which stone is an equal square on all its sides, and will also fit on all sides as soon as the work is brought to its full extent of Multiplying: It must be first put into the third degree of fire, whereon it must receive a proportionable substance, and strength of the Metallick particles: On this Cubical stone, as the fourth point or rule of the Scottish Master, you must try brother for the 4th time to place your foot thereon. Then at the last follows the 5th work, which is to us discovered by the flaming Star: after the work is brought to a proportionable substance, the same must be brought into the fourth and

[428]

strongest degree of fire, whereon it must remain three times twenty seven hours, untill it is thoroughly glowing with fervent heat, by which means it becomes a bright and shining Tincture, and becomes fit to charge the lighter metals, whereof a 1000 part of lighter metals are tinctured; since this flaming star shews us the fifth and last point of the scottish Master, So you must my brother for the 5th and last time put your foot on it, by which you have compleated the 4th scottish Masters Ste These 5 different installments you have performed only Ceremonial, but you should go through those 5 Master points and rules in the practical performance, and with one part of a 1000 part Exchange, and Ennoble them; so you may truly say in the practical way that you are 1000 years old which we as yet can Commumicate not other ways to you than Ceremonial. This great and noble art has in the time of Solomon and afterwards, untill the time of the Crusades remained amongst the brotherhood and more particularly reigned in Jerusalem after our Enlightened and most Honorable and Respectable Grand Master Hiram was murdered by three vicious and Villianous fellow Crafts: that art was Intirely forgotten and destroyed: this event is represented by the 2 overthrown and broken pillars, of which the Posture of the Basis and the Columns are still standing, but part of the Columns, Chapiters and Architrives are still missing, which gives us to understand that not only the foundation to the divine art is already laid, but that they have been also reared and raised to a considerable height, only that the

[429]

true measure and perfect height of Exaltation is still wanting: Out of all this my brother you must draw the following observation; that whatever art or work your Inclination leads you to, if you wish to be an Expert working scottish Master, you must be attentive to the real physical knowledge thereof, that you may thereby learn the principals or handy Craft of Chymistry, and that you may be the more Expert and handy in the use of the square and Compass, which you likewise see here in the draft, to build and Erect Edifices whererin you may with exactness proceed to the Philosophical works. Lastly you will perceive a sorrowful Emblem of the Tragical History of your respectable Grand Master Hiram Abiff, nearly at your Entrance. The Rope round your neck which you wear, for the honor and Immortal memory of our Enlightened and Noble Grand Master, will be soon taken from you and I will in recompence thereof decorate you with a more brilliant and glittering token of a Jewel. Further you will here observe the Grave of our murdered and Respectable Grand Master with the sprig of Cassia fixed on it; this is to signify that our respectable Grand Master is buried in the holy and secret part of the Temple, likewise in the secret part of the scottish Mastership. Lastly I must inform you, that the scottish Masters through their great valour, they showed during the Crusades, were Associated with the scottish Knights of Saint Andrew they were honored with the Thistle, and were created Knights of the most honorable and Antient Order

[430]

of Knighthood, with all its formalities and fiery Ardor, which honor of Knighthood, I shall now Invest you with, as a reward for your valour, virtue fervor and Constancy. The new Initiated brother kneels down on a perfect square £, the Grand Master draws his naked sword over his back in the form of a Saint Andrews Cross, and says as follows.

1st I Create you Knight of the holy order of the great J.....h.

2d I create you Knight of the noble and honorable Order of Saint Andrews.

3d I create you Knight, Knight, Knight in the name of the most Grand, Worshipful, Scottish Elder Lodge and in the name of the whole Knighthood all over the Zenith of the Two Hemispheres.

N:B: at every Knighthood he confers on him, the Grand Master strikes him with the naked sword, over his forehead in the form of a saint Andrews Cross, all the Knights standing round the Knight brother (or Candidate) with their swords drawn during the Ceremony. Then the Grand Master raises him and kisses him 4 times, after which the Grand Master clothes him with the order, and says, "I decorate you, my Dear Brother with the Order of hope and Perfection"; after which follows the Consecration; which is thus performed.

The Grand Master puts both his hands on the head of the new Initiated brother, and says, "The Lord bless thee, and keep thee; the Lord make his face to shine upon thee; the Lord lift up the light of his Countenance upon thee, and give thee peace, Amen!" This benediction is said in a solemn Tone, as it is still practiced

[431]

in the synagouges on the festivals, by the Cohens, or the descendants of Aaron; after which the Initiated Knight makes himself known to all the Knights by giving them the Signs, Token and Words.

The Grand Orator makes then the following moral Declaration.

"To us my dear brethren as Grand Scottish Masters the Temple is open, and by our undertakings the whole work thereof is compleated; by this your care for the great preference we have to the Masters of the blue Order of Saint Johns Lodge to which it is only permitted to serve in the sanctuary, or in the middle part of the Temple: the 3 divisions of the Temple you observed here Viz[t] the out court of the sanctuary, and the Sanctum Sanctorum, signifies the 3 principals of our holy Order, which directs to the knowledge of Morality and teaches the most particular virtues which ought to be practised by mankind, therefore the 7 steps which leads up to the out Court of the Temple, is the Emblem of the seven fold lights we are in need of, before we ever can arrive to the height of knowledge, then in this consists the ultimate limits of our Order. Next to this we come to the Masonic pavement, which puts us in mind, that nature unpoluted; and men unperfect, takes to themselves so many different figures, as their disappointments, sorrows, and unperfectness drives them from one place to another, like these marble pavements, when put together by the hands of the artist, whose Colours and Arangements reflects now one way, and now the other. Also we find

[432]

our two pillars Boaz and Jachin, which signify strength and Establishment, but they are shortened and disfigured, because they have lost their Capitols, by the death of our most respectable Grand Master Hiram Abiff, now we will consider the table which is divided by three lines in the Length with a view to learn and understand the signification thereof. If we begin to the right, we find the Tower of Babel; It is well known that it was a foolish undertaking by men who were probably fearless of the Almighty God: This serves us as an Emblem, that we should never indulge ourselves with too high and Exalted notions, but that we must in all our undertakings and works, use the greatest foresight and Consideration with due moderation and at the same time it further Instructs us to be very careful and Circumspect; how we acted or attempted to act against the will of the

Great and mighty J.....h! that we may not like those inconsiderate men, find in our works (like those people) our destruction, our graves, and our Disanulation: Truly we find Comfort in the sprig of Cassia, upon the grave of our most Respectable Grand Master, Hiram Abiff for the errors commited by those who preceeded us; but this must not serve us for a security to enter again into such Idle matters. The moon is of itself but a Cold body, so that she can bring nothing forth from her own warmth, and this points to the imperfect state of mankind: the beauties of our order suffered also a two–fold shock; first by the burning of the

[433]

Babylonian tower and more by the Tragical end of our Respectable Master Hiram Abiff, for which the scottish Masters to remember that unhappy event (which is very affecting to the whole scottish Order) do represent the same. His death is by every true brother untill this day lamented, and who very humbly pray for the establishment of the order of J.....h: Let us now turn to the left, when you perceive the shortened pillar B: which leads us to the Ark of Noah. This signifies the wonderful escape and the Establishing of our order under a thousand dangers and difficulties, which is not unlike to the memorable Adventures, and dangers of our Godly fathers. The Cubic stone, signifies the Perfection of our Order as the Cube is the most regular body, equal on all sides, so is likewise the structure of our Order: If you consider its regularity, its unanimity, and its sacred connection, which is like the perfection of the Cube. Further we see the Draft of the Temple, as the most noble structure that ever Existed; which Almighty God had himself ordered and honored in a most particular manner, with his glorious presence, as a testimony of his favour, and of which we have the representation in our Assemblies. The sun signifies the former Glory of the Temple the fame of which was spread amongst all nations: The pillar J signifies the Establishment of the Order likewise suffered very much, but it is yet very large, and still makes

[434]

a very beautiful or brilliant appearance: It stands in a direct Line under the sun, the most heavenly and compleat body that we could choose. Now observe the middle road, whose steps leads us over, the Mosaic pavement, between the B: (strength) and the J, (Establishment,) to the brazen sea, where we must purify ourselves and wash off all pollutions, as well of those faults committed by unwarrantable deeds, as those by our Judgments and bad opinion; they both prevent us to arrive to the knowledge of the true word, and we must also be Clarified, and thoroughly purified from the bottom of our hearts, untill we can Contemplate with an unspotted heart, the flaming Star which is the Emblem of the Glory and Glorious Sheckaniah, before we are to approach the seat of the most Exalted Wisdom. The ark of Alliance and Covenant, wherein formerly the tables of the Law were deposited; serves us to remember that our heart is the present depository thereof, where those laws must be for ever engraved thereon. This Godly wisdom remained among the order unconsumed even in the most sorrowful periods. This we remark on the middle road, where not the least trait of Dimunition, shortning, darkness, or any remembrance of those sorrows are to be remarked: then God loved his Order and protected them openly, at a time when their destruction seemed to be nighest and unavoidable, he suffered them to fall that he might raise

[435]

them against with the greater Glory.

The Lecture.

Q: – 1st Are you a Scotch Master?

A: – I am of the old scottish, Worshipful brotherhood and acknowledged as such, being well acquainted with the Letters *M* and G.

Q: – 2d Where was you received in the Capacity of a scottish Master?

A: – In the Sanctum Sanctorum under the Cassia

Q: – 3d How did you come there?

A: – Through the porch, out Court and the sanctuary

Q: – 4th After you was received and brought to light, what did your perceive?

A: – I saw a Brazen sea.

Q: – 5th For what use was that Sea?

A: – To serve the scottish Masters, to wash and purify themselves therein; after the manner of the priests and Levites, who were obliged to cleanse themselves before they could enter the Temple.

Q: – 6. What else did you see there?

A: – Three Golden basons; In the first was the Letter *M*, in the second the letter G, and in the third, there was no character or engraving: those 3 basons were by the Scottish Elder Masters found in the ruins of the Temple.

Q: – 7. Did you see nothing Else?

A: – Yes I did; I saw the Ark of Alliance and Covenant wherein was deposited the 2 Tables of the Law.

Q: – 8. What does all this signifie?

A: – That the Scottish Masters must keep the Law of

[436]

God in their hearts, that they may have a Covenant with God.

Q: – 9. Have you seen any thing else?
A: – I have also seen a flaming Star.
Q: – 10. What signifies the flaming Star?
A: – The holy presence of the Almighty God.
Q: – 11. What brethren have you seen in the Temple?
A: – The Apprentices and fellow Crafts in the out Court the Masters in the sanctuary, and the Elder Masters in the sanctum Sanctorum.
Q: – 12. Is that all you have seen there?
A: – No. I have seen things there also, which I and all the scottish Masters keep in our hearts.
Q: – 13. How old are you?
A: – A Thousand years.
Q: – 14. How many pillars has a scottish Lodge?
A: – Four; 2 broken and shortened, and 2 which is overset and thrown down.
Q: – 15. What do they signify?
A: – That the Temple is in Ruins.
Q: – 16. What is the time?
A: – It is break of day.

To Close.

The Grand Master, then speaks to the Grand Senior Warden, "Most honorable Knights and brethren we are going to leave off, for the present, our holy work, which we are carrying on, through the merciful Assistance of the Almighty Grand Architect of heaven and earth, and am resolved to close this Scottish Lodge. I must ask you if our holy

[437]

Knights labours, were carried on, in such a manner as to procure us at all times praise and honor."

Grand Senior Warden says, "High exalted Grand Master and honorable Knights of Saint Andrew: This most right Worshipful Assembled Lodge of Valiant Knights and worthy brethren; Do honor and most submissively thank you for the high and commendable zeal, work and foresight which is so perfectly shewn, and taught to this holy Assembly: Your native greatness of Soul, gracefulness of mind, and brotherly Love, has filled our hearts with the sublimest veneration, and which for ever unites us to you. We now find more than ever its true Observation and doctrine, by your Knightly practice we desire now no more; only most Exalted Knights and Grand Master that you may henceforth never leave off Assisting us with your good Council and admirable Example, and to provide for our future Knightly works, that we may be Enabled readily to transmit to our successors, the true foundation of our Knightly labours, and the practice of our works that we may rejoice ourselves.

Then the Junior Grand Warden as follows.

"The Wonderfull secrets that the scotch Knights and brothers have discovered in clearing the ruins of the Temple at Jerusalem, made it to us highly necessary to consider the true use thereof, and that we may in future make a happy use of the same The Knights and Masters of this scottish Lodge request the most high Exalted Grand Master that our

[438]

Consideration and labours may be Assisted by his Great Wisdom and insight, that we may be able to make further beneficial discoveries, and through Wisdom, Beauty and strength, never fail in the happy undertaking of our most hallowed Masonry."

Then the Knight Grand Secretary speaks as follows,

"We most heartily thank our high Exalted Grand Master, for holding this Lodge; we are Unanimously resolved to regulate and fulfill every thing agreeable to his will: but now we must remember our duty towards our high Exalted Grand Master by 4 times 4 with all the Knight's honors &c &c &c to discharge our plight and duty: My brethren and Knights you must assist me therein"; All the Knights then arise, and clap with their hands 4 times 4: they then take off their hats with their left hands and draw their swords with their right hands, raising them up to their faces, and after holding them for a short time in that position, they then lower the points thereof to the Ground (in Tempo) or at one motion; takeing time from the Grand Master of the Ceremonies; then they make a low bow and remain standing.

The Grand Master then says, "My dear brethren and exalted Knights; I am happy to find, that you are not deficient in your Duty: but it is not to me that those honors are done; It is to the mighty and Grand Architect of the Universe, whose precepts and holy laws we practice in our Assemblys, all honor and

[439]

homage is due to him: let the fear of his great and mighty name, be always before your Eyes; his laws engraved on your hearts, and Imitate as much as possible his Goodness; be forgiving and merciful to your Enemies, benevolent, and bountifull to your friends and fellow; Do to every one as you would like to be done by: By which means you will propagate his holy Religion.

Blessed be his great and mighty name for ever and ever Amen! Retire my brethren in peace and friendship; and practice those virtues you are here taught.

The Lodge is Closed.

The brethren then put on their hats, sheathe their swords, and applaud by 4 times 4, and then give the Common Scotch sign.

Apron. The Apron must be Lined with Green, and bordered with the same and red: On the flap must be Embroidered or painted, a Deaths head and two Cross bones, above which is a sprig of Cassia; on the Æra of the Apron must be Embroidered, a flaming Star with 5 points full of rays, in the middle thereof the Letter G.

Order. The Order is a broad Green watered ribbon from the right shoulder to the left hip, to which must be appended by a red ribbon, a gold Saint Andrews Cross, Innamelled with Green and surrounded with Thistels.

Index

Prepared by S. Brent Morris, 33°, Grand Cross

The spelling of many of the words in the *Jamaica MS* is inconsistent, whether from variations in the original manuscript or the transcriber's inability to read or copy the original. Thus, as an example, we find the following variants of what is surely one root word: Jachinia, Jackania, Jackinai, Jackinia, Jakinai. We have tried to indicate variants in the index, but we urge the reader to try alternative and phonetic spellings when looking for unusual words.

A

Q

T

X

Y

Z

Arturo de Hoyos, 33°, Grand Cross, is Grand Archivist and Grand Historian of the Supreme Council, 33°, S.J. He was one of four people invited to the Vatican by the Roman Catholic Church to discuss Masonry. He has been featured on ABC, CNN, NBC, DC's FOX 5 News, WAMU Radio's "Metro Connection," Voice of America, The History Channel; interviewed by the *New York Times, US News & World Report, El País,* and others. He is a Past Master of McAllen Lodge No. 1110, Texas, an honorary member of John Blair Lodge No. 187, Alexandria, Virginia, and a full member of Quatuor Coronati Lodge No. 2076, London. He has both Mackey Awards in the SRRS, is Deputy Grand Abbot of the Society of Blue Friars, holds the KYCH, the IX° SRICF, and the Kt. Gr. Cross in the Allied Masonic Degrees and Grand College of Rites. A bibliophile, history and science geek, polyglot, and Musikliebhaber, he belongs to the Society of American Archivists, the NRA (Life), and the VCDL. Among his many vices are spicy foods, sweet deserts, horror movies, and Franzl Lang's yodeling.

Book layout by Elizabeth A. W. McCarthy.
Composed in InDesign CS6 using Adobe Jenson Pro, Cronos Pro, Bickham Script Pro, and Type Embellishments One LET.

Related Titles from Westphalia Press

Ancient Mysteries and Modern Masonry: The Collected Writings of Jewel P. Lightfoot, Edited by Billy J. Hamilton Jr.

Jewel P. Lightfoot. Former Attorney General of the State of Texas. Past Grand Master of the Masonic Grand Lodge of Texas. From humble beginnings in rural Arkansas, he worked to become an educated man who excelled in law and Freemasonry. He was a gentleman of his time, well-known as a scholar, public speaker, and Masonic philosopher.

Essay on The Mysteries and the True Object of The Brotherhood of Freemasons
by Jason Williams

This isn't a reprint of a classic. It's a new rendition with new life breathed into it, to be enjoyed both by the layperson trying to understand the Craft and Masonic scholars taking a deeper dive into the fraternity's golden years—when the concepts of liberty and equality were still fresh.

Female Emancipation and Masonic Membership: An Essential Collection
By Guillermo De Los Reyes Heredia

Female Emancipation and Masonic Membership: An Essential Combination is a collection of essays on Freemasonry and gender that promotes a transatlantic discussion of the study of the history of women and Freemasonry and their contribution in different countries.

Freemasonry, Heir to the Enlightenment
by Cécile Révauger

Modern Freemasonry may have mythical roots in Solomon's time but is really the heir to the Enlightenment. Ever since the early eighteenth century freemasons have endeavored to convey the values of the Enlightenment in the cultural, political and religious fields, in Europe, the American colonies and the emerging United States.

Freemasonry: A French View
by Roger Dachez and Alain Bauer

Perhaps one should speak not of Freemasonry but of Freemasonries in the plural. In each country Masonic historiography has developed uniqueness. Two of the best known French Masonic scholars present their own view of the worldwide evolution and challenging mysteries of the fraternity over the centuries.

Worlds of Print: The Moral Imagination of an Informed Citizenry, 1734 to 1839
by John Slifko

John Slifko argues that freemasonry was representative and played an important role in a larger cultural transformation of literacy and helped articulate the moral imagination of an informed democratic citizenry via fast emerging worlds of print.

Why Thirty-Three?: Searching for Masonic Origins
by S. Brent Morris, PhD

What "high degrees" were in the United States before 1830? What were the activities of the Order of the Royal Secret, the precursor of the Scottish Rite? A complex organization with a lengthy pedigree like Freemasonry has many basic foundational questions waiting to be answered, and that's what this book does: answers questions.

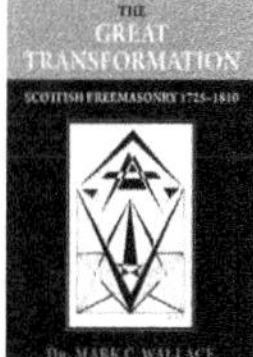

The Great Transformation: Scottish Freemasonry 1725-1810
by Dr. Mark C. Wallace

This book examines Scottish Freemasonry in its wider British and European contexts between the years 1725 and 1810. The Enlightenment effectively crafted the modern mason and propelled Freemasonry into a new era marked by growing membership and the creation of the Grand Lodge of Scotland.

Getting the Third Degree: Fraternalism, Freemasonry and History
Edited by Guillermo De Los Reyes and Paul Rich

As this engaging collection demonstrates, the doors being opened on the subject range from art history to political science to anthropology, as well as gender studies, sociology and more. The organizations discussed may insist on secrecy, but the research into them belies that.

The Great Transformation: Scottish Freemasonry 1725-1810
by Dr. Mark C. Wallace

This book examines Scottish Freemasonry in its wider British and European contexts between the years 1725 and 1810. The Enlightenment effectively crafted the modern mason and propelled Freemasonry into a new era marked by growing membership and the creation of the Grand Lodge of Scotland.

Getting the Third Degree: Fraternalism, Freemasonry and History
Edited by Guillermo De Los Reyes and Paul Rich

As this engaging collection demonstrates, the doors being opened on the subject range from art history to political science to anthropology, as well as gender studies, sociology and more. The organizations discussed may insist on secrecy, but the research into them belies that.

Freemasonry: A French View
by Roger Dachez and Alain Bauer

Perhaps one should speak not of Freemasonry but of Freemasonries in the plural. In each country Masonic historiography has developed uniqueness. Two of the best known French Masonic scholars present their own view of the worldwide evolution and challenging mysteries of the fraternity over the centuries.

Worlds of Print: The Moral Imagination of an Informed Citizenry, 1734 to 1839
by John Slifko

John Slifko argues that freemasonry was representative and played an important role in a larger cultural transformation of literacy and helped articulate the moral imagination of an informed democratic citizenry via fast emerging worlds of print.

Why Thirty-Three?: Searching for Masonic Origins
by S. Brent Morris, PhD

What "high degrees" were in the United States before 1830? What were the activities of the Order of the Royal Secret, the precursor of the Scottish Rite? A complex organization with a lengthy pedigree like Freemasonry has many basic foundational questions waiting to be answered, and that's what this book does: answers questions.

A Place in the Lodge: Dr. Rob Morris, Freemasonry and the Order of the Eastern Star
by Nancy Stearns Theiss, PhD

Ridiculed as "petticoat masonry," critics of the Order of the Eastern Star did not deter Rob Morris' goal to establish a Masonic organization that included women as members. Morris carried the ideals of Freemasonry through a despairing time of American history.

Brought to Light: The Mysterious George Washington Masonic Cave
by Jason Williams MD

The George Washington Masonic Cave near Charles Town, West Virginia, contains a signature carving of George Washington dated 1748. This book painstakingly pieces together the chronicled events and real estate archives related to the cavern in order to sort out fact from fiction.

Dudley Wright: Writer, Truthseeker & Freemason
by John Belton

Dudley Wright (1868-1950) was an Englishman and professional journalist who took a universalist approach to the various great Truths of Life. He travelled though many religions in his life and wrote about them all, but was probably most at home with Islam.

History of the Grand Orient of Italy
Emanuela Locci, Editor

No book in Masonic literature upon the history of Italian Freemasonry has been edited in English up to now. This work consists of eight studies, covering a span from the Eighteenth Century to the end of the WWII, tracing through the story, the events and pursuits related to the Grand Orient of Italy.

westphaliapress.org

www.ingramcontent.com/pod-product-compliance
Lightning Source LLC
LaVergne TN
LVHW010602100826
845148LV00014B/2816

* 9 7 8 1 6 3 3 9 1 9 4 7 1 *